Al-Maghred, The Barbary Lion

A Look at Islam

Nat Carnes

iUniverse, Inc.
Bloomington

Al-Maghred, The Barbary Lion
A Look at Islam

iUniverse books may be ordered through booksellers or by contacting:

iUniverse
1663 Liberty Drive
Bloomington, IN 47403
www.iuniverse.com
1-800-Authors (1-800-288-4677)

ISBN: 978-1-4759-0342-3 (sc)
ISBN: 978-1-4759-0343-0 (ebk)

Printed in the United States of America

iUniverse rev. date: 07/18/2012

Chapter One

The pure force and ear-shattering sound of the explosion was beyond simple description. It was heard from as far away as San Juan, Puerto Rico, the capital city of this U.S. Caribbean Commonwealth.

One man—drinking an early morning coffee with friends—immediately came out with the first thought that came to mind. And he knew instinctively it would be a wild guess at best.

"It must have been an atomic blast of some kind."

Besides the almost ear-shattering sound, the ground trembled slightly, suggesting a possible earth quake. The island is part of a Caribbean earthquake zone.

Thinking immediately of many ways all life could be brought to an end, the man did, however, try to apply some restraint on his own reaction to the sound and the small earth movement.

He refused to say aloud another part of his thinking: "This could be a part of a very large terrorist plot." Using those words could have provoked unnecessary panic.

Looking around quickly at the others seated near him, he guessed most likely they were going over similar mental options.

It was also probable they would have agreed to remain quiet until they had more concrete information. If they could have been asked, he guessed they would have all said that would be the only sure way to control wild and out-of-control thinking.

*　*　*

Immediately, a U.S. Coast Guard helicopter was ordered to the scene. Those aboard had been asked to visually confirm the explosion site and to determine as much as possible what may have happened.

At best, the fly over would only be the first step of a long and complicated investigation to find out what had set off the blast on that bright and sunny Caribbean day.

A search and rescue vessel was also involved. If the explosion had been set off by an accident of some kind, there could be survivors in need of immediate attention.

Or worse yet: floating dead bodies would have to be recovered.

*　*　*

Within what seemed like seconds, news reports about the so far mysterious explosion came quickly. Those men and women reporting were careful not to speculate on what may or may not have caused the blast.

They reported on only what they knew for sure.

There had been a single loud explosion somewhere north of Puerto Rico, the U.S. Coast Guard was investigating and their findings would be reported as quickly as possible.

Coast Guard Captain Bryson Whitlock faced a crowd of reporters who had gathered at the guard's pink-colored station in the part of the city known as old San Juan.

"At this moment, we know nothing for sure," Captain Whitlock said. "As soon as we have something more substantial, we'll pass along any and all definite and reportable information."

He warned: "This looks like a situation where it will take time—perhaps a lot of it—to determine what set off this terrible blast and why."

*　*　*

Within the hour, a helicopter pilot reported debris covering a large area at sea. Instead of it being north of Puerto Rico, it was found northwest of the island towns of Aguadilla and Isabella near a body of water known as the Mona Passage. It covered what is believed to be the deepest part of the Atlantic Ocean.

"What do you see?" demanded the pilot's commander.

"As best as I can tell, sir, there are at least a dozen suitcases there and a fairly large piece of metal with something printed on it. I can't see the letters clearly."

Later when a Coast Guard Search and Rescue vessel arrived, the slab was pulled out of the water. It read: 'The C.' There was nothing more, only the four letters and a jagged edge just to the right.

It was assumed the slab was part of a sign or the ship itself. For the moment, it was believed more complete wording had been painted, printed or placed there.

Immediately, the Coast Guard checked with Puerto Rico's government Ports Authority about the kind of shipping entering and leaving the Port of San Juan in the last 24 hours.

They came up with the name of a tourist cruise ship.

'The Caribbean' had set out hours earlier on a two-week voyage. The ship's first two scheduled stops were to have been made in the Dominican Republic and Haiti.

Puerto Rico and the Dominican Republic were separated by the Mona Passage, where the explosion apparently occurred.

Following quick checks by the Coast Guard and by the Associated Press, it was determined the ship had yet to dock in either one of those ports.

Within moments after that determination, skimpy details of what may have happened began to surface.

Captain Whitlock told news reporters:

"Again, I want to say. At this moment, we know nothing for sure. As soon as we have more, we'll pass along any and all definite information as quickly as possible."

He outlined what had been done to date.

"One our helicopters and a single Search and Rescue vessel were sent to the scene or very near to where we believe at least a single explosion or maybe more likely occurred."

Selecting his words carefully, the official knew it was not the time for needless mistakes or speculation.

Instead of attempting to take questions, he said firmly:

"Our first priority at this time . . . obviously . . . is to look for possible survivors."

It was a frantic, very tense moment.

*   *   *

Shortly afterwards, the Associated Press and other international news media were reporting a world class cruise ship may have encountered some kind of difficulty north of Puerto Rico.

Moments later, the full impact of what had happened was made public.

According to Captain Whitlock, "there is a report that an explosive charge was placed just below the ship's waterline. And we believe that single blast sent the 630-foot long vessel to the bottom."

He added: "We have more helicopters at the scene and a second rescue vessel is en route. We have advised any vessels in the area to help look for survivors."

At last report, some 900 people including passengers and crew were aboard. "So far none have been sighted," Captain Bryson Whitlock said. "It is feared all may be lost."

And at the same time, several news reports originating in the Middle East reporting on what happened repeated the phrase "Praise Be To Allah."

A news reporter added later: "We have just learned that a man identified only as the Barbary Lion claims responsibility for the sinking ship and the loss of lives."

*   *   *

Within 20 minutes, Jordon Frost and Colt McCoy received a telephone call. After Frost identified the office as Frost and McCoy Associates, the caller asked: "If possible I would like to speak to Mr. Frost or Mr. McCoy."

"May I ask who is calling?"

"Yes, of course. My name is Carl Frank. I'm President Hugh North's chief of staff. And I'm calling you from the White House."

"The what . . . !"

He was taken back. He'd never talked before to anyone so close to the president of the United States. Regaining a little self control, he asked bluntly: "Are you sure you have the right number?"

"I have the number right," the caller said patiently.

Immediately Jordon Frost identified himself as the speaker. "I'm here to serve the president anyway I can." Convinced everything was correct, his attitude changed dramatically.

"Thank you."

"You are more than welcome."

After a short delay, President Hugh North was on the line.

"This is President North."

"Good morning sir. Please tell me what I can do for you." He recognized the president's voice.

"I hope quite a bit."

"If possible, I will of course."

President North then asked a question.

"Have you heard about those still unexplained explosion or explosions going off on a cruise ship near Puerto Rico?"

"I just learned about them sir."

"Good. Your answer tells me I'm talking to the right man."

He had been advised by a security staff member that Jordon Frost and Colt McCoy were the best in the business. If anyone could find out the truth about what happened, they could.

Both were long time agents for the Central Intelligence Agency [CIA] and the Federal Bureau of Investigation [FBI]. And both took early retirement for the same reason. They reportedly wanted to operate independently as a team.

President North took immediate action after receiving a normally reliable tip that a vessel involved in terrorist activity between South America, the Caribbean, North Africa and Europe was steaming close or near Puerto Rico.

The first news of the explosion arrived only moments after he received the tip. He instinctively knew he had to prove or disprove the information without delay. He believed the security of the United States could be at stake.

Besides a security staff member's negative recommendation, he decided to go forward with Frost and McCoy for another reason.

Both—like their fathers before them—were long time agents working for the Central Intelligence Agency [CIA] and the Federal Bureau of Investigation [FBI]. And both took early retirement for a second reason.

They left over policy disagreements.

Once the President and Frost were talking on a secure telephone line, President North gave him more detail about the tip.

"The CIA reported a terrorist organization has claimed responsibility for an explosion of some kind in the Caribbean," the president explained.

Frost asked his first question.

"Who gave you the first report, sir?"

"We got it from our embassy in Rabat, Morocco, in northwest Africa."

"And where did they get that report?"

"First word apparently came from news reports in the Middle East."

"Does this terrorist organization have a name?"

"Yes and no."

"So what is it?"

"We don't have a name for the terrorist organization yet."

"So what do you know?"

"For the moment, we understand this person or terrorist may be called the Barbary Lion."

"And where is this alleged Barbary Lion located?"

"Somewhere in North Africa or 'Al-Maġhreb' as it's called there."

"Is Islam involved?"

"That's what we need to find out."

"I see."

"Can you help us?"

"And what is it exactly you want us to do?"

"Specifically, I want you to investigate what happened and why. And then report to me directly."

"What about the CIA and our other intelligence agencies?"

"They have also been assigned to the case."

"Not to be a wise guy, but why would you do that Sir? By that I mean . . . getting us involved."

"I've been looking over your father's file during his time with the CIA. And I learned you and Colt McCoy have been friends for a long time dating back to childhood."

"That's correct sir."

"I have a question."

"Not a problem sir."

"I see your father was not in agreement with the Church Committee findings released in 1975. And according to him the results ended up downgrading our intelligence gathering capability."

"That's true sir."

"Do you still agree with your father's decision to resign?"

"I do sir."

"Is that the reason you and Mr. McCoy formed your own private intelligence gathering company?"

"It is Mr. President. And I want to be very clear on this very important point. I want to have you hear me say that."

"I can respect that."

"My father and also Mr. McCoy's father are in fact the reason we did what we did. They were our advisors and remained so until their recent deaths."

"This may be a little late in coming for you . . . I just want to let you know I've always been in agreement with your father . . . not only yours but also Mr. McCoy's."

"Thank you sir. We both appreciate that obviously more than you can ever know."

"As a result," the president admitted, "I believe we lost our ability to know what was happening on the ground in critical areas of the world. I feel we still may be coming up short too many times because of cut-back decisions made at that time."

"And you now want us to help cover any possible gaps in the information collection process in this particular case."

"Yes. That's correct. Will you do it?

Again there was a moment's pause.

The pain and frustration of that past moment suddenly flooded his memory. And he never in his wildest dreams ever expected to hear such a statement from the President or from any President for that matter.

He then responded:

"I will help. And I'm positive Colt McCoy will join in this effort."

"I thank you and the nation thanks you. My chief of staff, Carl Frank, will provide anything you need at whatever cost. I know your rates. We will meet them and more, if necessary."

"Thank you."

"There is one other thing."

"Yes."

"If you need to talk to me, regardless of the hour, please do not hesitate. Carl will connect us."

"I understand."

"Time is short. We need as much information as quickly and as fast as possible."

"I understand, Mr. President. Again, thank you for letting us be a part of this operation."

*   *   *

Frank was back on the line.

"I have a request."

"Shoot . . . !"

There was no hesitation.

"We will need to see and review all official reports, memos, contacts official and unofficial prepared by the CIA, the FBI or any agency that makes you think this explosion or these series of explosions were set off by terrorists."

"We will setup a secure FAX line directly to your office. You should start getting what you need within 12 hours or less. Is that satisfactory?"

"Totally . . ."

"I have one other question."

"What is it?"

"Once we've had an opportunity to read and to review the reports, we'll need to come to Washington to meet with agency heads and all those directly involved or responsible for preparing this information. We'll undoubtedly have questions or will have need for some clarification."

"That can be arranged."

"Thanks."

"We'll send a plane to bring you here. The meeting will be held at the White House in two days."

*   *   *

He couldn't believe what had just happened or heard and he replayed the conversation again and again in his mind and from a recording.

It was a long ago formed habit. Push the telephone record button before every important conversation. It was his way of knowing and remembering exactly what was said without error or misunderstanding.

And each time that particular conversation was repeated, he and Colt would have a single regret. Their fathers could not hear what they could now listen to over and over again.

It was perhaps the beginning of putting an end to a memory of how past U.S. intelligence had been gathered.

Their fathers' recount of what happened in 1975 would never be forgotten. They had resigned in protest over the way the Democratic Party had handled the matter following President Richard Nixon's resignation on Aug. 9, 1974.

In his and his partner's view it was an unfortunate attempt to punish Republicans for Nixon and the Watergate scandal.

Burglars were hired by Nixon's reelection campaign officials to bug the offices of the Democratic National Committee at the Watergate Hotel in Washington.

According to Democrats, if Nixon and Republicans could be responsible for Watergate they were probably using the CIA and the FBI to do similar deeds not only domestically but internationally. If so . . . such wrongdoings had to be cut out at the roots for the good of the country.

After all, Sen. Edward Kennedy [D-Ma] had traveled to Santiago, Chile, after the Sept. 11, 1973 overthrow and death of Chile's President Salvador Allende. He reported back to Washington mistakenly that the CIA was responsible. They had tried but failed.

So what followed was even more scandalous and was the primary reason for their fathers' resignations.

In 1975, the Senate Select Committee on Intelligence, headed by Sen. Frank Church of Idaho, began hearings on the CIA and its activities. The result was a detailed report entitled "Alleged Assassination Plots Involving Foreign Leaders."

"Such an effort" he said "made it look like the Presidency and the CIA had formed an undercover company named MURDER INC."

He remembered pointing out there was no proof of U.S. involvement in connection with plots to assassinate five world leaders between 1960 through 1975:

1. Patrice Lumumba of the Congo.

2. Fidel Castro of Cuba.

3. Rafael Trujillo of the Dominican Republic

4. Ngo Dinh Diem of South Vietnam

5. Rene Schneider of Chile.

No mention was made of Salvador Allende of Chile.

They had resigned in protest believing America's ability to gather reliable on the ground intelligence information internationally had been compromised.

And when Jimmy Carter, a Democrat, was elected president in 1977 they were further outraged when Carter ordered a major shift in American gathering policy. Instead of talking to "bad guys" on the ground they would rely only on satellites.

A network of on the ground intelligence contacts that had taken years to build was destroyed in the blink of an eye.

* * *

While they worked for the CIA and the FBI until early retirement, Jordon Frost and Colt McCoy had made a clear and conscious decision to support their fathers publically before and after they left government.

Not only did they maintain a close relationship with their fathers, they considered them to be their teachers and a primary source of information about all things related to intelligence gathering for a reason. Between them, they had accumulated 60 years of experience.

After leaving the two agencies, the sons maintained contact with both and accepted special assignment cases from time to time but nothing like what had just been presented them at that moment.

While critical of what had happened in the past, they blamed the Democratic Party for the injury to intelligence gathering and not the agencies themselves.

After early retirement, Frost and McCoy developed their own way of investigation including a painstaking effort to establish an on the ground intelligence network. In short, they would apply what they believed were tried and tested methods to resolve the current problem: an intelligence challenge of a lifetime.

*   *   *

Something else was at stake.

If they were successful, they knew the CIA and the FBI would be open for the first time to take their methods seriously and to implement them over a period of time.

Otherwise they knew their intelligence collection philosophy would be set back for years. In other words the agencies might forever be locked into a Jimmy Carter type intelligence mentality.

*   *   *

Here is what President North knew about the two men, sons of former CIA and FBI agents and themselves agents for 20 years each.

Their company was headquartered in Puerto Rico, a U.S. Commonwealth, for a reason.

From San Juan, they believed it was the only place in the Western Hemisphere where one could view or look into the soul of Latin America and the United States at the same time.

Why?

The reason was a simple one: the island's political relationship with the United States.

In other words, they believed they were in the best place possible to start hearing and evaluating any political situation and going over intelligence coming in from any world location.

Here is what they did for a living:

For a fee they investigated and sold information to companies and governments dealing with or working in world trouble spots.

They placed what many thought were unusually strict standards on themselves. Those guidelines were thought the only way to penetrate large bases of knowledge outside the United States.

While they believed the English language was the best and most universal language and that the United States presented the best example to the world on how to build a structure providing the most opportunity for its citizens, they knew that alone was not enough.

So for them what were the basic tools needed to penetrate any challenge mixed in politics and more often than not with religious thought and belief?

President North had learned these men started with the basics. If those elements could be achieved, there was a chance of success. If not, their ability to penetrate was diminished.

What was their definition of basics, areas overlooked by many or simply rejected by others as impractical and inefficient and a huge waste of time?

Anytime anyone bothered to ask and they had a few minutes to listen, they would hear essentially the same story over and over again.

Some got bored hearing it and others were simply turned off by what was said.

Jordon Frost and Colt McCoy did not because of their belief without such basics their chance of success would be decreased by ten maybe a hundred times.

"Basics," they believed, "meant being aware of a second culture or cultures other than our own, knowing or learning a second language and acquiring knowledge of local and international politics."

There was one other important basic and maybe the most important: "For us, it's our belief in God."

Both were members of a Southern Baptist Church in San Juan, Puerto Rico.

They concluded this way:

"Once penetration is achieved, using those important tools to get inside the subject matter for an intimate look at people or an event, a true investigation could begin."

Confident their approach was perhaps the only way until proved differently, they warned: "Sometimes this turns out to be a very slow and maybe even a very painful process."

Chapter Two

Two days after receiving and looking at all the documents related to the case, Jordon Frost and Colt McCoy advised Carl Frank, the president's chief of staff, they were ready to travel to Washington.

As promised an Air Force One plane landed at San Juan's Luis Munoz Marin International Airport shortly before noon the next day. Moments later they were aboard and headed for Andrews Air Force base near Washington, D.C., the nation's capital.

*   *   *

The next morning at 10am sharp, Jordon Frost and Colt McCoy met with the President Hugh North and members of his National Security Council [NSC] in the Cabinet room located in the West Wing of the White House, adjoining the Oval Office. It looked out over the White House Rose Garden.

Ronald Brown, director of National Intelligence and Jack Kramer, the Undersecretary of Defense for Intelligence, flanked President Hugh North and Carl Frank, the president's chief of staff.

All 16 heads of the Intelligence Community (IC) were present. They included:

Air Force Intelligence, Army Intelligence, Central Intelligence Agency, Coast Guard Intelligence, Defense Intelligence Agency,

Department of Energy, Department of Homeland Security, Department of State, Department of the Treasury, Drug Enforcement Administration, Federal Bureau of Investigation, Marine Corps Intelligence, National Geospatial-Intelligence Agency, National Reconnaissance Office, National Security Agency and Navy Intelligence.

*　　*　　*

Jordan Frost and Colt McCoy were seated across the large table and directly in front of President North.

"We're more than delighted to have you both here on such short notice," said the president, who directed his vision and words directly at Frost and McCoy.

"Thank you Mr. President," said Frost, who looked every intelligence chief there in the eye by the time he finished his greeting. "We are more than pleased to accept your invitation to assist in any way we can to find and apprehend those responsible for this tragic and probably terrorist act."

*　　*　　*

It was the type of encounter they never tired of, regardless of the number of times they gathered to exchange ideas with those high-ranking officials. The names changed, but the thrill, the aura of being there would remain the same. Past differences, no matter how deeply felt, could not change that.

*　　*　　*

Chaired by the President, the seven-member NSC team advised him on national security and foreign policy. When Frost and McCoy were escorted into the room, they were already in their seats. They knew whatever they suggested, either now or later, would have to be approved by a majority.

They were the Director of National Intelligence, chairman of the Joint Chiefs of Staff, the Vice President, the Secretary of State, the Secretary of the Treasury, the Secretary of Defense and the Assistant to the President for National Security Affairs.

Carl Frank, the president's chief of staff, made sure they had good seats. They sat across the table from the president and they had a clear view of all those present. He didn't want to later hear excuses or complaints from two, old friends for whatever reason.

President North spoke first.

"Just to be clear, I'm the one who invited Jordon Frost and Colt McCoy to be with us today."

The president paused a moment to let his words sink in. It was highly unusual for anyone not connected to the intelligence community to attend this kind of meeting.

"And I've done so for a very good reason. I believe they may have something special to offer us in this very important investigation."

Looking around the room, he wanted to be sure everyone there was paying attention to what he had just said.

"I know all of you will cooperate and work with them when needed during this period of finding answers."

Again he paused.

"First, I want Mr. Frost to give us a little background on his approach to this kind of challenge. And then I'll ask Mr. Frank to bring us up to date on what may have happened to the ship."

So when President North gave him the floor, Frost hit on two points.

"First, I want to know what you know about this man called the Barbary Lion. And then I'll briefly cover how we plan to approach our investigation," something he knew would bring on immediate and likely strong disagreement.

Frost didn't ask anyone in particular. He wanted the person with the most knowledge to speak up.

Ronald Brown, director of National Intelligence, responded immediately.

"At this moment, we know very little," he said. "And frankly that's one reason my office suggested to the President to have someone like you and Mr. McCoy to help us out."

Pausing a moment to apparently let his words sink in, Brown added: "We know a little history, but I'm afraid that's about it."

Before going further, he repeated the first report coming out of the Middle East about the ship going down near Puerto Rico.

Frost said: "I'd like to hear whatever you have to say. Everything no matter how small will likely be important."

Brown followed up by saying:

"First the phrase, 'Praise Be To Allah,' was repeated a number of times on many Middle Eastern radio and television stations in reaction to reports of the ship going down in the Caribbean."

Later a news reporter working for the Associated Press added: "We have just learned that a man identified only as the Barbary Lion claims responsibility for the sinking ship and the loss of lives."

"Is that all?"

"We have asked our embassy in Rabat," the capital of Morocco in North Africa, "to confirm or deny the report and to provide us with more detail if available as soon as possible."

"So that means, I assume, the person or persons responsible could be found right there in Rabat."

"I do."

"Good."

"It might help to review a little history about this entire affair," Frost said.

"That can't hurt."

"The origin of all this, in my view at least, goes back to the 11th century."

"Really . . . that long ago? . . Is that possible?"

Ignoring the comment, he continued: "This all started as a terrible conflict between the Roman Catholic Church and Islam."

"Does that period have a name?"

"Yes, of course . . . the Crusades."

Stopping again for a moment to let the point sink in, Frost added: "So this is one way of connecting the then and the now."

Or he added: "It's perhaps at least a place to start, nothing more."

"Do you have anything more up-to-date to tie us to that long-ago period?"

"Perhaps . . . We do know a little about the term 'Barbary Lion' if you would like to hear it."

"I would."

"We think this man who calls himself the Barbary Lion is likely the head of a criminal group called Barbary or Maghreb Pirates."

"And these pirates do or did what exactly?"

"In the past, they destroyed and plundered British, French, Italian and Spanish ships for cargo and raided southern Europe's coastal zones for people to be sold later as slaves."

"Slaves . . . You did say slaves?"

"Yes."

"Do we know how many were taken?"

"Yes. An estimated 800,000 to 1.25 million Europeans were sold at Algerian and Moroccan slave markets."

"According to what you know, who were these pirates and where did they came from?"

"They were members of two groups, Muslims and privateers. The latter were paid to operate with the followers of Islam. And this alliance had at least three names: Barbary Corsairs, Ottoman Corsairs or Barbary Pirates."

"And this alliance operated where exactly?"

"They either raided separately or together along what was known as the Barbary or Maghreb Coast between the 16th and 19th centuries. This land at the time belonged collectively to the Berber people."

"Can you identify those land areas?"

"Yes I can. There are four: Algeria, Libya, Morocco and Tunisia. And out of that number Morocco was the most significant."

"Why?"

"Because of geography . . ."

"Does that mean the others were not important?"

"I didn't say that. All of them played individual and significant roles." He added: "Of the four, Libya was the furthest east, and Algeria and Tunisia were in the middle."

"What else can you add?"

"Maybe this will help."

"Okay . . ."

"These attackers headquartered in the capitals of those four countries. The first was Rabat in Morocco followed by Algiers in Algeria, Tripoli in Libya and Tunis in Tunisia."

McCoy broke in at that point. "The pirates wanted what exactly?"

"As I said before two things: merchant ships cargo from the sea and slaves from the land. Both were sold in America, Europe and sub-Saharan Africa."

"And this went on for how long?"

"The Barbary Coast existed four centuries, but the power block if we can call it that lasted a lot longer."

"Do we know how much longer?"

"Roughly it started in the 16th century and ended in the 19th."

"And the pirate problem ended when?"

"It started in 1815 and was brought to a halt following separate British and Dutch military operations. France then colonized the Barbary Coast to be sure nothing like that would ever happen again."

* * *

Once Ronald Brown, director of National Intelligence, covered general background needed to help identify the Barbary Lion and to know where he might be headquartered, Jordan Frost started to talk about how he and Colt McCoy would approach their investigation.

"First I want to thank Mr. Brown. What he has given us will no doubt play a significant role in our search for the truth behind this horrible event that occurred in the Caribbean, near Puerto Rico where we live."

He and McCoy had agreed on what should be said before the meeting. They reasoned it would be easier in the long run to determine early how badly the president and NSC members wanted to hear from them.

If their views were rejected, despite the President's personal invitation, they could make an early exit. Plenty of work assignments waited for them back at the office.

Taking a deep breath, Frost first looked the President straight in the eye and said:

"Thank you for this opportunity, Mr. President. My partner and I, Colt McCoy, are more than honored to be with you and these distinguished gentlemen this morning."

Before saying another word, he moved his sight around the room, making a point to look each one present straight in the eye as he had done with the president at the beginning.

For a brief moment, he was silent before he got to this crucial first point.

"I think we are in agreement in one general area: to be of service to our country."

His remark was greeted in the affirmative by all those present.

"But to do that following this very tragic and dangerous event occurring just off the northwest coast of Puerto Rico, we need to start somewhere. And I believe such a point is the island itself."

* * *

Immediately, there was a voice of dissent and it came from Charles Barkley, the Assistant to the President for National Security Affairs.

"I have a question."

"Of course, please go ahead."

21

"Puerto Rico?" he asked. "I don't understand despite the fact that it is near where this tragic and as you said perhaps terrorist event was staged."

"I'm listening."

"How can a small island a thousand miles from nowhere help us in any way at all? Any solution to what we're talking about is likely to start and finish somewhere in the Middle East?"

"I agree. That's a fair question," Frost said. His voice was calm and his words were well chosen.

"So what's your answer?"

"First. Let's understand our own location and our own back ground."

"And the answer to that is . . ."

"We're in the Western Hemisphere. In other words we live here."

"And . . ."

"We are Americans, you and I."

"No doubt about that."

"So what does that mean exactly?"

"Besides being born, raised and educated in the United States, we speak the English language, perhaps the most important speaking tool in the world."

"We can agree on that at least."

"Good. So let's go one step further by anticipating your next question."

"And that is . . ."

"If we both speak English and if our language is the most important in the world, why bother to learn a second or a third language?"

"I can't argue with that. In other words, I agree."

His tone switched suddenly. "So you want to give your adversary . . . if I may use the word . . . an advantage."

"I never said that."

"You just have."

"How could that be? . . ."

"That's simple enough. If you speak only English and the he or she you're talking to speaks English and Spanish, you are at a serious disadvantage."

Rearing back and stunned by the assertion, he exclaimed: "How can that be if we both are speaking English?"

By the time he finished his sentence, he was near shouting.

At that point, President North broke into the conversation. Not directing his comments specifically to Charles Barkley, he said:

"We . . . I mean . . . I invited Mr. Frost and Mr. McCoy to be with us this morning. I said that at the beginning of this meeting and I repeat it now. In my view, they have something important to say.

"I don't expect any of you to fully agree with them. I do expect, however, for all of us . . . including myself . . . to listen respectively to their presentation this morning."

"I understand, Mr. President," Charles Barkley said.

"Good. Please go ahead Mr. Frost."

*   *   *

Smiling to himself, Frost knew he had accomplished what he wanted, to quickly expose and control disruptive opposition right from the start.

Once that was accomplished, he moved on to explain how he and McCoy planned to start their investigation in cool, rational terms.

Frost started again by rephrasing the question that had enraged Charles Barkley.

"I assume none of us want to give this Barbary Lion or Barbary Pirate any kind of political or any kind of advantage for that matter. Is that correct?"

This time around, Barkley was quiet and so were the others. President North had set the tone for the meeting and it would continue that way.

*   *   *

Frost continued. "If we want the advantage, I suggest the following." Everyone listened without further hostile comment or questions.

"If we know how to penetrate or get inside something different in the western hemisphere, we might be successful in using the same system somewhere else . . . like in the Middle East."

"Okay. That seems to make sense for the moment anyway," one of the others said.

"Good. So we might approach the question in the following manner."

"I'm listening."

"If we understand what's needed to probe Puerto Rico, a simple proposition compared to the Middle East, we might be prepared to take on something more complicated."

"I admit. That sounds reasonable so far. In other words this is a first step."

"Exactly . . . we are now in agreement on what may be termed 'an important starting point.'"

"Okay. I'm ready to listen. Go ahead."

"In order to solve Puerto Rico, one needs knowledge in three areas."

"Just three . . . ?"

Barkley couldn't help himself. He had to ask the question. He would try anything no matter how slight to get Frost off track.

Gathering himself, Frost ignored what Barkley said. To have done otherwise, he would have lost his advantage.

So Frost calmly went ahead with his point again.

"In order to solve Puerto Rico, one needs knowledge in three areas. And those three parts are . . . culture, language and politics."

*   *   *

Barkley wasn't finished.

"So let's start with first things first. You mentioned language."

"Yes I did," Frost responded quickly in soft controlled speech. "And to get along there, one needs two, English and Spanish."

"But if this is a U.S. Commonweath, isn't English enough?" Barkley thought he had him there.

"For that reason, English is very important. So is Spanish. It's the language of schools, the local court system and the language of the major political parties."

"So you're saying, I'm not going to grasp what Puerto Rico is all about without Spanish."

"That's exactly right. You can get along granted. But you will be excluded from getting in on the ground floor."

"So anyone taking my position will be excluded. Is that what you just said?"

"Yes. I did. In other words, the Spanish language is the best reflection of Puerto Rico in general terms. By that I mean it's a mixture of Spain, the nearby Caribbean islands and Latin America in addition to the United States."

"That's a mouthful."

"Yes it is."

"Can you explain that a little more please?"

"Let's look at it this way," said Frost, who thought Barkley perhaps was beginning to get the point. "I believe it's the only place in the Western Hemisphere where one can look into the soul of Latin America and the United States at the same time."

The remark was met with silence.

Frost added immediately: "This is something I often repeat again and again. I never tire of saying it. If I have to say it a different way one or one hundred times I will."

"Why for you is that statement so important?" Barkley asked.

"It is for a very simple reason, Puerto Rico's political relationship with the United States."

"Can you explain that a little further please?"

"Rather than going into more detail, I'll tell you a true story. Sometimes that's the best way of getting a point across."

"I'm listening."

"My story may be the best way or at least one way of responding to your question."

"That's not a problem."

"I once asked an important businessman in Bogota, the capital of Colombia in South America, who would be his choice for a U.S. ambassador in his country if he had the power of selection."

"And what did he say?"

"I gave him two choices: one from Kansas City, Missouri; and the other from San Juan, Puerto Rico."

"What was his response?"

"Before answering, he asked me if this was a serious question." Frost waited a moment to let the tension build.

Barkley couldn't wait any longer. He blurted out: "What did you say?"

"Yes, of course. For me it was a very easy answer." Again Frost waited a moment as he had done moments before.

"And he said . . ." Barkley was beginning to lose patience.

"Kansas City was his response."

"Kansas City? Is that what you said?"

Rather than answering the Barkley question, Frost responded this way: "I must admit to you I couldn't believe what I was hearing either. So I asked him simply. Why?"

After a short pause, apparently needing more time to collect his thoughts, he said: "That's an easy answer."

"You said 'an easy answer.' Frankly I don't understand."

"'Yes . . . I'll say it again . . . that's an easy answer. I said Kansas City for a reason. We can manipulate him.'"

"Admittedly Mr. Barkley, I was stunned. So I asked him again. You are talking about the man from Kansas City? I just want to be clear."

"You heard me correctly and I will repeat what I've just said. We can manipulate him."

Barkley then asked: "What was your response?"

"And that could not be possible with an ambassador say from San Juan?"

"That's right. It would not be possible. A Puerto Rican knows us from A to Z. In other words . . . No manipulation there."

"So the reason for you telling me the story might be the following. By recognizing Puerto Rico in the way you have just described, we might be in a better position to crack the Middle East."

"Exactly . . . I couldn't have said it better myself."

*   *   *

"Let me put it another way," Frost said. "If we can identify a connecting link in the Middle East like a Puerto Rico to Latin America, we might have a chance of penetrating."

He wasn't finished.

"And if we can penetrate, we'll be in a better position to understand. If we understand, perhaps we can begin to solve some of those now seemingly unsolvable challenges."

*   *   *

At that point, the President asked a question.

"If we are faced with a challenge say like in a Middle Eastern country like Morocco . . . would it be necessary to speak Arabic?"

"Yes, Mr. President that's correct. A speaking knowledge of Arabic is extremely important."

"Is that the only language spoken in Morocco?"

"No there is Spanish and French. French is probably the most important second language there."

"So . . . what would you suggest is needed in that country?"

"We'll need French, which we have, and we'll need to find a Arabic speaker we can trust."

There was another question, related to the "Praise to Allah" comment and the mention of the "Barbary Lion."

"Does any of that mean anything? Should we be concerned about either one or the other or both?"

"Both are something to be concerned about."

"I hope you will not blame all Muslims for what happened to the ship."

"As I said," Frost continued, "Islam's role in all of this will have to be examined just like everything else."

The remainder of the time was spent reviewing faxed material sent to them from Washington.

Chapter Three

Jordan Frost and Colt McCoy returned to San Juan that same evening. Once there, they agreed finding the Barbary Lion or Pirate or whatever terrorist name he responded to would be a long and painful path.

"If so," Frost said, "we need to shorten our time investigating as much as we can."

"I agree," McCoy said, "but how are we going to do that?"

"Without him knowing it, I believe Ronald Brown," director of National Intelligence, "helped more than he perhaps realized."

"What do you mean by that exactly?" asked McCoy.

"He gave us a short history or general background about the Barbary Lion, who he might be and where he might be found."

"He gave us all something to think about. There's no doubt about that."

"All of that tells me a lot about the direction and points to be covered by our investigation."

"I'm listening."

"To find this terrorist, we're going to have to look at places where this man may be hiding. And if everything is done correctly, I believe our investigation will show us exactly where to look."

"Where might those places be?"

"Our first hint, I believe, may come looking at terrorist-attack history; getting a list of terrorist organizations; by taking a closer look at known terrorist organizers like Osama bin Laden; find out sinking details of other ships; get a list of past terrorist bombings; and interview the owners of the ship that went down near Puerto Rico.

"From there we need to go back and look at the reason for the Crusades. Once that's established, we should review why we are Southern Baptists. Afterwards, we should look at the Roman Catholic Church and finally Islam."

"I have a question and a doubt."

"Please go ahead."

"In this kind of terrorist investigation, do we need to go into why we are not only Southern Baptists but members of the Southern Baptist Convention?"

"Look at it this way. If our terrorist is involved with Islam, a government-religious mix, we will likely be in better position to understand him if we are clear on what we believe and what we do not."

"I see."

"Does that mean you are suggesting our investigation exclude those points you covered in our Washington, DC, meeting?"

What was covered there combined with Brown's review will or should sharpen our probe into the explosion and sinking of the ship.

* * *

They concluded real progress had been made in Washington, DC, more than they ever could have expected.

This opportunity, in their minds, was probably far more important in the long run than solving what looked like a very complicated case.

At stake, they thought, was a major switch in methodology. If accepted, the use of culture, language and politics would be inserted or would become an integral part of all probing methods used for investigating and solving international crime in the future.

Until now, they believed governments and institutions investigating criminal activity believed such skills were important—if available—during the normal investigation process of international crime. But too many times, in their view, such crimes went unsolved or large parts even unrecognized without a conscience presence of culture, language and politics.

It was too easy to base all assumptions on their own definitions of culture, language and politics. To do what they were suggesting, Frost and McCoy accepted as fact it was a difficult barrier. Too many times it was too much of a rigid mental block to cross and look beyond self-imposed barriers to examine crime or parts of a larger wrong doing.

And in facing almost predictable failure, they had agreed to continue on. It was what their fathers had taught them and why they had resigned those high and well paying posts years ago.

In their mind, it was a challenge that confronted all countries, not just one or two, but all of them regardless of size, wealth or importance. It would have been too easy to place such a burden on the United States alone.

So why did Frost and McCoy tell President North and his intelligence leaders what they did?

They believed the potential of learning what happened and finding those responsible for the ship's sinking would be slowed down drastically using only accepted methods.

For them, it was a question of enriching current procedure, not rejecting it.

*   *   *

Before leaving Washington and returning to San Juan, Frost and McCoy told President North and Frank they believed the explosion may have been directed by small international political units whose leaders shared a common goal: discredit the United States and her western allies.

One—extremist Islamic terrorists—may have been the driving force behind those events.

Frost and McCoy had learned such reasoning was the same in other cases they had investigated.

In other words, this was perhaps a good starting point unless proved otherwise.

WHY?

Because of other possible connections these terrorists reportedly have with world slave traders as an example.

If slave trade could be confirmed, other criminal activity was likely present.

That included money laundering, drug trafficking and illegal arms sales.

Within the president's intelligence circle, it was more than clear most of them, if not all, opposed the kind of approach proposed by Frost and McCoy.

Lyndon Collinsworth, who represented the CIA at the meeting, said so emphatically. "It's simply too early in this large of an investigation to make such statements even if true. We've not even had an opportunity to examine all the evidence yet."

Frost and McCoy remembered their response to his statement was not appreciated.

"While Mr. Collinsworth has a point, we have enough investigative parts to go in more than one direction to find answers. At this stage of the game, we all should be probing in our individual areas of expertise and knowledge."

McCoy followed up. "There is a why and an answer to such a question. And the why is simple enough in our view. In this room, we have men of many investigative skills and talents, perhaps some of the best in the world, if not the very best."

"Yes, that's true," Collinsworth admitted.

"If we are in agreement, logic tells us anyway, to make every attempt to take advantage of every available source to find answers. The president has told us clearly: 'time is short.'

Frost and McCoy realized immediately at the time this was an internal power play, the kind that had caused their fathers to resign and form a private investigation company. At that moment, there was no other alternative for White House insiders but to agree at least openly with men like Collinsworth.

It was no different on this occasion. They were voicing conflicting opinions openly in front of the president and the nation's best intelligence minds. They knew their fathers would be more than proud of them. It was after all their moment.

It was not the first time they had spoken out.

After today, they hoped they would continue to have the ability to repeat their position and to be heard. They could never expect total victory nor did they want it.

Victory was what had occurred in Washington, although Frost and McCoy weren't willing to admit or say that openly.

With the president's blessing, they would probe the terrorist possibility. Collinsworth and the CIA would look for evidence. The FBI would look for known criminals with a record of explosive skills.

Their findings, together with what the CIA and FBI turned up, would guide the investigation. In the end, they believed they would find those responsible and bring them to justice.

*   *   *

Once back home, Frost and McCoy began their work to prove or not prove what they thought could be true. They would report their weekly findings back to Carl Frank as would the CIA and the FBI.

They needed to determine if the ship's sinking was part of a general attack against the WEST: Europe, Israel and the United States.

To do that, Frost and McCoy concluded, they needed to start by gathering a list of past terrorist attacks, where they were carried out and to know when possible the attackers' intent.

"Here is one."

"Good."

They laid out the papers on a table and began to read, examine them.

"Where did you find such a large amount of material so quickly?" Frost asked. "I'm impressed."

McCoy's response came without hesitation. "On the Internet, that's where."

"Really . . . that's interesting. I'd like to know how you did that."

"By running a simple search on the Web, that's how. I got it by typing in the following: 'List of Islamic Attacks.' After I clicked the button near the entry, I got an immediate answer. Most of what I was looking for appeared right there in front of me not in days but immediately."

Frost was shocked. He felt sure his partner found it after hours of search in a government library. "I guess that means I'm getting really old not to have known that."

Ignoring the comment, McCoy said only: "It was enormous." He continued by giving his partner a quick summary of what he had in hand.

One source listed 12,319 world-wide Islamic attacks after Sept. 11, 2001, when two American Airlines commercial jets were hijacked and crashed into the twin towers World Trade Center in New York City.

Thousands have been killed in those confrontations by the intermingling of extremist Islamic and leftist political groups, parties and organizations.

Israel, the West including Europe and the United States were all primary targets.

In their view, it all had started with the Russian 1917 Revolution that spread largely to Middle Eastern governments. Also touched were world dictators including those in Cuba and Socialist leaning want-to-be dictators like Hugo Chavez in Venezuela.

"You know what we must do immediately."

"I think I do, "McCoy said. "Even though they may have found these lists, we have to tell our friends at the CIA and the FBI about it."

"Exactly . . ."

"It will be done immediately. We don't want them to accuse us of holding back on anything."

*   *   *

Once done, Frost and McCoy got back to work on their own.

*   *   *

"In order to move forward, we need our own starting point, a kind of outline to follow," Frost said.

"Agreed . . . what do you suggest?"

"For starters why don't we question each other like when we worked for the CIA and the FBI."

"If you think it will help, why not."

"How about using Puerto Rico?"

Both laughed at the suggestion.

It was the same proposition offered to the Washington intelligence community. Frost and McCoy agreed later what was said was good, even bordering on excellent. At the same time, they felt their position should be revisited and sharpened.

So they covered or repeated many of the same questions—sometimes word for word—mentioned during the Washington meeting.

"Where do we start?"

"That's easy. Since we want to practice what we preach, we'll start exactly where we did before . . . right here in Puerto Rico."

McCoy began by bringing up questions doubting what they had said in hopes of better grasping those concerns and better understanding how best to respond to them in the future. If successful, they hoped to be better able to find answers to critical and complicated political questions like in the Middle East.

Here was one response they remembered about Puerto Rico.

"I don't understand. How can a small U. S. Caribbean island help us solve something with a possible Middle Eastern origin or connection?"

Frost asked how he could have better answered the question. As simply as possible," McCoy said. "First, let's understand our own location and our own back ground."

"Why is that kind of response important?" After making the statement, Frost then reversed himself with McCoy. "What would be a better answer?"

"What do you have in mind?"

"In Washington, as I recall, you stated we're in the Western Hemisphere."

"And . . ."

"Why not shift that just a bit."

"Okay."

"Instead of saying 'we are Americans, you and I,' why not use the term 'roots'?"

"Roots? . . . I don't understand."

"Yes. Simply put anyone including ourselves is rooted in a single spot. For us that means we were born, raised and educated in the United States."

"What if we decide to live in say Paris, France? What would that mean?"

"It would mean our base or our roots would remain the same without change."

"Even say if we never return or see those original beginnings again?"

"Exactly . . ."

"If that's true, how should I approach the French language and culture?"

"I think we all have three choices."

"Only three . . . ?"

Smiling for a moment, McCoy responded:

"In France, we could take our roots to the extreme and refuse to learn anything French. After all, we speak the English language, perhaps the most important speaking tool in the world."

"I see. What's the second option?"

"Total immersion into everything French . . ."

"Total . . . ?"

"Yes by declaring you are abandoning one culture for another. It's like converting from one religion to another."

"That sounds serious."

"It is. In short, you are announcing your acceptance of French and ridding yourself of everything American including the English language."

"And option number three. What on earth could that ever be?"

"While in France, remember your roots, where you come from and never ever deny such a reality under any circumstances."

"Is that all?"

"No, it is not. Learn French and as much of the French culture as possible."

"And where did you learn all that?"

"This shouldn't surprise you. Right here in Puerto Rico."

"So this is what I think you are saying. Correct me if I'm wrong."

"Okay . . . Go ahead. I'll listen."

"In order to penetrate another country, remember who you are, learn their language and their culture."

"You've got it, but that doesn't surprise me at all."

"Is there anything else?"

"Yes, there is now that you mention it. Learn all you can about their politics."

"About politics . . ."

"I'm not talking about left or right. It means having a working knowledge of all political parties and what they stand for."

"We can agree on that at least."

"Good. So let's go one step further by anticipating your next question."

"And that is . . ."

"I want to back up a little on the language issue if I may. I want to be totally clear."

"Okay."

"If we both speak English and if our language is the most important in the world, why bother to learn a second or a third language?"

"I can't argue with that. In other words, I agree."

"But there is a BUT in there somewhere. I can feel it coming."

His tone switched suddenly like was done in Washington. "So you want to give your adversary . . . if I may use the word . . . an advantage."

"I never said that."

"You just have."

"How did I do that? I would never knowingly do that."

"That's simple enough. If you speak only English and the he or she you are talking to speaks English and Spanish, you are at a serious disadvantage."

Rearing back and pretending to be stunned by the assertion, he exclaimed: "How can that be if we both are speaking the very same language . . . English?" By the time he finished his sentence, he was near shouting on purpose. He wanted to drive home the point.

So you really want to give your competitor a definite advantage. Is that correct?"

"Is that a serious question?"

Ignoring the comment, Jordan Frost added:

"The point being might be . . . If we know how to penetrate or get inside something entirely foreign right here in the western hemisphere, we might be successful in using the same tool anywhere say like in the Middle East."

"Okay. That seems to make sense for the moment anyway."

"Good. So we might approach the question in the following manner."

"I'm listening," McCoy said.

"If we understand what's needed to probe Puerto Rico, a simple proposition compared to the Middle East, we may be prepared to take on something more complicated."

"I admit. That sounds reasonable so far. In other words this is a first step."

"Exactly . . ."

"Okay. I'm ready to listen. Go ahead."

"In order to solve Puerto Rico, one needs knowledge in three areas."

"And those three areas are . . ."

"As we've said before and I will repeat them."

"Good."

"They are language, culture and politics."

"And that's the third time you've said exactly the same thing. Aren't you pushing the obvious a little too far?"

"If it were that clear, I would agree totally."

"So it is not, according to you."

"No it is not."

"Okay. For now, we are in accord."

"So let's start with first things first. You mentioned language."

"Yes. To get along there, you need two languages, English and Spanish."

"But isn't this a U.S. connected island? Isn't English enough?"

"For that reason, English is very important. So is Spanish. It's the language of schools, the local court system and the language of the major political parties."

"So you're saying, I'm not going to grasp what Puerto Rico is all about without Spanish."

"That's exactly right. You can get by . . . granted. But you will be excluded from getting into and seeing reality on the ground level."

"You mentioned culture."

"Yes. I did. It's a mixture of Spain, the nearby Caribbean islands and Latin America in addition to the United States."

"That's a mouthful."

"Yes. Let's look at it this way. I believe it's the only place in the Western Hemisphere where one can look into the soul of Latin America and the United States at the same time."

"Why?"

"It is politically tied to the United States."

"Can you explain that a little more please?"

"Maybe a story will get us started."

"I'm listening." He braced himself for another repeat of the same old one.

"I once asked a businessman in Bogota, the capital of Colombia in South America, if he had the power of selection, who would be his choice for a U.S. ambassador to serve in his country."

"And what did he say?"

"I gave him two choices: one from Kansas City, Missouri, and the other from San Juan, Puerto Rico."

"What was his response?

"He first asked me if what I wanted to know was a serious question."

"And I said: 'yes.'"

"And he said . . ."

"Kansas City."

"I didn't believe what I was hearing. So I asked. Why?"

After a short pause, apparently needing to collect his thoughts, he said:

"That's an easy answer."

"Easy. I don't understand."

"We can manipulate him."

"We're talking about the man from Kansas City. Am I correct? I just want to be clear."

"Yes, of course."

"And that could not be possible with an ambassador say from San Juan?"

"That's right. It would not be. A Puerto Rican knows us from A to Z. In other words . . . NO manipulation there."

"So the reason for you telling the story again might be the following. By recognizing Puerto Rico in the way you have just described, we might be in a better position to crack the Middle East."

"Exactly . . . I couldn't have said it better myself."

"Let me put it another way. If we can identify a connecting link in the Middle East like Puerto Rico to Latin America, we might have a chance of penetrating.

"If we can penetrate, we'll be in a position to understand. If we understand, perhaps we can begin to solve some of those now seemingly unsolvable challenges.

"And if we penetrate . . . I mean really penetrate . . . we'll be in a better position to find the who, what and where behind the sinking of that ship just a few miles from here."

"I agree," McCoy said. "Part of our job will be getting this vital point across to the FBI and the CIA."

There was no need for Frost to respond.

Chapter Four

Once the Internet terrorist information was downloaded, Frost and McCoy got back to work on their own list.

"In order to move forward, we need a starting point, a kind of outline to follow," Frost said.

"And that point is . . ."

"Puerto Rico . . ."

"It was the same proposition offered the Washington intelligence community and what we covered earlier."

"I don't think we need to review the culture, language, politics and roots things again."

"No. If we don't understand that by now we never will."

"Agreed . . ."

*   *   *

"Here's where we want to look at first," Jordon Frost said.

Colt McCoy asked: "And what is that?"

"If we think the sinking of the ship near Puerto Rico may be related in some small or any way to the USS Cole attack, we should confirm or eliminate the point from consideration."

"Why?"

"According to the Central Intelligence Agency [CIA], Al Qaeda based in Afghanistan is likely to have been involved in the October 2000 bombing of the USS Cole in Aden, Yemen.

"This same group bombed U.S. embassies in Nairobi, Kenya, and Dar es Salaam, Tanzania, in August 1998. A total of 301 were killed and more than 5,000 injured."

Al Qaeda, he said, also claims to have shot down U.S. helicopters and killed U.S. servicemen in Somalia in 1993, and to have conducted three bombings that targeted U.S. troops in Aden, Yemen, in December 1992.

"Are they connected to other terrorist organizations?" Colt McCoy asked the question.

"Yes, Al Qaeda has cells in a number of countries and has ties to Sunni extremist networks."

"But bin Laden and his top associates are hidden away in Afghanistan. Is that correct?" McCoy wanted to know as much basic information as possible.

"Yes, it is."

"Osama bin Mohammed bin Awad bin Laden and top associates are believed to be based somewhere in the vast Hindu Kush mountain range and deep valleys of Afghanistan in Central Asia. Terrorist training camps also operate there."

"If you don't mind, tell me a little bit more about Afghanistan," McCoy said. "I know it exists and I can find it on the map. But admittedly, I'm a bit short after that."

Smiling, Frost said: "Afghanistan, approximately the size of Texas, is at an important geographical center. It is bordered on the extreme northeast by China, on the east and south by Pakistan, and by Iran on the west.

"While seemingly isolated, poor and insignificant, Afghanistan is part of a global conflict against world terrorism."

He added: "It's not the first time Afghanistan has attracted such attention."

"Really . . . I didn't know."

"Three wars were fought there between Britain and Russia during the 19th century.

"That was followed by the Cold War between the Soviet Union and the United States after World War II."

"What we're talking about now is more current. Is that correct?"

"Yes, that's true. Fierce popular resistance opposed the Soviet-backed Afghan government."

"Did you say 'popular resistance?' I don't understand."

"It's simply enough. A guerrilla force, called the Mujahideen, was an important factor in helping end Soviet occupation in Afghanistan in 1989."

*   *   *

"Can you tell me a little more about al-Qaeda and Osama bin Laden?"

"First in simple terms, al-Qaeda means 'the base' in the Arabic language. And from this base Osama bin Laden created an extremist and very dangerous network.

"Bin Laden did two things in Afghanistan.

"One, he reorganized Al-Qaeda and two, he did so in part by copying a tried and proven tactic used on more than one occasion by the Soviets."

The comment peaked McCoy's interest.

"As Al-Qaeda's leader and chief organizer, bin Laden invited Middle Eastern Muslims to defend fellow Muslims in Afghanistan."

"I'll ask perhaps a silly question. Did the tactic work?"

"Thousands volunteered. Does that answer your question?"

"Yes."

"And they—the volunteers—were called the MUJAHIDEEN or WARRIORS."

"I thought you said this was an old communist tactic? The term MUJAHIDEEN doesn't sound very Communist to me."

"Let's look at a little history."

"Okay."

"This kind of idea first surfaced in Moscow in September 1936. The Soviets asked international Communist Parties to recruit volunteers to fight in Spain."

"In Spain . . . I don't understand . . . Why Spain?"

"A Socialist leader, Francisco Largo Caballero, backed by Spain's Communist Party, was challenged by another Spaniard, a fascist."

"And he was . . ."

"General Francisco Franco. A stronger force was needed for a simple reason. Franco was supported by Germany's Adolf Hitler and Italy's Benito Mussolini.

"At the time, those volunteers were called INTERNATIONAL BRIGADES."

"I see."

"So instead of Muslim, as we are talking about now, they were communist volunteers."

"Yes."

"Did the invitation work?"

"An estimated 32,000 Communists from more than 50 nations including the United States fought in the Spanish Civil War between 1936 and 1939."

"I just want to be sure about something."

"Of course . . ."

"Were those two examples the only time this kind of volunteer strategy was used by the political left?"

"No. There was one other time and it was applied right here in the Western Hemisphere, a bit south of us."

"Really . . ."

"This same call for volunteer help was used during the early 1970s."

"Where . . . ?"

"It all happened in South America . . . in Chile to be exact."

"I didn't know. Either that or I have just forgotten."

Jordan Frost went on to explain what happened there.

"Thousands of Latin-American Communists flooded the country in support of leftist President Salvador Allende and close friend Fidel Castro, Cuba's Communist dictator. They were all volunteers.

"The announced intention at the time was to help convert Chile into a second Cuba."

"So how did all of this turn out?"

Laughing, he said, "Franco won in Spain and Chile's Army General Agosto Pinochet eliminated the communist threat and ended Allende's term of office on Sept 11, 1973."

"I see." He could not resist making another point. "So this was our first 9-11 . . . an early indicator of things to come."

"Yes, it was just that. Now we are dealing with a similar situation all over again. We can only hope and pray our investigation will end forever this kind of volunteer terrorism."

"I've got another question."

"Shoot."

"Just how important . . . or how dangerous . . . is this terrorist organization?"

"Let's put it this way. After 9-11 in New York City, al-Qaeda became the world's most threatening terrorist organization."

"That's quite a statement. Does that include the IRA and Hamas?"

"Without doubt . . ."

"So we are facing a very difficult task at best."

"Exactly . . ."

* * *

Jordon Frost and Colt McCoy decided to review how dangerous al-Qaeda sees itself.

"One thing is clear. It has been upfront about what it wants to accomplish."

McCoy asked. "What are you talking about exactly?"

"They want to destroy the West and Israel."

"How do we know that?"

"The organization declared a Holy War or Jihad against the West and Israel on Feb. 23, 1998.

"It's important to note," Frost said, "that Jihad or Jihadism is at odds with nearly all Islamic religious thought."

"What's your point?"

"We just can't lump all Muslims and believers of Islam into the same al-Qaeda package."

"I see what you mean. That would be very, very dangerous."

"It would be without doubt. Bin Laden would be more than happy if we all thought that way."

*   *   *

"What comes next?"

"The [Holy War] declaration was signed by Osama bin Laden, head of al-Qaeda; Ayman al-Zawahiri, head of Jihad Group in Egypt; and three other Islamic terrorist leaders."

"Besides their names, do we know more about these people?"

"Yes. Ayman al-Zawahiri merged his organization with al-Qaeda at the time this statement was announced and he likely wrote the declaration.

"Described publically as a bin Laden lieutenant, he is second in command but he could be described as co-leader."

"Why?"

"Besides being a qualified surgeon, he is an Islamic scholar and like bin Laden is a member of an Egyptian upper class family. He joined the country's Islamist movement in the late 1970s.

"He and not bin Laden is thought to be the brains for the movement. And saying this again because it's worth repeating these two important bits of information, he is an Islamic scholar and a qualified surgeon."

"Do we know anything more about this man?"

"Yes. Here is a very significant and important point."

"I'm listening."

"His terrorist credentials jumped considerably on October 5, 1981," the day Egypt's president Anwar Sadat was assassinated.

"How was that possible?"

"He was involved in the Sadat shooting death. After conviction, he served three years in jail."

"We are indeed dealing with a very dangerous man."

"Yes we are," and the other three signers were:

1. The Egyptian Refa'i Ahmed Taha or Refa'i Ahmed Taha Musa or Ahmed Refa'i Taha, alias Abu Yasser al-Masri and successor of "The Blind Sheikh" Omar Abdel-Rahman following his arrest in 1993 and imprisonment for life two years later in the United States.

    "He was named as an unindicted co-conspirator in the current indictment of 21 members of al-Qaeda and affiliated groups for their role in the 1998 bombings of U.S. embassies in Africa."

2. Sheikh Mir Hamzah, secretary of the Jamiarul-Ulema-e-Pakistan; and

3. Fazlul Rahman, leader of the Jihad Movement in Bangladesh.

In part the HOLY WAR declaration said:

"Praise be to God, who revealed the Book, controls the clouds, defeats factionalism, and says in His Book: "But when the forbidden months are past, then fight and slay the pagans wherever ye find them, seize them, beleaguer them, and lie in wait for them in every stratagem (of war)"; "and peace be upon our Prophet, Muhammad Bin-'Abdallah, who said: I have been sent with the sword between my hands to ensure that no one but God is worshipped, God who put my livelihood under the shadow of my spear and who inflicts humiliation and scorn on those who disobey my orders."

Such action was needed because:

"First, for over seven years the United States has been occupying the lands of Islam in the holiest of places, the Arabian Peninsula, plundering its riches, dictating to its rulers, humiliating its people, terrorizing its neighbors, and turning its bases in the Peninsula into a spearhead through which to fight the neighboring Muslim peoples.

"Second, despite the great devastation inflicted on the Iraqi people by the CRUSADER-Zionist alliance, and despite the huge number of those killed, which has exceeded one million . . . despite all this, the Americans are once again trying to repeat these horrific massacres, as though they are not content with the protracted blockade imposed after the ferocious war or the fragmentation and devastation.

"Third, if the Americans' aims behind these wars are religious and economic, the aim is also to serve the Jews' petty state and divert attention from its occupation of Jerusalem and murder of Muslims there. The best proof of this is their eagerness to destroy Iraq, the strongest neighboring Arab state, and their endeavor to fragment all the states of the region such as Iraq, Saudi Arabia, Egypt, and Sudan into paper state lets. If done this would guarantee Israel's survival and the continuation of the brutal occupation of the Peninsula.

"All these crimes and sins committed by the Americans are a clear declaration of war on God, his messenger, and Muslims.

"On that basis, and in compliance with God's order, we issue the following fatwa to all Muslims:

"The ruling to kill the Americans and their allies—civilians and military—is an individual duty FOR EVERY MUSLIM who can do it in any country in which it is possible to do it, in order to liberate the al-Aqsa Mosque and the holy mosque [Mecca] from their grip, and in order for their armies to move out of all the lands of Islam, they are to be defeated and thus unable to threaten any Muslim.

"We—with God's help—CALL ON EVERY MUSLIM who believes in God and wishes to be rewarded to comply with God's order to KILL THE AMERICANS and PLUNDER THEIR MONEY wherever and whenever they find it.

"We also call on the Muslim Ulema [scholars trained in Islam and Islamic law], leaders, youths, and soldiers to launch the raid on Satan's U.S. troops and the devil's supporters allying with them, and to displace those who are behind them so that they may learn a lesson."

*　　*　　*

Once announced, Osama bin Laden became the prime financial backer for al-Qaeda to recruit Muslims from mosques around the world.

At the beginning of his struggle against the West, bin Laden ran al-Qaeda in Khartoum, Sudan. But after being expelled from there in 1994, bin Laden moved to Afghanistan.

There he was the "guest" of the Taliban until driven from power by the United States in November 2001. Al-Qaeda set up terrorist training camps in the war-torn nation, as it had in Sudan.

*　　*　　*

"It's important to note, al-Qaeda operates as if it were a business franchise," Frost said.

"What does that mean exactly?"

"Besides acquiring name recognition, any terrorist operation adopting the al-Qaeda name could get financial and logistical support. Or even without direct support, they can act in the name of al-Qaeda.

"And they [al-Qaeda] operate in places like the Philippines, Algeria, Eritrea, Afghanistan, Chechnya, Tajikistan, Somalia, Yemen, and Kashmir.

"Al-Qaeda and their followers embrace "jihadism."

"And what does that mean exactly?"

"In short, it is a willingness to kill any 'apostate' or anyone who rejects their point of view."

"Is that a belief shared by all Muslims? I know we discussed this earlier. I bring it up again. I just think we should be very clear about what we are talking about as we get deeper into this investigation."

"That's a good point. I agree."

"So what's your answer?"

"No it is not. Jihadism is at odds with nearly all Islamic religious thought."

"If that's true, who specifically supports that kind of thinking?"

"Two so-called modern Sunni Islamic thinkers stand at the front of the line."

"And they are . . ."

"Mohammad ibn Abd al-Wahhab and Sayyid Qutb."

"Can you explain further?"

"Al-Wahhab was an 18th-century reformer who claimed Islam was corrupted after the death of Mohammed. In doing so, he rejected more than 1,000 years of religious scholarship. In short, he called any theology or customs developed after that time as non-Islamic."

"That's rather strong talk."

"Yes, it is."

"Where is this kind of thinking practiced?"

"It's done in Saudi Arabia primarily. And there 'Wahhabism' as it is called remains the dominant school of religious thought."

"You said there was a second so-called reformer."

"Yes, I did. He is Sayyid Qutb, who surfaced not that long ago."

"And what did he say or do?"

"A known radical Egyptian scholar pronounced Western civilization as Islam's number one enemy."

"Did he stop there?"

"No, he did not. There is a lot more. He charged leaders of all Muslim nations had failed to properly identify the enemy or recognize it."

"So what did he suggest they do?"

"His words were clear and simple. They had to get their heads straight so to speak and actively accept JIHAD. And most importantly, they had to be ready and willing to apply it."

"Can you define that further please?"

"Yes. Jihad should be used in two ways. One is to defend and two is to purify."

"So in his view, the proper application of JIHAD is the only way to defeat the enemy or the West."

"Yes, of course."

*   *   *

"This may be silly but I have to ask. Is there more?"

"As a matter of fact, there is one more point to remember?'

"Just one . . . ?"

Laughing he said: "Maybe."

"Okay, I'm ready."

"Al-Qaeda also serves as an umbrella organization for a worldwide terrorist network that includes many Sunni Islamic extremist groups, such as Egyptian Islamic Jihad, some members of al-Gama'at al-Islamiyya, the Islamic Movement of Uzbekistan, and the Harakat ul-Mujahidin."

"And tell me one more time. Who is bin Laden?"

"What we have here is typical of many political movements. Their leaders are many times rich and connected to families with influence."

"If you have a point, what is it?"

"Too many times, they end up thinking they're smarter than anyone one else in the world, barring none."

"Why?

"That's easy. And here is an example. If their family has power and wealth at the same time, they think they are smarter politically than anyone else."

"Do they think that way even if they have no political or religious experience at all?"

"They do. It doesn't matter. They believe most sincerely they can be capable in any area including politics and even Islam because of wealth and power."

"So that means they believe they are capable of operating anywhere in the world and can accomplish anything even without exact or hands on knowledge."

"Yes."

"Is there anything else I need to know?"

"Yes, one more but important point."

"Just one . . . ?"

"Yes, for the moment, just one."

"Okay, let's hear it."

"On the basis of what you have just said, they can place themselves as an equal or even above God himself. In this case, I'm talking about Mohammed and Allah."

"As stupid as this may sound to you or anyone else, the answer is 'yes.'"

"So briefly, what do we have and where do we go from here?"

"We have the son of a rich Saudi family who thinks he has a brilliant political idea. In his mind, he can put his plan and philosophy into play for a very simple reason."

"I think I know what you're going to say but I can't or will not believe it."

"Believe it. He thinks he is intellectually and spiritually ahead of anyone based on his family pocketbook not his mental or religious capability."

"Is his family money the only stable source of income?"

"No. His basic inheritance is used to finance Al Qaeda, the base organization. From there, Al Qaeda operates money-making front organizations, solicits donations and illicitly siphons funds from donations to Muslim charitable organizations."

"So what we have here is a misguided rich kid, causing a lot of mischief and real damage."

"That's one way of putting it."

*   *   *

"I still want to know more about bin Laden. You've given me bits and pieces. I would like, if possible, to have a complete package."

Chapter Five

Jordon Frost started the explanation. Colt McCoy listened and asked questions.

"Bin Laden was born and raised in Saudi Arabia, a Middle Eastern country that occupies most of the Arabian Peninsula, east of the Red Sea and the Gulf of Aqaba and west of the Persian Gulf."

"I understand there is a lot of sand there. Is that correct?"

"Yes, the Arabian Desert is called the world's largest sand desert and most of it is located in Saudi Arabia. It extends into Egypt, southern Iraq and southern Jordan."

*   *   *

McCoy insisted. "I want to hear more about bin Laden himself."

"Fine . . ."

Frost provided general background.

"Born in Riyadh, the capital of Saudi Arabia, Osama bin Mohammed bin Awad bin Laden or Osama bin Laden was the son of Mohammed bin Awad bin Laden, a wealthy businessman.

"His mother, Hamida al-Attas, was Mohammed bin Laden's tenth wife, Hamida al-Attas. Mohammed bin Laden divorced Hamida soon after Osama bin Laden was born."

"That was quick. So what happened next?"

"Interestingly enough Mohammed made an incredidble switch."

"This I've got to hear."

"He passed her off to an associate, Mohammed al-Attas."

"And he accepted that?"

"He did. Al-Attas married Hamida in the late 1950s or early 1960s. The exact date is not known."

"So what happened? Did the associate get rid of her after awhile?"

"No. They are still together."

"Anything else . . . ?"

"The couple had four children."

"So what happened to bin Laden?"

"Simply put, he lived in the new household with three half-brothers and a half-sister."

"I understand bin Laden was wealthy. Where did he get his money? Did he work for it or what?"

"Good question."

"I'm listening."

"Bin Laden got it from his real father. In all, he inherited between $25 million and $30 million. His father's construction business was worth an estimated $5 billion.

*   *   *

"With that out of way, I want to know something else."

"And what is that?" Frost asked.

"I want to know about his religious beliefs. And I want to know who he believed in . . . Allah, God or what?"

Frost answered the question this way:

"Osama bin Laden was from the start and remained a devout Wahhabi Muslim until this death," Frost said. "In other words, bin Laden was driven by what is known as Islam's Wahhabi Doctrine."

"The Wahhabi Doctrine . . . that's news to me. What does that mean exactly?"

"It was named for Muhammad ibn Abd al-Wahhab, the first modern Islamic fundamentalist and extremist. Born in 1703 and died in 1792, he was an Arab scholar who sought to return Islam to original thinking."

"What else do we know about this man?"

"Al-Wahhab made a name for himself by defining what he deemed correct Islamic thought. And that could be found only, he declared, in the original Koran dating back to the seventh century."

"And if something else was added, what was his position?"

"Any such ideas or new interpretations of the Koran would be declared false. And if declared false, they should be eliminated."

"In other words, according to Muhammad ibn Abd al-Wahhab, true Muslim belief started from the beginning and could not be progressively changed or added on to."

"Yes. And according to him, Islam's Wahhabi Doctrine is the only true reflection of Islam as favored by the Prophet Muhammad, Islam's founder."

"Can anything be added to that?"

"Yes, something very important."

"And what is that?"

"Anyone rejecting the Wahhabi Doctrine does not believe or does not follow Allah. In other words, they are not true Muslims."

"That sounds a little political to me."

"And it is . . ."

"How?"

"It all has to do with how one defines Muslims in a very key area."

"Where is that?"

"Simply put Muslims are forbidden to kill other Muslims."

"And that's according to Islamic law I presume."

"It is."

"So what changes?"

"The definition of a believer is changed."

"I don't understand."

"Here it is. Anyone not following Wahhabi Doctrine is a non believer. Once defined that way, Muslims or anyone else can be legally killed in war or during a terrorist attack."

"I want to be very clear on this point. Does that mean if a fellow Muslim dies under those circumstances, Wahhabi Doctrine followers will not be considered in violation of Islamic Law?"

"That's correct."

"So what does that mean for us and our investigation?"

"We must keep in mind at every step along the way of how much bin Laden was driven by Islam's Wahhabi Doctrine."

*   *   *

Frost added a general statement in an attempt to further clarify his point.

"Bin Laden favored Wahhabi Doctrine for a simple reason. It followed traditional Islamic law and it was the bringing together of government and religious belief.

"And Wahhabi Doctrine, as bin Laden understood it, was the only direct connection to the Prophet Muhammad, Islam's founder."

*   *   *

McCoy then asked Frost to provide, if he could, an example on how this government-religious philosophy was put into practice.

"Here is a quick answer. Bin Laden moved forward at a very rapid pace."

"What did he do exactly?"

"He combined his money and his Islamic belief to build a terrorist organization able to strike in any part of the world. And it was called al-Qaeda."

"And what did this terrorist group you call al-Qaeda do exactly?"

"Al-Qaeda organized and carried out the Twin Towers attack on Sept. 11, 2001 in New York City leaving an estimated 3,000 dead. And that's the group's big accomplishment to date."

McCoy added: "In other words, it was the kind of thing all non-believers living in Islamic states and, of course, all enemies of Islam in the WEST can and should expect."

"Yes."

*　　*　　*

McCoy wasn't finished with his questions.

"But the tide finally turned on Osama bin Laden," he said. "Is that correct?

"Yes."

"So what happened?"

"After New York, U.S. President George Bush declared a War on Terror and bin Laden was a major target. The Federal Bureau of Investigation [FBI] offered a $25 million reward for his capture after bin Laden was placed on the FBI's Most Wanted list."

"So what did that get us?"

"Bin Laden's end came May 2, 2011 in the Islamic Republic of Pakistan." A part of the Indian subcontinent, Pakistan is bordered by the Arabian Sea to the south, India to the east, Afghanistan to the north and China to the northeast.

Frost concluded by saying: "He was shot and killed by U.S. Navy SEALs and CIA operatives on the order of U.S. President Barack Obama."

Chapter Six

"Before moving a step further, I think we've got to define Islam, what it is and what it is not," Jordon Frost said.

Colt McCoy responded quickly: "That should be easy."

"Maybe not . . ."

"What is a good definition?"

"I'll make this as brief as I can."

"I'm listening."

"We have to divide this into two parts: one, militant extremists; and two, the large majority."

"Is it that easy? All we have to do is divide Islam by two?"

"Actually, it's a bit more complicated than that. The large part has five divisions along the lines of Sharia or Islamic Law. And each section or division is headed by a strong man, a political leader."

"In other words, you are talking about a dictator."

"Yes."

"So we have a classic example of the fusion of political power and religion."

"Yes, of course. So we have an extremist strong man who thinks he is superior to the others, politically and spiritually. So his aim is to have all followers accept a single leader to guide them over all affairs having to do with Islam and to how to serve Allah best under a single definition of Sharia law."

"And his next step. What will it be?"

"That's an easy one. He will invoke the notion of JIHAD or military engagement by quoting the Koran again and again. It says: 'Those who die in battle for Islam more certainly will obtain Salvation when compared to others.'"

"And why would he say that?"

"In other words, those who die in battle have the greatest or perhaps best opportunity to be saved or gain the presence of Allah over the rank and file after death."

"What else do we know about these 'extremists' or what might be called 'fanatics.'"

"They consider themselves freedom fighters. If they are that, they believe themselves to be the primary carriers of all supreme ideological causes in Allah's service. Many believe, despite the many parts in the body of Islam, that this minority has reshaped everything important in the Middle East and North Africa."

"And how have they done that?"

"It's by what they believe will be accomplished in the future."

"What is that? I don't understand."

"This minority has had a degree of success in provoking a general anger against the WEST in general and against the United States in particular."

"How exactly did they do that?"

"By claiming the West and the United States are jointly responsible for what they call cultural invasion, economic exploitation, political oppression, military superiority and alleged imperialistic greed."

"That's a mouth full."

"And there is more."

"I'm listening."

"Much of this anger at the U.S. government is because of what they believe is our unconditional and excessive support of the state of Israel."

"WHY?"

"For devout Muslims, Jerusalem is an extremely important place. It is their third holiest city after Mecca and Al-Madina or Medina, both in Saudi Arabia."

"And for them it's not an open place to visit like Mecca and Medina."

"That's correct."

"And why are they having success, if any, in pushing arguments like that?"

"It's one of the main ways they have of deflecting or attempting to deflect criticism for not providing more opportunity for their people."

"Their people . . . ?"

"Largely they have little or nothing. So it's easier to convince them to resent the level of materialism, hedonism and affluent consumption of those who "have a lot and plenty.""

"Does that stop there?"

"No. They also attempt to equate Christianity with the WEST. One way of doing that is bringing up the Crusades, which they believe was an invasion of the Arabic region and the Muslim world."

"Is there more?"

"There is another button to push: they harp on what they call corrupt lifestyles, products, items, and movies of the WEST shown in the Middle East."

"So that completes the circle?"

"There is something else, and its importance can never be overlooked."

"And that is . . ."

"They [the extremists] are willing to link up with any political group of like thinking to achieve victory."

"What does that mean exactly?"

"It means these people are really dangerous and are very hard to track."

"So that means we have our work cut out for us."

"Yes. So let's get to work going over this information. We can't waste any more time."

Chapter Seven

With Islam out of the way for way for now, Colt McCoy made the following suggestion:

"We've got a lot of bits and pieces of what happened to our cruise ship," 'The Caribbean.' "Why don't we try to put everything together as much as we know and go from there?"

"I agree," said Jordan Frost.

The desk top of their San Juan office was a mess. It was covered with maps, Coast Guard reports, the ship's design, photographs of the sunken vessel and no telling what else.

Maybe it could be cleared once their investigation had an organized direction. That was likely an impossible dream.

Here is what they said they knew:

Two brothers, Bruce and William Younger, owned three hotels, two in Florida and a third in Puerto Rico. In 1966, they decided to expand the business by acquiring a single cruise ship, 'The Caribbean'.

If successful, they planned to add a new ship annually. They reasoned those same businessmen and tourists staying in their hotels should be given a Caribbean cruise opportunity or option. The ship had scheduled stops in Haiti, the Dominican Republic, Puerto Rico, St. Martin, Guadeloupe and Martinique.

But unfortunately for them, the cruise ship part of the business began to lose money almost immediately. It was a plan, at least for them, that didn't work out.

So Instead of heading into bankruptcy in January 2001, they elected to lease the vessel to a company headquartered in Tortola, the British Virgin Islands. It was incorporated there as `Ships Inc.'

"And did it show a profit?" Jordan Frost asked.

McCoy answered: "It did . . . right from the start."

"Maybe if we can learn why the company made such a quick turnaround, we'll be in a better position to know `the why' of what sent their ship to the bottom of the Atlantic."

"Why? One could argue those who leased from the Younger brothers knew more about the cruise business."

"Perhaps, but perhaps not . . ."

"I don't understand."

"Right now, we need a basic assumption touched by reality. In other words, in order for us to move ahead and quickly, we should have a proven starting point."

"What have you seen or discovered to bring on such a statement?"

"You're right. There is something and it is a name . . . Francisco de Jesus."

"And where did you find or discover this name, Francisco de Jesus?"

"His name and signature was on company papers filed in the British Virgin Islands or the BVI."

"So what's so significant about that?"

"His is the only Hispanic name on the list."

"So? We live in the Caribbean surrounded by Spanish names and speakers."

"I did a little independent research."

"And you found what?"

"Francisco de Jesus was born in Spain and raised in Caracas, Venezuela."

"And you believe that means something?"

"Frankly, I don't know yet. I just think we should keep his name in mind. As we know more, we could find out more about Senor de Jesus."

*   *   *

Jordan Frost thought another direction might provide more information for now. "Let's examine other ships that sunk or nearly went down to determine possible links with what happened to 'The Caribbean.'"

Frost described what happened to the U. S. Navy destroyer USS Cole [DDG 67] anchored inside the North African port of Aden in Yemen on Oct. 12, 2000.

In short, the 630-foot long ship was struck with a shape bomb carried on a red rubber motor launch.

The suicide attack organized and planned by al-Qaeda left 17 sailors and two suicide attackers dead and 39 injured. It was the deadliest against a U.S. Naval vessel in 13 years. The USS Stark (FFG-31) was the victim of a 1987 attack in Iraq.

"Just to be clear in our own minds, do you believe the sinking of 'The Caribbean' and the bombing of the USS Cole is part of a general attack against the WEST?

"By that I mean Europe, Israel and the United States."

It was the same question Frost and McCoy had brought up earlier. They wanted to cover it again now as it would probably be considered again later in an attempt to better frame their investigation.

Frost provided a simple clear answer with no hesitation based on his gut feeling and what he believed at that moment their investigation was likely to conclude.

"Yes I do."

He then asked McCoy: "Was there doubt in your mind?"

"None at all . . ."

It was not the first or second time Al-Qaeda had been involved in such a dare-devil attack. The terrorist organization had taken responsibility for the 1993 World Trade Center bombing in New York City, a series of 1998 U.S. embassy bombings and the Sept. 11, 2001 attack in New York City.

"What makes you think the sinking of 'The Caribbean' and the bombing of the USS Cole could be linked?"

"Think about this," Frost said. "Before the Younger brothers acquired the vessel, the ship was used to evacuate families of British servicemen out of Israel to Cairo on June 1, 1967."

"So why do that? I'm talking about the evacuation."

"They [the families] were about to be caught up in the Six Day War."

"By Six Day War, do you mean the war fought in June of 1967?"

"Yes. It's sometimes called the 1967 Arab-Israeli War, the Third Arab-Israeli War or the June War."

"And the Arabs were . . ."

"The neighboring states of Egypt, Jordan, and Syria attacked Israel. It's worth noting Algeria, Morocco, Iraq, Saudi Arabia, Sudan and Tunisia contributed troops and arms."

"And who won?"

"Let's put it this way. Israel ended up with large tracts of Arab territory: Sinai Peninsula, the Gaza Strip, the West Bank, East Jerusalem, and the Golan Heights. The idea at the time was to destroy the Jewish state."

"And that failed!"

"Yes it did, big time."

"So one can most certainly assume those Arab countries have never recovered from such a dramatic and emotional political reverse. They more than likely thought it would be a push over."

"Yes."

"So the sinking of 'The Caribbean' was a payback for a long-ago past deed? Is that what you're saying?"

"Maybe, maybe not . . . We need an answer."

"What could that response be?"

"I think our investigation could show a direct link between the Cole and 'The Caribbean.' Maybe the same people are responsible."

"And if so, regional geopolitical conflicts of that period are alive and well to this day."

"If they attacked New York City, why couldn't they do the same to a ship near Puerto Rico?"

*   *   *

"Now let's move to another part of the U.S. Coast Guard's report," Frost said. "It could demonstrate the global picture of terror is much larger than we dared think and much more sophisticated than we would want to know or even to admit."

"Okay."

"We know 900 passengers died."

"Yes, we do."

"Two hundred more bodies have been found and they remain unidentified."

"There is no record of them anywhere?"

"No."

"So what do you think this might mean? Could it mean more income for someone?"

"Could be . . . but for who and what for?"

"Just off hand, I'd put bin Laden and al-Qaeda at the top of the list."

"My first reaction is to agree."

"But . . ."

"We're talking about a ship sinking near Puerto Rico. That's a long way from Afghanistan, bin Laden's home at the time."

"Again I repeat. If they organized an attack against New York City on Sept. 11, 2001, sinking a ship near here would be duck soup for that kind of mentality."

"Okay. I get the picture. We've got a lot of ground to cover."

"Yes.'

"No argument there."

"Before moving further ahead, those bodies need to be identified. Once done, we can begin to move forward."

"Agreed . . ."

*   *   *

Within two weeks they learned those unidentified bodies were mostly young women and children bound for Morocco where they were to be sold into slavery in other parts of Africa.

"Who were these women?"

"They were to be prostitutes."

"And the children . . ."

"Most likely they would have been killed later for their body parts."

"That kind of business makes money."

"Yes and lots of it, unfortunately."

"So what do you think? Did the Younger brothers benefit? Did they lease the vessel with human trafficking in mind?"

Frost didn't attempt to answer the questions at that time. Instead, he said: "There's one other thing."

"And that is . . ."

"A large amount of refined, high grade cocaine was also found aboard the sunken ship."

"So if slaves were headed for Africa, the drugs were headed for Spain and the rest of Europe."

"I think so . . . most likely."

"We now have a rather good idea of what happened to 'The Caribbean.' Or at least we think we do unless proved wrong at some point down the line."

Even though their investigation was far from complete, they agreed they should provide the U.S. President a summary of their findings to date.

*   *   *

"Mr. President, here is a very preliminary report," said Jordan Frost during a computer-visual telephone call. Colt McCoy sat beside Frost ready to provide additional information or comment if needed.

"Based on our examination of the U.S. Coast Guard's report here in San Juan and our own preliminary conclusions, we believe the following is likely."

McCoy nodded in agreement.

They told the president the sinking of `The Caribbean' was probably not an isolated event. "It seems to be part of a larger world-wide terrorist attack pattern," Frost said.

"Can you provide any more detail at this time?" the president asked.

"Let me say this Mr. President, we believe this explosion was most likely planned by organizers of the USS Cole bombing and the Sept. 11, 2001 attack in New York City."

The assessment was greeted with a long moment of silence.

"Mr. Frost, Mr. McCoy . . . are you absolutely sure?"

"We are not 100 percent sure of anything at this point. As we told you at the beginning, this is a very preliminary report."

"I see."

"Despite our lack of clear proof, Mr. McCoy and I feel it is our duty to give you our best assessment.

"Why is that?"

"Because as you so eloquently instructed us in Washington, our `time is short'. In fact, it's very short."

"I remember," he said. "Time is still short. But don't call us again until you have something concrete to report."

"We understand, Mr. President."

With that the conversation was over.

"So what do you think?" McCoy asked.

"I think we have brought ourselves some time. Obviously, his entire investigation team is working on this. So from now on, we'll move forward at our own pace until we have something concrete."

"As far as I'm concerned that's very good thinking."

"I thought you might agree."

*　　*　　*

"To get to the heart of this part of the investigation," Jordan Frost said, "we have to know the business history behind the sinking. Without that, we can't begin to put together the parts."

"If that's true, where do we start?" Colt McCoy asked.

"We need to know what it is exactly, how it expanded and why."

"I'll now ask what may be another one of my silly questions."

"But you'll ask it anyway . . . right?"

"That's Right! . . . You are absolutely correct."

"So?"

"Why do we need to do all of that?"

"If we don't . . . we'll never find answers."

"Okay. Let's get started."

*   *   *

"Do we know how to contact the ship's owners?"

"And they are . . ."

"The Younger brothers . . ."

"I don't think that will be a problem."

"Okay, let's do that. Yesterday would not be too soon."

"I understand."

After running an Internet search, Colt McCoy found that their Main office is in Kansas City, Missouri. They have two smaller ones in the Caribbean, one in San Juan, Puerto Rico; and the other in Tortola, in the British Virgin Islands.

"We're really in luck. I called Kansas City and learned William Younger is currently in San Juan. And I reached him and we have an appointment with Mr. Younger in two hours."

"You are indeed a miracle worker."

"Thanks. Let's get moving. I don't think we want to be late."

"No we don't."

*   *   *

William Younger was a pleasant man, who was they guessed to be six-feet-two inches tall. His black hair was beginning to show grey streaks. And he'd obviously been coming to the Caribbean long enough to know when to ditch a white shirt, tie and jacket for a guayabera.

Popular in Latin America, the Caribbean and Puerto Rico, the guayabera or shirt has two or four patch pockets in front and two vertical rows of tiny pleats running along the front and back of the garment.

After spending a few moments exchanging pleasantries, their conversation turned more serious.

"So what can I do for you?" William Younger asked.

Jordon Frost picked up immediately on the question. "We want to know your management role in the running of the cruise ship, 'The Caribbean.'"

"That is a question that may or not be any of your business. I think I need to know a little more about you first."

Colt McCoy jumped in quickly and gave him brief summary of their interest and listed credentials.

"Again . . . I don't want to be rude by seemingly cutting you off short. But, frankly I don't know you and my brother and I have just lost a very important part of our business."

"So what do you suggest?" Jordon asked. He attempted perhaps badly to cover his irritation with the response.

"I've got to check you out first. If you are who you claim to be . . . we'll meet again at 10 a.m. tomorrow. My secretary will call you if the meeting is off." He asked for their telephone number and they supplied it.

Later that day they received a confirmation call. The meeting was on.

Frost and McCoy showed up at Mr. Younger's office promptly at 10 o'clock the next morning. His secretary welcomed and said without hesitation: "Please be seated. Mr. Younger will see you shortly."

Within two minutes, William Younger came out of his office and said: "Please come in gentlemen."

After being seated, Younger said: "I see you identified yourselves correctly. I'm particularly impressed on one point."

Frost asked: "Do you mind expanding on what you mean?"

"You have direct contact with President North."

Without bothering to ask how he knew that, Frost restated the question he had asked 24 hours earlier.

"We want to know your management role in the running of the cruise ship, 'The Caribbean.'" He didn't bother to mention what had happened to it near Puerto Rico.

"We own the cruise ship and we plan to buy another one shortly, if possible."

"Can you tell us who currently runs, manages or who is the ship's captain?"

Laughing quietly for a moment, he asked: "Don't you know?"

McCoy was puzzled by the question. "Don't we know what?"

"The owners and directors were among the 900 dead."

"They what . . . ?" Frost asked. The statement took him and his partner by complete surprise.

Again Mr. Younger repeated what he had just said: "The owners and directors were among the 900 dead. To be clear, my brother and I are investors . . . nothing more."

"And you know that how?" McCoy asked. "I'm talking about the owners and directors being fatalities and that they were aboard the exploding ship."

"We just got word from the U.S. Coast Guard yesterday shortly after noon."

"I see."

"Did they [the Coast Guard] tell you anything else?"

"Should they have?"

"I'm asking you."

"You'll have to be more specific than that."

"What kind of cargo was aboard 'The Caribbean?'"

"It was a cruise ship until a few days ago. The passengers were tourists."

"There were other bodies found aboard belonging to women and children. They were not tourists."

"I was as shocked by that information as I'm sure you two gentlemen must have been."

"What does that mean?"

"It means I know no more than that."

McCoy added: "Why was the company [Ships Inc.] based in the British Virgin Islands?"

"As far as I know, it was a business decision. That's where the company wanted to be headquartered. My brother and I had nothing to do with that."

"I suppose the Coast Guard will tell you later if they learn more. In the meantime, I wonder if you would be kind enough to supply us with the names of those dead officials who went down with the Caribbean."

"Yes, of course." Reaching into his desk, he got an envelope.

Handing it to them, he said: "Here are their names, titles and where they lived."

"Thank you."

"Those same names are listed in the British Virgin Islands Tortola office."

Frost accepted the envelope and opened it so both he and McCoy could view the list at the same time. It read:

1.   Manuel Santos Espinosa, President, Caracas, Venezuela.

2.   Ismael Torres Torres, Vice President, Bogota, Colombia.

3.   Carlos Jose Rodriquez Aguilar, Treasurer, Panama City, Panama.

"I see these men are all from the same general area of South America. What does that mean if anything?"

"It means exactly what is says. They are residents of Bogota, Caracas and Panama City."

Frost's questioning was more pointed this time. "Were the dead women and children slaves?"

"I guess next question could be if they were part of a criminal drug and illegal arms ring. And of course, money laundering could be added to the mix."

"For now, let's stick to the African slave trade part."

Taking on a more critical tone of voice, Younger asked:

"Why would you even suggest such a ridiculous possibility? I was under the impression you were serious people and that folks like yourselves would ask smart questions not dumb ones."

"Mr. Younger . . . this is a very serious question," Frost said. Turning to his bag, he pulled out a world map and placed it on a table separating them.

"Would you be kind enough to point out the tourist stops made by 'The Caribbean?'"

"Frankly, I must say I don't know. I don't or didn't follow their business decisions that closely. My brother and I were primarily interested in whether or not the ship's business was turning a profit or a loss."

McCoy said: "Let us help you then. They had scheduled stops here, here and here." With his finger, he pointed to:

1. Caracas, Venezuela.

2. San Juan, Puerto Rico

3. Cap Haitien, Haiti

4. Las Palmas, Canary Islands

5. Rabat, Morocco

6. Algiers, Algeria

7. Barcelona, Spain.

Suddenly, Mr. Younger said: "I see no need to carry this conversation further."

"We will return, sir. I can assure you that."

* * *

As they left the Younger office, Frost told McCoy:

"Even after the fall of the [Berlin] wall in 1989, there were many who bought the illusion that everything was better now, that the story was over. 'Dreams are the guardians of sleep,'" said Freud. "We incorporate anything that might disturb our sleep into our dreams so that we don't have to wake up. There are many guardians of sleep. The thinker's task is to fight against them."

In response, McCoy said: "I guess that means you think we don't live in better times."

"As bad as I hate to admit it, we don't."

Chapter Eight

After their interview had concluded, Jordon Frost and Colt McCoy regrouped and attempted to refocus.

Trying not to dwell on how little William Younger had given them, they had hoped he would have provided a lead to work on. They knew, however, he would be given another chance at some future time.

Needing something substantial to act on before any reliable answers could be found, they realized their only hope at this point would be to start again from scratch.

*   *   *

Frost started out by reviewing conclusions they believed to be fact.

"For better or worse, this is a mix of religious belief and politics," he said.

McCoy asked . . ."So where do you suggest we go?"

"Let's begin with the religious part first."

"So you believe it's absolutely necessary to begin there before moving forward?"

"Unfortunately, yes. Why? In general terms, any political discussion usually does not cover the spiritual and it should."

"I can't argue with that. So where do we begin?"

"If we believe our thought process starts with our view and our belief in God, we may be in better position to understand the enemy or the adversary if he or she says they are doing the same thing only better."

"So that means we should review who and why we are Southern Baptists."

"Of course . . . Number one on such a list is our belief in God. Number two is why we are Southern Baptists and why we are members of the Southern Baptist Convention [SBC].

"Yes."

"We're spiritually conservative or traditional. In other words we believe the Bible is the inerrant word of God or that it was written without error. Everything else comes from there."

"And that means?"

"It's simple enough."

"Okay."

"First and foremost, it's our relationship with God. Once we accept Jesus Christ as Savior, our relationship is permanent. And we believe in the Great Commission, which means God's word should be spread to all peoples regardless of where they live."

"And we are members of the Southern Baptist Convention [SBC]."

"Yes. What does that mean exactly?"

"The SBC is the largest U.S. Christian denomination and the world's largest Baptist denomination."

"Is that all?"

"No. The SBC has 42,000 autonomous churches with 16 million members spread over all 50 states and the U.S. Commonwealth of Puerto Rico."

"I didn't know."

"Those members use their belief as the basis for all logic. In other words, God makes it possible for us to relax in that knowledge. When we do that we are in the best position possible to examine information and find answers."

"You might add there was an attempt recently to push the SBC away from that kind of base. If it had been accepted, our thought process would have moved to the left or in a more moderate or liberal direction."

"Yes, that's true."

"And when did that happen? And why did it happen?"

"Such an attempt was turned back between 1980 and 1990. And many refer to what took place as the most profound and significant course correction in the history of American Christianity."

"Why do you say that?"

"It was what happened and the way such a correction was brought about."

"I guess you mean change resulted after a hard and fast power play."

"No, that's not what happened at all."

"I'm listening."

"It was a long, slow application of Baptist polity by Baptist people working to address a Baptist challenge in a Baptist way."

"Why or how did the process start?"

"It all started when grassroots SBC churches grew concerned about the leftward theological drift of Convention institutions."

"Can you give me an example? One or two will be fine."

"I'll give you two from Texas. There are more."

"Two will be fine."

"And that has to do with two prominent institutions: Southwestern Baptist Theological Seminary in Fort Worth and Baylor University in Waco."

"If possible can a label be placed on what happened?"

"Some have called it a 'Conservative Resurgence' and I agree."

"And what does that mean exactly?"

"Those Institutions and others were drifting to the left. The idea was to anchor them firmly in historic Baptist theology."

"Can we back up a little bit. You mentioned all of this covered a 10-year period starting in 1980. Exactly what did happen?"

"Maybe this is the best way of saying it."

"Okay."

"SBC Convention messengers or representatives of local churches decided on a strategy to bring those institutions back on course during annual conventions."

"Why?"

"Here is what one of those participating in that long process concluded:

"A convention of fifteen million people had been managed and controlled, not by its membership or even by one thousand trustees, but by a very small handful of paid employees combined with a few elected officers of the various boards and commissions."

"Who said that?"

"Judge Paul Pressler did in his book, 'A Hill on Which to Die,' or 'One Southern Baptist's Journey.' The quote can be found at the bottom of page 175 and on the top of page 176."

"And the strategy was . . ."

"Put conservatives on SBC committees to bring about change."

"Why do that?"

"It was believed to be the best way to avoid open conflict. That's about as simple as I can put it."

"And conservatives won all the votes during that period. Is that what you are saying?"

"Yes, I am."

"I see."

"After winning 10 consecutive Southern Baptist Convention [SBC] assembly votes, the eleventh and most significant came during the 1990 New Orleans SBC Convention."

"I'm listening."

"Dr. Morris Chapman, pastor of the 7,700-member First Baptist Church of Wichita Falls, Texas, was elected to the first of two one-year terms as SBC president."

"Why was this crucial?"

"Doctor Chapman scored a significant victory over the moderate candidate, the Rev. Dr. Daniel Vestal, pastor of the Dunwoody Baptist Church of Atlanta, Ga."

"Significant? What does that mean?"

"Chapman won 57 percent of the vote compared to 43 percent for Vestal," he said. "A 14 percent margin is in my view at the very least overwhelming."

"What happened next?"

"These people weren't satisfied with just winning."

"They weren't? Can you explain exactly what you mean by not being 'satisfied with just winning' the vote."

"They went a step further. A Peace Committee was named in an attempt to bring both sides together."

"So what happened?"

"One Peace Committee member, Cecil Sherman, called the process 'unacceptable'."

"Was this committee open, democratic and above board?"

"Yes."

"So what did he do?"

"He resigned in early 1992."

"And that was it?"

"No. He helped organize what is now known as the Cooperative Baptist Fellowship [CBF]. And immediately he was named the CBF's national coordinator."

"So what happened next?"

"Something very interesting did occur but it was not surprising."

"And that was . . ."

"Daniel Vestal was named CBF executive director."

"And he was the one defeated by Morris Chapman during that historic 1990 SBC vote."

"Yes."

"I have one other question."

"Okay."

"I understand why the CBF was created, but do we know how their leaders feel today after their position had been turned aside time and time again over an 11-year period."

"Yes, we do."

"I'm listening."

"Immediately following the final vote, Baylor President Herbert H Reynolds refused to take SBC telephone calls. At the same time, he sought and changed the school's charter in 1990 to limit Baptist General Convention of Texas control of the university.

"And former Southwestern Seminary president, Russell H. Dilday, in his book, "Glimpses of a Seminary Under Assault;" and four prominent CBF members, writers of a second book entitled: 'The Fundamentalist Takeover in the Southern Baptist Convention [SBC],' share a similar conclusion:

"The SBC now can be compared to ISLAMIC EXTREMISM" or to those responsible for the World Trade Center Sept. 11, 2001 attack in New York City.

"So that means they didn't react very well to a democratic process."

"Unfortunately, you are more than correct."

*   *   *

"We're covered the SBC. Now what comes next?"

"We have to know something about two more parts of the puzzle, if we can call it that."

"Is that all . . . just two parts?"

"Yes, part one is the Roman Catholic Church or Catholic Church. Many Catholics reject the word 'Roman.' Part two is Islam."

"Okay. Let's start with number one."

"The Roman Catholic Church as we know it started in 313 AD."

"How did that come about?"

"Rome's Emperor made it possible, the one who served from 306 until his death in 337."

"Can you spell that out a little better please?"

"Roman Emperor Constantine the Great or Caesar Flavius Valerius Aurelius Constantinus Augustus brought it about in 313 AD when he sanctioned Christian worship. Until then the Roman Empire was pagan and it played a major role in crucifying Jesus Christ."

"Why?"

"They feared mistakenly Jesus wanted to replace the Roman Empire with one of his own."

"So what happened exactly?"

"While Constantine served as emperor, he also moved the Roman capital from Rome to Constantinople. It would have been more difficult to recognize Christianity in Italy at the time."

"There are those who doubt that version. You do know that, right?"

"Yes, I do."

"So how do we approach this obviously delicate subject?"

"As objectively as possible . . . that's how."

"I agree."

"So here is what we have."

"I'm listening. Believe me I am on this one."

"If Constantine's history is correct, this means Peter was not the first Pope and that the Catholic Church was not launched until more than 300 years after the birth, crucifixion and resurrection of Christ."

"So how do we define Peter?"

"Peter was one of the 12 disciples who served Jesus. Eleven of them excluding Judas who betrayed Jesus worked after Jesus returned to Heaven and leaving behind the Holy Spirit."

"And what does that mean specifically?"

"In short, the Holy Spirit was the direct contact the disciples had with Jesus and God, his father. And it's this same Holy Spirit afforded anyone who confesses their sins and accepts Jesus as their Lord and Savior."

"Is there more?"

"According to the teachings of the Old and New Testaments and the message the disciples began to spread that the relationship between Jesus the Savior and each believer was permanent.

"Jesus was a Jew and the disciples worked to spread the Gospel to all people, not just one race.

"The New Testament tells us Calvary or Golgotha is where Jesus was crucified outside what was then the wall of Jerusalem, part of the Roman Empire at the time.

"The exact place where this happened still is unknown perhaps for a reason. If there was an exact site, undue attention could be given to where Jesus died rather than the resurrection. It was a complete package: the death, burial and resurrection.

"While important, the pure act of death on a cross like Jesus did was common place in those days. Criminals died on one daily during that period.

"It was the resurrection of this man who was human and who was God at the same time that made the difference.

"The combination of being the SON of GOD born to a human mother made it possible for him to live a perfect life without sin, according to God himself as recorded in the BIBLE."

"No other can make such a claim. Is that correct?"

"Yes it is. He was the one and only being to enter the world like he did, return to his father and then come again to the world to be a part of every believer.

"That miracle occurs daily when a sinner—any man or woman—accepts Christ as their personal savior."

"Why is it necessary to make that kind of statement just in that way?"

"Another miracle occurs once that individual God-Man-Woman permanent relationship is established."

"And what is that?"

"The HOLY SPIRIT or God's presence becomes a part of every believer for eternity."

"That's an incredible reality."

"Let's look at all that another way."

"Okay."

"Jesus, our God, walked among us so all men and women had the opportunity to touch him and know him to be the REAL THING. By touching him and by seeing him, they had clear unquestioned evidence of God's existence."

"So the idea, the thought was not an abstraction. It was real and it was living."

"Exactly . . . And that experience was recorded in the New Testament and reported to all of those who have a copy of the Holy Bible so believers could know him in the same way his disciples did."

"What about those who lived before Jesus?"

"Yes, they were saved if that's what you mean."

"How . . . ? I don't understand."

"They believed this would happen as was recorded and was promised in the Old Testament."

"Who were the main carriers of this message?"

"The Jews were. And that's why at that time they were referred to as the 'Chosen Ones.'"

In other words, those who believed at that time were saved in advance of what would happen later."

"Yes, that's correct."

"Why?"

"Because they believed the death, burial and resurrection would take place."

"There was a practical aspect of all that."

"A practical aspect . . . I don't understand."

"All people before and after Christ lived should and could have the opportunity to accept or to reject him."

"I see your point."

"Later, the actual death site was reportedly found by St. Helena, the mother of Emperor Constantine in 325AD. The spot is now enshrined inside the Roman Catholic Church of the Holy Sepulcher built by her son."

"So what happened next?"

"Nearby, Helena said she identified the location of the Tomb of Jesus and at the same time claimed she had discovered the True Cross.

"Her son, Constantine, then later built the Church of the Holy Sepulcher around the whole site.

"Despite her claim and despite the building of the church surrounding that sacred spot, the most famous and most difficult identification is that of Calvary itself."

"Why?"

"Jerusalem, located west of the Dead Sea and the Jordan River, is a holy city for Jews, Christians, and Muslims. And the city, just to repeat, was part of the Roman Empire at the time."

"And is this where Constantine makes his appearance?"

"Yes. Constantinople, now called Istanbul, was founded (A.D. 330) at ancient Byzantium as the new capital of the Roman Empire by Constantine I, after whom it was named."

"And . . ."

"And this is when the Roman Catholic Church started, not before."

"I see."

"This version makes sense for a couple of reasons."

"I'm listening."

"The Catholic Church would have been talked about over and over again as essential well in advance of that moment. There is no mention of the church in the Bible's 66 books. And this one reason is why the Catholic Church has played down the Bible."

"Is the Bible denied?"

"Of course not . . ."

"So how is it described?"

"Very simply . . ."

"And what is that?"

"Catholics must accept BIBLE truth as handed down by the POPE and BISHOPS. In other words, this is not left up to individual church members."

"I have a question."

"Shoot . . ."

"Does the Holy Spirit play a role in helping Catholics understand the Bible? Or taken a step further, can individual Catholics look to the Holy Spirit to help them understand the Bible?"

"The short answer is the Catholic Church is the only source for Biblical interpretation."

"Why?"

"Roman Catholic Church members or adherents must accept the church as possessing the fullness of revelation, and the church, according to the Roman Catholic catechism, is the only Christian body that is 'one, holy, catholic, and apostolic.'"

"How does that compare with our belief?"

"Catholics do not accept our interpretation of the Holy Spirit. By that I'm talking about New Testament Churches. In other words, the Holy Spirit alone can't be counted on as the primary source for understanding Scripture or the Holy Bible."

"That's a hard way to say it."

"Yes, it is. Obviously, we are not in a position to judge them. And at the same time, they shouldn't judge us or anyone else in such an unwavering way."

"Here is another question."

"I'm listening."

'How do Catholics define salvation?"

"First, here is their way of defining for us how we should see and understand salvation."

"That ought to be interesting."

"The doctrine of salvation for non Catholics is God affords each human being sufficient light to attain salvation."

"So far so good . . ."

"This may be the most interesting part of the definition."

"The most interesting part of the definition is what we're talking about. Is that what you're saying? I just want to be clear on the point."

"Yes. All will be saved who persevere in what they believe to be good, regardless of ignorance."

"Is that all?"

"No. Only those will be damned who persist in what they know to be wrong."

"And who are those?"

"They are those who resist or deny the church."

"Is there more?"

"Yes. They are talking about men and women who resist and who deny the church when they know it to be the one, true church."

"How large is the Catholic Church?"

"The "Catholic Church" or "Roman Catholic Church" is the world's second largest single religious body after Sunni Islam."

"In terms of numbers, how large is the church?"

"Catholics number over half of the 1.1 billion people who call themselves Christian. And that total is about one-sixth of the world's population."

"One final question . . ."

"I'm listening."

"Who heads the only church or the Roman Catholic Church?"

"The Pope does."

"Is that true?"

"Not according to the Bible."

"So what do the scriptures say?"

"The 18th verse of the first chapter of Colossians in the New Testament is very clear on the subject and says the following:

'And he [Jesus] is the head of the body, the CHURCH: who is the beginning, the first-born from the dead; that in all things he might have the preeminence.'

Chapter Nine

"Okay, that's good. What's next?" Colt McCoy asked.

Jordon Frost responded: "Part two about Islam."

"Correct me if I'm wrong, but didn't we discuss that before."

"We did. Earlier we defined Islam and its parts. Now, I think it's time to take a closer look at the man who put it all together. I'm talking about Muhammad, Islam's founder."

"That sounds like a good idea to me."

"First it's good to remember Muhammad is considered by Muslims to be God's last and greatest prophet."

"I'm ready."

"Born into the Quraish (Quraysh) clan in Mecca, he was orphaned early," Frost said. "His father [Abd Allah] [Abdallah ibn Abd al-Muttalib] was dead six months before his birth in 570. And his mother, Aminah, died soon afterwards."

"That's terrible."

"And there is more."

"I can't believe it."

"He lived with a Bedouin family, his foster-mother, Halimah bint Abi Dhuayb, and her husband, until he was two years old."

He stopped for a minute to take a breath.

"Please don't tell me this is not the end to this part of the story," McCoy said.

"It is not. For another two years, he was passed on to his paternal grandfather Abd al-Muttalib, of the Banu Hashim clan a part of the larger Quraysh tribe. When Muhammad was eight, his grandfather also died."

"If I may so it sounds like our friend Osama bin Laden had a lot in common with Muhammad in early life. By that I mean both experienced a lot of instability growing up. It's amazing both survived."

"I agree."

"So when did stability settle in? It obviously did at some point."

"That came from an uncle, Abu Talib, the new leader of Banu Hashim family at the time."

"So what happened?"

"He became a trader."

"A trader . . . I don't understand."

"Still in his teens, Muhammad accompanied his uncle on trading journeys to Syria. He acquired experience in commercial trade."

"Why trade? Why that? Why not something else? That doesn't sound too religious to me."

"As an orphan, it was the only career open to Muhammad."

"That meant he was on the road a lot. Is that correct?"

"Yes. He really got to know the territory between the Indian Ocean and the Mediterranean Sea."

"Perhaps realizing his chances at life were slim indeed without something, he took the work very seriously."

"Enduring so much personal family tragedy, I can see why."

"Does that mean Mecca was an important trading center and crossroads?"

"Yes, by that time the merchants of Mecca had monopoly control over such commerce."

"He was really alone. I had no idea."

"Here is another interesting fact. As a minor, he was unable by Arab custom to inherit anything."

"So what saved him, so to speak?"

"Believe it or not it was a rich widow, Khadija, also a trader between Mecca and Syria. Fifteen years older, she met him when he was 25 when he started working for her. And believe it or not, she later asked him to marry her."

"Why would she do that?"

"Here might be a reason. It may have been connected to his nickname, `Al-Amin.'"

"And what did that mean?

"It meant Muhammad was faithful, trustworthy and that he was sought out when there was a need for an impartial arbitrator."

"So that must mean Muhammad accepted her proposal."

"He did in the year AD 595. And by all accounts it was a successful and happy marriage."

"Was that his only wife?"

"Until she died . . . yes. In all, he was married 12 times."

*   *   *

"So when did the religious part or Islam first surface?"

"Good question. First, it should be of no surprise to know Muhammad was a loner."

"Why?"

"It was a means of escape—his way of copping—after so much family upheaval so early in life. He began to spend time alone."

"I see."

"So where did it all get started?"

"Believe it or not it all began inside a cave."

McCoy had difficulty believing what he had just heard.

"The story goes something like this," Frost explained. "Inside the cave, according to all accounts, the angel Gabriel appeared."

"Did you say `an angel'?"

"I did. Gabriel told him he was to become a prophet. And those first words would become part of the Koran, Islam's Holy Book."

"I'm having difficulty believing this."

"So did Muhammad."

"You've got to explain that."

"One report said he became so distressed during his first contact with Gabriel that he considered throwing himself off the top of a mountain."

"I can believe that after all he had been through."

"Another report said his revelations were accompanied by mysterious seizures."

"So how did he survive all that?"

"Gabriel told him he was chosen to be God's messenger. Back home, Muhammad was consoled and reassured by his wife, Khadijah, and her Christian cousin, Waraqah ibn Nawfal."

"Let's back up a little."

"Okay."

"Where did all of this take place?"

"Inside a Mount Hira mountain cave north of Mecca."

"So what happened there exactly?"

"A voice, later believed to be the angel Gabriel as I told you earlier, spoke to him."

"And this voice allegedly said . . ."

"One, Allah is the only God; two, he [Muhammad] should adopt the name 'Prophet'; and three, his job as Prophet would be to convert others into accepting Allah as the only and true God."

"That's a mouth full."

"Yes it is."

"Were there more of these so-called divine visions? If so can you give me an example?"

"All 114 chapters of the Koran [Qur'an] are the result of Muhammad's divinely inspired revelations."

"So these visions launched Islam. Is that correct?

"Yes."

"So what does all that mean exactly?"

"There is another point here . . . a very important one . . . a view that must be considered and understood."

"So where does Muhammad fit into this picture?"

"According to Islamic teaching, Muhammad was the final Prophet and that Allah is the true God dating back to the beginning of time. Everything else is secondary."

"So what happens to Jesus?"

"He is a Prophet."

"Does that mean Jesus was reduced in title? By that I mean he could no longer be called 'Our Lord and Savior.'

"Yes . . ."

"So does that mean they reject the idea that he is 'A Savior' as we see and understand him to be? I just want to be clear on this very important point."

"Let's look at it this way. The Koran, as believed by Muslims, is God's final revelation. Allah, according to that position, is the only God and the only True God."

"So they reject the idea Jesus was God and Man simultaneously, that he died on the cross in payment of all past, current and future sin."

"Yes."

"And that Jesus was God's only son."

"Yes."

"And that his son—Jesus—died on the cross carrying the entire burden of sin for all men and women."

"Yes."

"Three days later, he was raised from the dead victorious over all sin."

"Yes."

"And he did that so every man and woman cleansed of sin can have an internal relationship with God."

"Yes."

"So what do we have to do to be clean of sin and to know an eternal relationship with God is secure?"

"Just say 'yes.'"

"That's all?"

"We have a choice. We are free to tell God 'YES' or 'NO.'

"And he will accept our decision?"

"Yes."

"No amount of effort on my part, like say a life-time of GOOD WORKS, will or can buy my or your way into his presence or will gain his favor?"

Nat Carnes

"No."

"So Muhammad and believers in Islam reject all of that?"

"Unfortunately, they do. In other words, Muhammad or the Koran and their definition of Allah are incomplete for one reason: salvation is not secure. Allah will decide that when we enter heaven. In other words, it's a combination of BELIEF and GOOD WORKS."

"Yes, yes and yes. That's how it is."

"Anyone who thinks that way is in constant fear. There can be no peace, no tranquility."

"Absolutely . . ."

*   *   *

"Now let's look at Imperial Islam. In other words, let's look how Islam combines church and state," Frost said. "Once we understand that, in my view anyway, we'll be closer to grasping the why of what sunk that ship off the coast of Puerto Rico."

"Okay."

"In about 613 Muhammad began to preach in public. There he emphasized how Allah called on the rich to use their wealth to help the poor."

"Why?"

"He warned—if they didn't—they would be judged by Allah on the Last Day according to their deeds."

"And the result would be . . ."

"It would be Heaven or Hell, either one or the other."

"So did anyone respond to that kind of message?" McCoy wanted to know.

"An estimated 70 did at the beginning."

"And they were" . . . McCoy was so astonished he was unable to finish the sentence. Catching his breath, he started again.

"Do we know who these people were and if so where did they come from? I assume they did not just drop out of the blue somewhere?"

92

"They were believed to be mostly sons and brothers of Mecca's richest men in the country of Saudi Arabia."

"So what did they call themselves?"

"This new religion was called Islam, meaning 'surrender to the will of God.' And those believers were named Muslims."

"So what happened next? How did they spread the word? Did they preach or what?"

"Until the death of his wife and uncle, Muhammad was able to express his views about Allah and Islam without fear. They provided him needed protection."

"But that changed?"

"Yes. Another uncle, Abu Lahab, the new head of the Hashim clan, saw things differently and withdrew protection."

"Why?"

"While Muhammad's preaching was basically religious, he was thought to be far too critical of Mecca's rich merchants."

"So what happened next?"

"In 620, Muhammad reached a new agreement with Medina clans and moved from Mecca to Medina two years later in 622. His move is remembered as HIJRAH."

"So there he was able to preach and practice Islam without fear. Is that what happened?"

"Yes. Medina was different from Mecca. It was an oasis where date palms flourished and cereals could be grown."

"So the difference was economic?"

"There was another element, an important one, having to do with culture."

"I didn't know."

"Agriculture there had been developed by Jewish not Arab clans and they had the best land."

"And this caused a serious conflict?"

"Yes. The Arabs didn't like that at all. Since it was essentially Arab territory, they figured they should have the best or at least share it equally with the Jews."

"I see."

"They hoped Muhammad, this new religious leader, could settle the conflict between the clans."

"And why would they think that?"

"They had learned from the Jews about Jesus. So they reasoned Muhammad—the Arab Prophet—could reason with them."

"I see."

"They figured or hoped Muhammad would free them of what was termed Jewish oppression and that he could provide proper justice with the making of a new Arabic kingdom."

"Obviously, that didn't work."

"No it did not. A serious outbreak erupted in 618. They clashed, much blood was spilled and peace was never fully restored."

"So what happened next?"

"They tried to move beyond the Medina conflict."

"How was that possible?"

"With Muhammad's approval, Arabic clans began to attack caravans from Mecca passing near Medina en route to Syria. Muhammad participated in three."

"So there was no chance for Arabs and Jews to cooperate or just get along."

"No. Something else more significant happened, though. Muhammad fully became an Arab Prophet."

"How did that come about?"

"From that moment on, Muslims would look to Mecca, where Islam started, and not Jerusalem during prayer time."

"So that was the moment Muhammad moved himself ahead of Jesus and the Jews in the Arab world."

"Yes."

* * *

"So what did Muhammad accomplish?"

"He founded a state [Arabia], a religion [Islam] and launched Islamic imperialism combining church and state."

"How did he create the state?"

"He used Islam to unit Arab tribes, a difficult procedure on any terms."

"In the years ahead, Islam spread out of Arabia in three directions."

"Where did that occur exactly? . . ."

"The first was across North Africa and eventually into Spain. From there, Islam moved through the Middle East forward into Europe to the gates of Vienna."

"That's impressive."

"Here's another way of putting it. By the end of its first century, Islam stretched to the western borders of China and to the southern borders of France. North Africa was dominated completely."

"You did say there was a third direction. Is that correct?"

"Yes, that's right. It spread east across Asia to the Pacific Ocean."

"That's huge. No doubt about that."

"But it could have been larger."

"Larger. I don't understand."

"They tried and were stopped in the year 732."

"Can you explain that please?"

"Charles Martel, known as Charles the Hammer, a brilliant Christian army general, directed 'The 732 Battle of Tours' victory.

"It has been called one of the most important battles ever to be fought in history."

"Why?"

"After the Arabs and Islam had taken and occupied Spain for more than 700 years, Martel expected them to attempt a takeover of all of Europe."

"Martel saw this coming?"

"He did and it was a loss Arabs remember and regret until this day."

"Tell me more about this general, the man named Martel."

"Sensing the expansionist move was coming, Martel began to prepare for it early."

"Okay."

"By 721, he knew Arab Emir and General Abdul Rahman of Córdoba in Spain had a strong army made up of troops from Morocco, Syria and Yemen and that this military force was there for only one reason: conquer Europe."

"In other words, our general had some rather clear evidence."

"Yes. And General Rahman's first move was successful. His June 9, 721, Battle of Toulouse victory took place just north of the Spanish border in southern France."

"I'm listening."

"By that time, Charles knew it would only be a matter of time before the Arab force would regroup and would attempt to move further north for more territory."

"So what did he . . . Martel . . . do exactly?"

"He began by forming a fulltime, year-round standing army, something that was unheard of at the time."

"So he did the correct thing?"

He answered the question this way. "And as predicted the Battle of Tours took place in 732 somewhere between Tours and Poitiers, France, southwest of Paris."

"So what was the size of Martel's force at the time?"

"Martel's veteran infantry, numbered between 15,000 and 75,000 men. And after the Toulouse victory, the Muslims expected to easily sack Tours."

"So what happened next?"

"General Rahman moved his army into place and ordered the attack after waiting seven days."

"And he lost."

"Not only did the advance fail, General Rahman was killed."

"Unbelievable . . ."

* * *

"To realize the importance of the victory, it's good to know what the Islamic force had accomplished up to that moment."

"I take it you are about to tell me how successful they had been leading up to the Tours loss."

"After Muhammad's death, Arabic leaders moved to create an Arabic Islamic Empire powered by Islamic Imperialism."

"So . . ."

"By the end of its first century, an Islamic empire stretched from the Atlantic Ocean in the west to Central Asia in the east to the Pacific Ocean."

"That's huge."

"Yes. In other words to repeat in part what was said earlier, Islam stretched to the western borders of China. They completely dominated North Africa, Southwest Asia and had gained control of Spain and Southern France."

"And it could have been larger had it not been for Martel."

"Maybe even the world as it was known at the time."

"Yes."

"And you believe Islam still wants to conquer the world."

"Yes I do. The Islamic extremists do without doubt."

Chapter Ten

"Is there anything more we need to know about Islam? We've covered quite a bit. I just feel like there is something else we need to know about."

"And you would be correct."

"So what more needs to be said?"

"Mecca is the holiest city of Islam. The city was an ancient center of commerce and a place of great sanctity for idolatrous Arab sects before the rise of Muhammad."

"What more can be said of Mecca?"

"Plenty . . . At the center of town is the Great Mosque. And a square surrounding the Mosque can hold more than 300,000 Muslim pilgrims.

"More than two million pilgrims reportedly visit Mecca each year during a tradition called HAJJ, believed to date back to the time of Ibrahim (Abraham) and Muhammad."

"What is HAJJ?"

"HAJJ means Muslim solidarity and submission to Allah or God and is scheduled from the eighth to 12th day of Dhu al-Hijjah or the 12th and last month of the Islamic calendar or usually in November."

"Do all Muslims make the trip?"

"All Muslims, if financially and physically able, are required to make the trip once."

"So what happens?"

"The HAJJ is a series of rituals carried on inside and outside the Kaaba. The main event is staged 10 miles from Mecca, where the Prophet Muhammad spoke to followers during his last pilgrimage. They later visit the Prophet's Mosque in Medina."

"Is that all?"

"No.

"Once HAJJ ends, they celebrate the Festival of Sacrifice, called Eid al-Adha, when an animal is killed."

"Why sacrifice an animal?"

"In memory of Abraham, that's why. When he was ready to use his only son, he was instructed by an angel to substitute a ram caught in a nearby bush for Ishmael. The story can be found in the first book of the Old Testament, Genesis chapter 22, verse 13."

"Is there more?"

"Muslims believe Arabs descended from Abraham and Hagar through their son Ishmael. Abraham is further regarded as an ancestor of Muhammad. According to the Koran, Abraham and Ishmael built the Kaaba in Mecca."

*   *   *

"Anything else . . . ?"

"This perhaps is small but none the less important. Those completing the pilgrimage can add the phrase al-Hajj or Hajji at the end of their name."

"Could you and I visit what you are talking about? I mean is it possible for either one of us to actually walk inside and examine for ourselves all parts of these so-called holy sectors of Islam?"

"The short answer is 'no.'"

"I see."

"Besides that it's meaningful to point out where the holy elements or places are located in Mecca."

"I agree."

"First there is the Haram."

"What is that exactly?"

"It's the title for the restricted for Muslims only zone of Mecca."

"How large an area is the Haram?"

"It's not a perfect square but part of it extends out as much as 12 miles."

"Okay. We're inside the zone. What's next?"

"The Kaaba, sometimes called the House of God, is a shrine built in the shape of a square inside the Grand Mosque."

"The Kaaba . . . ?"

"Yes, that's correct. It means the 'Cube' or the 'House of God.' The site predates Islam. Tradition says it was built by Adam and rebuilt by Abraham and the descendants of Noah."

"What does this shrine look like?"

"The Kaaba is made of grey granite with four corners pointing north, south, east and west."

"And it's size. Do we know?"

"Yes we do. It measures 33 feet long, 50 feet wide and 45 feet high."

"What else should I be aware of?"

"There is only one way to get inside."

"Only one . . . ? You're talking about getting inside the shrine itself if I understand you correctly. Am I right?"

"That's true. It's located on the northeast side of the structure and believe it or not it's 2.3 meters above ground."

"What's it look like inside?"

"Bare may be the best description."

"A bare interior . . . ?"

"They apparently want no distractions."

"What does that mean exactly?"

"I think it's easy enough to understand."

"Why?"

"Nothing should take away from what is called 'the Black Stone of Mecca.'"

"And this Black Stone is inside the Kaaba. Is that correct?"

"Yes, it's been placed in the eastern corner and is elevated about 1.5 meters off the ground."

"And that's it? There's nothing else?"

"Yes. There are small exceptions."

"And they are . . ."

"For one, there are three supporting wooden pillars. And for two, so to speak, there are a number of gold hanging lamps."

"Do we know more about the Kaaba's history?"

"Yes. According to Muslim tradition, Adam built the original Kaaba as a copy of and directly below God's throne in heaven."

"Just to be clear . . . you are talking about the same Adam as the Adam and Eve described in the Old Testament book of Genesis."

"I am. This is where Islam and Christianity cross paths so to speak."

"I see."

"There is something else. A gilded cage near the Kaaba contains a stone that allegedly preserves a footprint of Abraham."

"And why is that important?"

"By establishing this ancient pedigree for the Kaaba, Muhammad could better connect his new faith from the start along with Judaism."

"Interesting . . ."

"So yes . . . if that's what you have or had thought to ask . . . Muhammad had something clearly in mind and that was it."

"What else do we know about the Kaaba?"

"When Muhammad received his revelation, the Kaaba was under the control of one of the most important tribes of Mecca, the Quraysh.

"It was used as a shrine for pagan idols, especially al-Lat, al-Uzza, and Manat, known together as al-Gharaniq (Daughters of God), and Hubal, a marriage god."

"So what was Muhammad's reaction?"

"When Muhammad took control of Mecca he cleaned out the idols and dedicated the Kaaba to God."

"So I guess we must be careful at this point how we define things related to Christianity and Islam."

"Without doubt . . ."

"Islam claims the Bible's telling of Adam and Eve reflects negatively on women."

"In what way . . . ?"

"For starters, woman was created from Adam's rib that is crooked and cannot be straightened."

"Anything else . . . ?"

"Yes. The woman is wicked because she tempted man. So there is only one conclusion: man is innocent and woman is feeble."

"I thought followers of Islam believed that way."

"Unfortunately, according to Islam, this concept has touched the conventional `Muslim' as well."

"So what can we conclude?"

"As long as the concept of Eve being created for man prevails, according to Islam, women can never be free in the true sense of the word."

"So what does Islam think of Adam?"

"Adam is a symbol of mankind. The story of Adam explains the status of human beings."

"The status . . . ?"

"Yes. Man has the faculty of will and choice and he can say NO to the Laws of God. The NO part is known as the influence of evil or the "devil"."

"So what do the Koran and Islam teach?"

"Both men and women exist on their own right. A woman is neither weak nor wicked simply because she is a woman. In Surah 2, Verse 36, it proclaims both men and women are equally susceptible to temptation."

*   *   *

"So what's next?"

"For now, we leave the Koran and return to the Bible to better understand what occurred next."

"Okay."

"After Adam and Eve were cast out of the Garden of Eden, they lived with the knowledge of right and wrong. And not too long afterwards, God destroyed the World to rid it of out-of-control evil."

"I assume you are talking about Noah and the Great Flood, also recorded in Genesis, the first book of the Old Testament."

"Without doubt . . ."

"So what was the next step?"

"With Adam and Eve out of the Garden, a perfect environment had ended and it had to be replaced with a new one."

"If the known world at the time was destroyed, what happened next?"

"A new type of structure was launched based on spiritual values."

"A new type . . . ?"

"Yes."

"And who was responsible for doing all of that?"

"God himself . . ."

"I don't understand."

"It was a slow process, this change from the Garden of Eden to the current day environment. In the beginning, Abraham (Ibrahim) and his son Ishmael (Ismail) were the main human building blocks of this new spiritual structure."

"And it was completed when?"

"At the moment of the death, burial and resurrection of Jesus Christ, Jesus concluded what Abraham had started."

* * *

"That was it. There was nothing else?"

"Actually, there was something else."

"I'm listening."

"Jesus spent 40 days and nights with his followers and friends to repeat again what had gone on during his life leading up to his death, burial and resurrection."

"He must have thought they could not or would not understand all that had taken place."

"In other words he dotted every 'I' and crossed every 't' so to speak.'

"So what did he do exactly?"

"He met twice with his disciples."

"Why?"

"The man named Thomas said he could not believe."

"He was that blunt?"

"Yes. He said and I quote: 'Except I shall see in his hands the print of the nails and put my finger into the print of the nails and put my hand into his side, I will not believe.'"

"So that's why Jesus appeared to five or six other groups in different parts of Palestine."

"Yes, it is. He wanted all questions settled."

"Can you provide at least one example of how he accomplished all of that?"

"I'll give you two. Jesus met with seven fishermen disciples on the shore of the Lake of Galilee and later with a group of 500 in Galilee itself."

"And then he left."

"Yes."

"From where . . . I think I know but refresh my memory."

"Mount Olivet . . . After saying goodbye, Jesus was taken up by a cloud until he was out of sight and returned to his Father in Heaven."

"And what were his final words?"

"He gave them what we call the GREAT COMMISSION."

"And that is . . ."

"They were commanded to take his 'good news' all over the world, to make disciples, to baptize believers and to teach them to observe all that he had commanded."

"So in your own words, what did that mean?"

"In simple language, the 'good news' means each living man and woman can either accept or reject God."

"Obviously, a world like a perfect Garden of Eden or a totally imperfect one like the world destroyed by the Great Flood was far from satisfactory."

"That's correct."

"So what did happen?"

"There had to be a new plan, one that would give all men and all women a logical and a permanent way out: a life with a way of dealing with good and evil."

"And that means . . ."

"In Biblical terms, anyone who accepts Jesus as Lord and Savior can live the good life. Once done, each individual has the only instrument available to adequately deal with and to conquer evil."

"Are we or anyone for that matter required to do anything on our own beyond saying 'yes' to God to obtain permanent salvation?"

"No. You, I or anyone are not good or powerful enough to earn any part of salvation."

"So good works will not help?"

"Once saved, the positive things we do are a product of a relationship with God, the father of Jesus Christ."

"I know I'm repeating myself, but I must. I need to have a clear understanding on this simple but important point."

"I don't mind saying part or all of that as many times as necessary."

"Okay. Here it is again. Good Works alone or in part does not earn or obtain salvation for me, you or anyone. Is that correct?"

"There are two points here."

"Two?"

"Yes. If Good Works were necessary to secure salvation or an eternal relationship with God, we would be placing ourselves on a level with God himself."

"And two . . . ?"

"Even if that were true and it is not, we by ourselves could or can do nothing to obtain salvation."

"Why not . . . ? I don't understand."

"From a practical point of view, what happens to such a 'good works' process when we commit error or fall into sin regardless of how minor?"

"In other words, to obtain salvation by asking for it is the only way of realizing and overcoming our short comings . . . that there is nothing we can do to receive something that is only God's to give to you, me or anyone."

"That's correct."

"So once there or once we have salvation, we can relax and allow God to produce Good Works through us."

"Again, that's correct."

"Thank you for your patience."

"You are most welcome."

Chapter Eleven

"It's time now to interview William Younger again," said Jordon Frost to Colt McCoy, his partner. "You will remember I'm sure that he cut off our earlier conversation when I asked him if the dead women and children found in the ship's lower decks were slaves."

"I do," McCoy said. "I have total recall of his words: 'I see no need to carry this conversation further.'"

Frost added: "Maybe we'll have better luck this time. Perhaps we can finish our conversation without being booted out."

"And hopefully, we'll be able to meet his brother, Bruce Younger at the same time."

"And if we are fortunate enough perhaps we should ask softer questions at the beginning. And if we're lucky he might tell us about the 'slave' part without being asked."

"Good idea. One thing is for sure, he knows we have slaves on our mind and that he must realize we won't stop probing until we get an answer."

"Before we tackle the Younger's again, let's review what we think we know about them."

"That's a very good thought."

Frost started the review.

"As I understand it the two brothers own and operate the business."

McCoy added: "As I recall Mr. Younger told us they were investors in 'Caribbean' cruise ship, not actual owners."

"I do remember now that you mention it," Frost said. "But if my memory is correct, he also said they planned to buy a second cruise ship before the sinking of the first."

"We will need to clarify the point, obviously."

Immediately, they were granted an interview. There was no waiting around this time and they were grateful. They learned Bruce Younger was traveling and would be back later.

"His answers, I'm afraid, would be similar to mine," William Younger said at the beginning of the interview. "He sends his best wishes and regrets about not being here at this time. Hopefully you will meet later on."

With that short introduction, they started to talk.

Again when asked Mr. Younger repeated what he had said earlier: "The owners and directors were among the 900 dead. To be clear, my brother and I were investors . . . nothing more."

Apparently feeling they weren't listening or did not want to understand what he had just said, he ended up going over what had been said for a third time:

"The owners and directors were among the 900 dead. To be clear, I like my brother were investors . . . nothing more."

"And just for the record, please name the two investors." A recording device had been clicked on moments before.

"First, I will introduce myself again. I am William Younger, one of the main investors in the ship. The other is my brother, Bruce Younger."

"And the Younger brothers own what exactly?"

"For starters, we control three hotels, two in Florida and a third in Puerto Rico."

"So you have been interested in the cruise ship business for a while. Is that correct?"

"Yes. We invested in the vessel a few years back."

"And that was the one that sank off Puerto Rico's northwest coast line?"

"Yes."

"What was the ship's name?"

"The Caribbean . . ."

He accepted his routine answer without attempting to probe too deeply this time around. Again, he was hoping the owner-investor would be more relaxed the longer they talked and that he would give them more information than he may have planned on providing.

With that in mind and after a brief moment of silence in hopes he would say more than repeating the ship's name, he asked another question.

"What does the future hold?"

"As I understand it, if successful, we had planned to add a new ship annually."

"So that means . . . when that occurs . . . you will be owners of a cruise ship for the first time?"

"Actually, we owned the first one until it was leased. If successful this time, it will be our second one to own. For now, we don't want to lease anymore."

"So why did the Younger brothers want to get in the cruise ship business in the first place?" It was a question he had asked earlier. He repeated it thinking a second opportunity to respond might provide more information.

"That's an easy one. And I think I may have mentioned it to you before."

"Frankly, I don't remember," Frost said on purpose. "If you wouldn't mind repeating yourself we'd appreciate it very much."

William Younger said without a moment of hesitation: "We wanted to give businessmen and tourists staying in our hotels an added travel option."

"I see." Again disappointed that Younger's answer was not a broader response, he took another approach.

"Before the sinking, the ship had scheduled stops in Haiti, the Dominican Republic, Puerto Rico, St. Martin, Guadeloupe and Martinique."

"Yes."

"So the cruise part of the business was paying off."

"I think it would have in time. But before the accident or whatever caused it to sink, the ship was losing money."

"So what did you do . . . if anything . . . to earn rather than continue to lose money?"

"We made a decision in an attempt to put ourselves in a better economic position."

"And that was . . ."

"Instead of declaring the business bankrupt, we elected to lease the vessel to a company headquartered in Tortola, the British Virgin Islands."

"Is there a corporate name?"

"Yes . . . `Ships Inc.'"

Finally, Frost got a new piece of information.

"So, I think, the next step will be to define the British Virgin Islands [BVI] and then to know something about the now three dead men in charge of the operation."

"Good."

"As you may know they [BVI] are east of us [Puerto Rico] and just on the other side of the U.S. Virgin Islands."

"And the three men . . ."

"They are Manuel Santos Espinosa, President, Caracas, Venezuela; Ismael Torres Torres, Vice President, Bogota, Colombia; and Carlos Jose Rodriquez Aguilar, Treasurer, Panama City, Panama."

"Do those names appear on any official document at the Tortola office in the British Virgin Islands?"

"Yes."

"Sorry, but I've got to ask. Why would anyone want to locate in such an isolated place?"

"Good question."

"We're listening."

"Off hand, I'd say it all depends on who you are talking to."

"I want to know your response."

"It's in an isolated region, easy to control."

"Why is that exactly?"

"In my opinion it's mainly because of geography."

"I see."

"Again, just to be clear, the BVI are east of us [Puerto Rico] and just on the other side of the U.S. Virgin Islands."

"Is there more?"

"Yes. There are a total of 30 islands and only 16 of that number are inhabited. Road Town, where the ship is registered, is the capital on the island of Tortola, one of three major islands. The other two are Anegada and Virgin Gorda."

At least, Frost thought, he was being a little bit more open despite the fact the information he provided could be found in any reference book.

"Before we go further, you said these islands are part of the British Virgin Islands."

"I did."

"Does that mean the British are involved somehow?"

"They are."

"How . . . ?"

"History tells us the BVI were first acquired from the Dutch in 1666."

"That's a long time ago." Frost admitted to himself Younger had at least done his homework as far as geography was concerned.

"Yes. They were granted autonomy in 1967 and are currently governed by their own constitution written in 2007. And 13 voting members serve four-year terms in the BVI unicameral House of Assembly."

"Is there more?"

"Yes, the government is headed by a premier, and the monarch of Great Britain and Northern Ireland, represented by a governor, is the head of state."

"So what do people do there to earn a living?"

"There are roughly three sources of income. Tourism, as you might expect, and light industry, which you might not expect."

"And the third . . . ?

"They offer financial services, like to this cruise ship corporation."

"And is this international in scope?"

"It is."

"So it could be called a tax haven or the main office for an international bookkeeping operation. Is that correct?"

"That's a good starting point, obviously."

"Can you tell us more about the three main officers of Ships Inc.?"

"To start with they have one thing in common. They are agents for the sale and export of their products."

"Okay."

"So let's begin with the corporation's president, Manuel Santos Espinosa, of Caracas, Venezuela, and then follow with the other two."

Slowing down a moment, Younger asked Frost and McCoy a question.

"What do you want to know about Santos Espinosa?"

Frost was almost shocked when Younger asked them a question. Maybe it was his way of somehow changing the direction of their probe.

"Not much I'm afraid. We'd appreciate any background information about him, of course. But mainly we'd like to know of his interest in such a project."

"Perhaps part of the answer can be found by just be looking at Venezuela itself."

"I agree. That's a start."

"We can do the same with all three by knowing more about each one's country of origin."

"Good."

"Here they are:

- Manuel Santos Espinosa, chairman of the board, lives in Caracas, Venezuela. He learned his trade dealing in coffee—the major income producer before oil—plus iron ore, gold and diamonds, rubber, tropical hardwoods and cattle.

- Ismael Torres Torres, the company's vice president, lives in Bogota, Colombia's capital city. He learned about coffee, high-grade coal reserves, grains and cattle, iron, coal, and emeralds and light crude oil.

- Carlos Jose Rodriquez Aguilar, Treasurer, Panama City, Panama. He learned how to administer the Panama Canal, a 51-mile long and 10-mile-wide strip across the isthmus that connects the Caribbean Sea with the Atlantic Ocean to the north and the Pacific Ocean. A New York-San Francisco sea journey is cut from 14,000 miles to 6,000 miles or more than half by using the canal.

After hearing the background, Frost got more direct with his questions.

"Now let's get back to the Younger brothers, Bruce and William, for a moment."

"I'm listening."

"Did either one of you know the kind of hidden cargo the cruise ship carried?"

"You are obviously talking about the dead women found in the cargo area of the vessel."

"I am."

"And as you might guess, we don't have an answer."

"We'll need one before we can move ahead or find out what's really going on here."

"Without a doubt you are more than correct."

The interview ended on that point.

*   *   *

Later Jordon Frost and Colt McCoy found out Santos Espinosa and the other two company officers were very much alive. They had not gone down with the ship.

And they later learned William Younger told them what he thought to be true.

Why the mistake?

From Kansas City, Younger called Santos Espinosa in Caracas. His secretary told Younger her boss was out to lunch and would be back shortly.

With his limited knowledge of Spanish, William Younger understood instead Santos Espinosa and the others went down with the ship. He didn't ask for a repeat or any kind of clarification at the time in fear the telephone conversation could have been taped by federal authorities after what had happened to the ship.

And because it was obviously a sensitive issue, Younger didn't bother to confirm the report elsewhere for a reason. At the time, he wanted to distance himself as much as possible from the explosion and the loss of 900 lives.

Frost and McCoy also remembered Younger was slow to answer their questions in their last interview. Maybe at the time he realized his information about Santos Espinosa might not have been correct.

Chapter Twelve

In Caracas, Venezuela, Manuel Santos Espinosa, gets a telephone call from Madrid, Spain. Santos Espinosa is president of a shipping company called, Ships Inc, headquartered in Tortola, the British Virgin Islands, in the Caribbean.

Based in the South American country, Santos Espinosa, worked with two other company officials. They were Ismael Torres Torres, Vice President, Bogota, Colombia, responsible for drug movement; and Carlos Jose Rodriquez Aguilar, Treasurer, Panama City, Panama, responsible for moving slaves.

One of their vessels, called 'The Caribbean', made scheduled stops in Haiti, the Dominican Republic, Puerto Rico, St. Martin, Guadeloupe and Martinique before heading to France, Morocco and Spain.

The unidentified caller asked a question. "Are you ready to make the shipment?"

"It was prepared and was en route," Santos Espinosa responded.

"I don't understand. What do you mean? Did something happen?"

"Yes."

"What?"

"Something very dramatic took place!"

"How dramatic . . . ? I need to know."

"Not only did our cruise ship sink . . . so did everything else including our goods."

There was a long moment of silence. It took a little time for the harsh reality to take hold.

Finally, they started talking again.

Both men spoke in general terms about what was aboard the vessel. They did so for a reason. U.S. authorities in Puerto Rico or elsewhere could be monitoring their telephone conversation.

"Where exactly did the ship go down?"

"The incident occurred in the Caribbean, near the U.S. Commonwealth of Puerto Rico."

"So all was lost? Is that correct?"

"Yes. Nothing was recovered."

"Just so I'm clear in my own mind, I'll ask the question again."

"Not a problem."

"So does that mean all cargo and all those aboard are not only gone but unrecoverable?"

"Yes it does."

"In short, every member of the ship's crew and passengers drowned. And that includes all cargo. Is that correct?"

"That's correct."

His next question came instantly. "How soon can we launch a new one?"

"Quickly and that means as soon as possible, obviously."

"What does that mean exactly?"

"One, we have to acquire a new ship. Two, we need a new cargo."

"How much time will that take?"

"At least 30 days . . . maybe a little longer . . . but not much more than that. I'll start to work on it immediately."

"Good. I may be able to help with the ship part."

"That's good. In fact, that's very good."

"I believe our friends, the Younger brothers, will be able to provide one."

"Really . . . ?"

"How and when?"

"They have the connections and the money to get the job done."

"The money . . . ? I thought something this large would have left them without or almost without resources."

"Fortunately for all of us there is insurance. With that in hand, there should be enough to get the operation started again and quickly."

"Do you know that for sure?"

"No. But I know how they think and operate. They would not leave themselves uncovered for any reason."

"I hope you're right."

"If not, we'll consider other options."

"So for now, you will work on the ship and I will see about putting together a new cargo. Am I correct in thinking that?"

"Yes, I think that about covers it."

"Good."

*   *   *

Their fathers—supporters of Spain's dictator Francisco Franco—had migrated to Venezuela in the late 1930s. They made up only a small percentage of immigrants who thought that way.

Most chose to leave Spain to escape the Franco-inspired chaos of the Spanish Civil War and World War II and attempt to start again in a freer environment.

They had grown to detest dictatorships and the misery and suffering associated with such governments.

So that meant they were part of a mass immigration leaving Europe for the Western Hemisphere. It was estimated more than one million traveled to Venezuela alone including a half-million Spaniards, 400,000 Portuguese and 200,000 Italians. As many as two million Spaniards ended up in Argentina.Santos Espinosa, his associate and Franco had something else in common, their Roman Catholic faith.

Franco was buried in the Valle de los Caídos or Valley of the Fallen near Madrid. In 1960, Pope John XXIII declared the underground crypt a basilica, larger in size than St. Peter's Basilica in Rome.

And they came for another reason.

They wanted more dictators like Franco in Latin America. And it didn't make any difference if such leaders were either to the extreme political left or right.

Santos Espinosa and his friend were men of their word. They played a role in bringing Hugo Chavez to power in 1999. He was encouraged to be like Cuban dictator Fidel Castro.

And they believed Venezuela was the historical place to launch such a movement.

Under the leadership of Simón Bolívar, Venezuela was one of the first Spanish colonies in South America to declare political independence from Spain in 1821.

Federated at first with Colombia and Ecuador as the Republic of Greater Colombia, Venezuela became a republic in 1830 all on its own.

From there dictatorships flourished.

Antonio Guzman Blanco governed from 1870 to 1888. Gen. Juan Vicente Gómez followed from 1908 to 1935.

The trend was broken when Rómulo Betancourt and the Democratic Action Party won a majority of seats in the South American country's government assembly.

A new constitution was drafted in 1946.

Rómulo Gallegos, the candidate for Betancourt's party, became Venezuela's first democratically elected president in 1947.

That didn't last long, however.

Within eight months, Gallegos was toppled by a military-backed coup led by Marcos Peréz Jiménez, who himself suffered the same fate in 1958.

Beginning in 1959, Venezuela became one of the most stable democracies in Latin America.

Betancourt returned to serve as president from 1959-1964 and he was followed by Rafael Caldera Rodríguez from 1969 to 1974.

*   *   *

His story was not an unusual one during that troubled period. Forced moves brought on almost unbearable stress for him and his mother and father.

Born in Sevilla, Spain, Santos Espinosa lived with his family three years in the Spanish Canary Islands just west of Morocco near the northwest coast of Africa in the North Atlantic Ocean.

His journey from Europe to South America started when his father applied and received travel visas for himself and family from a Venezuelan Consular office in the town of Santa Cruz de Ternariffe in the Canary islands.

With travel documents in hand, they returned to Sevilla to wait for the first available ship to take them to Venezuela—an ocean away—on the north coast of South America.

Almost immediately, he learned his father's name was bumped up on the list. Later, he learned why. His father agreed to report periodically back to the Franco government about Spaniards and other Europeans who fled their homes.

Franco planned it that way. It was the dictator's way of keeping his father and others totally occupied with his spy business not his family at the start.

For his father and the others, their role was easy to hide because of the high dislike level for Franco, Adolph Hitler of Germany and Benito Mussolini of Italy. Even if they would have let it slip about favoring Franco, the chances were good no one would have believed such an option as possible.

And with such a political advantage, his father traveled ahead of his family to Venezuela.

The remainder of the family followed 18 months later. In all, they lived 12 years in Caracas, Venezuela's capital.

During that period, the family paid a heavy emotional price for the long, disjointed journey from one continent to another and the adjustment to a new environment.

It was a too familiar story.

Fearing the worst at the start, it was decided to leave their 10-year-old son, Santos Espinosa, behind with an aunt, his mother's sister.

Problems erupted right from the start.

Coupled with uncertain times and an inability to communicate properly, the family endured an overpowering wave of personal stress in Caracas.

As the only child left behind, Santos Espinosa learned years later his parent's marriage had ended in divorce.

Communication between Spain and Venezuela at the time was virtually impossible.

In fact, he didn't know if his mother, father, his two older brothers and a sister were dead or alive. And all of that information was gathered by word of mouth and nothing of what he thought could be true was ever confirmed.

According to those versions, his mother had returned to Spain, his father may have traveled to Italy and his brothers and sisters remained somewhere in South America.

Despite the family separation, he retained his father's view of Franco and dictatorships in general. And he supported them whenever and however possible.

And as an adult, over a period of 10 years, he managed to establish firm relationships with extremists who funded their political agenda from money earned from drugs, money laundering and slavery.

They operated in both four major connecting points in two hemispheres: Madrid, Spain; Rabat, Morocco; Caracas, Venezuela; and Bogota, Colombia.

Chapter Thirteen

He lived in apartment four, at the Rommana Residence, in Rabat, Morocco. It served as his home and as an office from where he directed all activity linking activity between South America, North Africa and Europe.

Armando de la Cruz and his trading group had decided to locate here for a reason. Rabat was a political center for all things coming and going in northwestern Africa, the Mediterranean and southern Europe.

De La Cruz was a businessman—turned criminal and terrorist organizer—who spoke English, French and Spanish and who knew the cultures and politics of those countries where those languages were dominate.

Subconsciously, he regretted not knowing Arabic, a communication tool he would be required to dominate if he chose to remain in Morocco and deal with the Middle East over a longer period of time.

For the time being, he elected to concentrate on the business at hand and not spend a great deal of effort acquiring a fourth language.

Rabat, the Moroccan capital, he reasoned, would be most friendly to those without Arabic because the zone had been washed in French and Spanish colonialism.

Both France and Spain had two of the large world empires. France was larger in Africa than Spain.

*   *   *

It started in the 19th century when France established a new empire in Africa. Some of these colonies lasted beyond the invasion and occupation of France by Nazi Germany during World War II.

As early as 1624, France began to establish trading posts in Senegal in West Africa. Their influence extended to Algeria in 1830, Morocco in 1844 and Senegal in 1854.

France used and applied a simple straight forward cultural and political philosophy: bring civilization to people who were considered intellectually or morally ignorant or simply unenlightened.

To those Africans adopting French culture, learning to speak fluent French and converting to Christianity were granted French citizenship.

The 33 million people living in Morocco were given ample opportunity to convert. French Institutes provided language study, complete libraries and the frequent showings of French-language films in eight Moroccan cities. They were Agadir, Casablanca, Fèz, Marrakech, Meknès, Oujda, Rabat and Tanger.

Gradually, French control was established over much of Northern, Western and Central Africa by the turn of the century including the modern nations of Benin, Chad, Central African Republic, the east African coastal enclave of Djibouti (French Somaliland), Côte d'Ivoire [Ivory Coast], Guinea, Mali, Mauritania, Niger, Senegal and the Republic of Congo.

*   *   *

Morocco became a French protectorate in 1911.

Spain had a different African history.

In 711, the Muslims known as Moors conquered the entire Spanish peninsula except for Asturias and the Basque Country.

The Muslim advance was stopped 732 by Charles Martel during the Battle of Tours (732-33). Then they were driven out of Spain by Ferdinand and Isabella in 1492.

Charles Martel, known as Charles the Hammer and grandfather of Charlemagne, ruled Austrasia, parts of current day Eastern France, West Germany and Netherlands.

Spain went on to become the world's first power in the 16th century. And the chief rival was France.

A small part of that empire exists today in Africa and those small parts—called enclaves—are found in Morocco, just over 30 miles south of Spain. The two countries are separated by water, the Mediterranean Sea and the Atlantic Ocean to the west.

Two of those enclaves are the Spanish municipalities of Ceuta and Melilla. Ifni, formerly a Spanish-held enclave on the Atlantic coast, was ceded to Morocco in 1969.

The two cities, Ceuta and Melilla, and several small islands off the Mediterranean coast remain part of metropolitan Spain. Morocco claims and administers Western Sahara although sovereignty remains unresolved.

In 1956, Spanish Morocco became part of the independent state of Morocco; in 1968, Spanish Equatorial Guinea became independent; in 1969 Ifni was ceded to Morocco; and in 1976 Spanish Sahara was transferred to Morocco and Mauritania.

In 1968 Spain closed its frontier with the British colony of Gibraltar, just north of Morocco.

Rabat is Morocco's capital and Casablanca is the country's most populous city.

*   *   *

Politics—sometimes violent—were part of the Spain-Morocco relationship.

In 1967, Spain's colonization was challenged by a peaceful—protest movement called the Harakat Tahrir. Its failure resulted in the creation of a more radical group, the Polisario Front, organized in 1973 and later backed by Algeria.

Before the death of Spanish dictator, Francisco Franco in 1975, Spain was confronted by territorial demands from Morocco and to a lesser extent Mauritania, a second North African west coast country located south of Morocco.

In the end, Spain left Morocco and Mauritania in control of the region. Mauritania later surrendered its claim after fighting an unsuccessful war against the Polisario Front.

Backed by Algeria, because Algeria was using the Front to gain control for itself, the Front continued to oppose Morocco until a 1991 cease fire. A political solution has yet to be found.

* * *

De la Cruz clearly understood the politics involved and agreed with a Moroccan intellectual, Ahmed Moatassime, that France's political view of Morocco and North Africa is 'underdeveloped.'

In other words, the French view of that part of the world or anywhere else for that matter had a lot to do with themselves but little to do about African culture, language or politics.

He had learned the lesson in Colombia from Spain. These were the same reasons Latin American countries used to begin a break with the Spanish-speaking European country in the early 1800s.

And it was basically the same political interpretation learned at home from his father, Guillermo de la Cruz, an organizer of political leftists in Latin America. Thousands had traveled to Chile in the early 1970s in a failed attempt to convert that South American country into a second Cuba.

Guillermo's son, Armando, hoping to have learned from that experience carried this kind of leftist political agenda to Africa. He vowed to help or support any group—regardless of name or location—taking up the anti-colonialist or anti-imperialist cause.

For him, a violent response was the only avenue open to correct or rectify what seemed to be a clearly untenable political situation.

*   *   *

Armando claimed to be a recent convert to the political part of Islam, turned to Muhammad—the founder—for guidance now and in the future. He did so to gain the confidence of Islamic Extremists.

Here is what he did.

He announced publically he had accepted Islam's five pillars of faith, beginning with repeating the "Shahada," the Islamic acceptance statement. "I testify that there is no true god (deity) but God (Allah), and that Muhammad is a Messenger (Prophet) of God."

The other four pillars are: Salah (prayers), Zakah (Giving of Alms), Saum (Fasting during Ramadan) and Hajj (pilgrimage to Mecca at least one during his lifetime).

There was something else that caught Armando's interest. It was Muhammad, Islam's founder.

Muhammad had become a wealthy slave trader of men, women and children. This was the part of his life he wanted to learn more about and if possible adopt some or all of his methods to make himself a better slave trader.

So he decided to spend time studying Islam's founder.

Armando knew it would take some patience on his part to learn about the man who lived so long ago and how best to make his thinking about slavery his own in a totally different time frame.

*   *   *

Muhammad's early life was filled with personal tragedy. His mother and father died by his sixth birthday. A third family member, his grandfather, cared for him until his death. Abd al Muttalib was the patriarch of the family's Quraish tribe and was responsible for the pagan Holy Ka'bah Santuary, the home of 360 idols.

A fourth family member, Abu Talib, an uncle provided Muhammad his first long-term family stability beginning at age 12.

The uncle—a trader—put him to work immediately and allowed him to be on trips to Syria to the north, to Egypt to the northwest and to Yemen to the south.

* * *

It was a tough business for the Arab or any trader. They had to know and understand the Sahara desert, the largest in the world.

Bordered by the Atlantic Ocean to West, the Mediterranean Sea and the Atlas Mountains to the North and the Red Sea to the East, the desert extends across North Africa to Southwest Asia.

The Atlas Mountains start in southwest Morocco and continue through the northern parts of Algeria and Tunisia. The highest peak, called Jebel Toubkal, is in southwest Morocco.

In all, the Sahara Desert covers 3.5 million square miles and measures more than 3,000 miles from the Atlantic to the Red Sea.

This means the desert not only touches current day Saudi Arabia but also Algeria, Chad, Egypt, Libya, Mali, Mauritania, Morocco, Niger, Senegal, Sudan, Tunisia and most of the Western Sahara.

To penetrate this isolated and huge land mass during Islamic times, traders turned to large camel caravans. The number of animals used in a single caravan ranged in size from 1,000 to 12,000 camels for protection from attackers wanting gold, ivory and slaves and whatever else they carried to market to sell for themselves.

* * *

And while learning how the business worked, Muhammad learned something else.

In time Muhammad concluded successful traders could and did undermine traditional Arab tribal values of solidarity, mutual help, and magnanimity.

There was something else he didn't like. Too many times he witnessed traders telling potential buyers their pagan Gods would be pleased when they traded with them.

Muhammad made a personal decision based on what he would do once he was an independent and full-fledged trader on his own. He vowed to treat everyone fairly and honestly, using moral sensitivity.

His approach impressed a rich widow [Khadija], who commissioned him to take charge of her caravan trade. Again, liking what she saw and the results, the woman, though a family friend, asked Muhammad to marry her and he accepted. At the time he was 25 or 15 years younger than his new wife and business partner.

From that moment on Muhammad was known as a wealthy merchant in Mecca.

*   *   *

After becoming rich, Muhammad had more time to think about fairness, the key he believed to his economic success.

During one of those quiet times of contemplation spent inside a Mount Hira cave north of Mecca, he experienced a vision. The first one turned out being one of many that would change his life forever.

There Muhammad would learn he had been called to found a new expression of religious thought to later be called Islam.

It all started this way.

At 40, Muhammad believed he had been commanded by Allah (God) to be the first Arab prophet, an important cultural sales tool in the Middle East, and to preach what he had learned in the mountain cave.

It was the logical conclusion.

At the beginning, Muhammad preached submission and the approach failed. His position was weakened when he lost his protection.

First his wife, Khadija, died. And his greatest benefactor, Abu Talib, followed her in death. From that moment on, he was called a lunatic, a liar and demon possessed. Abu Talib, leader of the Quraish tribe, had been asked to replace Muhammad with another so they would be free to kill him.

Left alone, Muhammad could be openly challenged by rich merchants. They didn't want to be questioned about their use of the Ka'aba, a stone where offerings were made to 360 pagan Gods.

After all the rock, later to be called the House of Allah, a huge square building where Muslims now turn to pray, was a symbol of Arab pagan beliefs and a major source of income.

From that moment forward, Muhammad added a new dimension to Islam: politics and the use of force. It was a new starting point for the Islamic faith.

This expanded definition of Islam started when Muhammad was forced in 622 to leave Mecca and move to Medina, where he lived the rest of his life. It was later named City of the Prophet.

The decision was made after the Angel Gabriel warned him of a murder plot.

The warning was delivered by Gabriel who visited and instructed Muhammad over a 23-year period.

On one of those visits, Muhammad traveled with Gabriel on a night flight lasting several hours. It started and ended at the Mosque near Ka'bah.

In between, they stopped at a second Mosque in Jerusalem and heaven where he reportedly met the major prophets including Abraham, Moses and Jesus.

* * *

In Medina, Muhammad also decided to use force to replace the Byzantine and Persian empires with an Arab one.

Part of that conquest in the name of Allah included Mecca in 630.

His Arab military didn't stop there.

Between 634 and 650, the army was used to expand Islam and the Arab Empire into North Africa, Iraq, Persia and Syria.

Later, Islam moved into Asia, Europe and Spain.

Islam has been described as a blend of paganism and twisted Bible stories.

Muhammad, its lone "prophet", who made no prophecies, conceived his religion to satiate his lust for power, sex, and money.

In all, Muhammad was married 12 times and had sex with a child, slaves and concubines.

He has been called a terrorist.

*　　*　　*

Armando de la Cruz learned Muhammad institutionalized slavery in North Africa by making it Islamic doctrine. Under those terms, followers were given slaves starting in Medina as a reward for fighting in the name of Allah.

Local warfare, kidnapping, plus the manipulation of religious and judicial institutions produced slaves. That meant West African military, political, and religious authority determined controlled access to the Atlantic slave trade.

It was a well developed practice by the time France, Great Britain, the Netherlands, Portugal and Spain moved to dominate African slave trade.

And the practice continued and continues today in secret. An estimated 27 million slaves exist worldwide.

Muslim states and tribes attack non-Muslim groups or non-believers for slaves.

According to Islamic jurisprudence, slaves are to be treated well. But abuses have been reported from the start until now.

*　　*　　*

Two main trans-Saharan caravan trade north-south routes developed. Caravan routes linked sub-Saharan African peoples with North Africa and the wider Mediterranean and Middle Eastern worlds.

The first ran south through the desert from Morocco, across western Algeria, to the Niger Bend or to the town of Bourern on the Niger River in Mali. Niger is east of the West African coastal nation of Senegal.

The second ran from Tunisia in the north to Lake Chad in western Chad, near the northern point of Cameroon and east of Nigeria.

In all, between the 10th and 19th century, an estimated nine million slaves were moved north to serve as domestic servants or concubines.

*   *   *

Armando de la Cruz learned something else.

The buying of black African slaves in Africa and selling them in Europe started in the 15th century. From there, West African trade was built on gold, ivory and slave trade.

When white traders entered the market, they considered themselves competent international traders. Instead, as far as the slave business was concerned, they were shocked and surprised for a couple of reasons.

They discovered black African rulers, merchants, and middlemen—not white Europeans—set the rules for slave trade along the West African coast two reasons: coastal geography and disease.

There was another unknown reality.

It was a business Muhammad had started 15-hundred years before in 642.

They found out Arab and black Africans made slaves of culturally foreign groups, enemies, the poor and rivals. Other factors made slavery easier. Africans were divided by class, ethnicity, gender, language and religion.

At the very beginning of their learning process, European traders made most of their slave deals aboard ship for a simple reason. They feared dysentery, malaria and yellow fever.

The West African coast became known as the "white man's grave."

Hazardous offshore reefs and sandbars also complicated trade.

So it took time for white newcomers to enter the market, learn how to trade and then get them back to Europe.

And once a deal was closed they faced another significant challenge: getting slaves on board ship for the return trip home.

Here was the solution.

Slaves had to be transported to waiting slave ships anchored off shore in canoes because safe harbors to dock ships largely didn't exist.

It was not until the 19th century that Europeans gained a significant bargaining trade advantage. They were able to send enough military force ashore on a consistent basis.

* * *

Despite the fact Armando de la Cruz knew slavery was outlawed worldwide, at least officially, he elected to use the Islamic approach, the one started and encouraged by Muhammad.

He had long admired Muhammad's way of drawing the sword to rob, conquer and make slaves of non-Muslims and even black Muslims.

Slavery, as he understood it, was in complete harmony with Islam. And if acquired in armed conflict, Christians and Jews could be made slaves regardless of color.

Plus, he knew, slaves from China, India, and Southeast Asia had been traded in slave markets across the Islamic world. And until this day they can be bought and sold in a Mecca back alley market.

And there was something else.

He admired the way Muhammad mixed political and religious thought into Islam. It started in 622 when Muhammad left Mecca for Medina, called the City of the Prophet. There he began to build a theocratic state and to rule over an Islamic Empire.

It was the kind of combination, the mixing of politics, religion and slavery, he believed, that would make it easier to connect and cooperate with other international extremist and political groups.

Their goal would be a simple one: defeat the WEST.

Chapter Fourteen

It was a reasoned conclusion for Armando de la Cruz.

To gain support from the international political left, he would look to Muhammad for guidance. Those rejecting Islam would be treated today like infidels were dealt with centuries ago.

Should they say `no,' according to Islamic law, they could be arrested, enslaved and sold to the one who would bid the most for the individual and their belongings.

De La Cruz pledged money generated from the slave trade would fund a radical way to govern. He or someone like him would rule with an iron hand not only over one country or regime but the WORLD.

All residents would be forced to bow and declare such a leader the most important and only sovereign. He would be like an African tribal leader, reflecting again to Muhammad's time, subject to no one but himself.

At the beginning, de la Cruz would publically announce such a world government would be Islamic as called for by Allah. It would a mixing together of a kind of religious orientation and government. In more practical terms, it would be making church and state one.

Once done, there would a dramatic shift in political direction, something more significant, a more up-to-date vehicle to make the journey.

At the start, Muhammad used camels to spread Islam. Now, a new carrier was needed to move at a faster pace. Instead of a camel, it would be a cruise ship, according to de la Cruz.

And once his political definition was established, he would make two other radical changes.

First, anything religious would be eliminated from consideration. That meant Muhammad, the Prophet; and Jesus Christ, the son of God.

Both Muhammad and Jesus, according to de la Cruz, were imposters and needed to be totally discredited and removed from all levels of society once and for all.

Second, the world should be ruled by a single charismatic leader. He and not a popular vote would make the selection.

He would get to that point by proclaiming Islam and Allah and make the switch once established as not only the chief but also a self-proclaimed descendent of Muhammad.

He would get there by telling anyone willing to listen that this was the way to be fair to all people, a philosophy he learned from Muhammad, and expanded upon by Jesus Christ.

In the end, however, he or someone to be named at a later date would be patterned after Fidel Castro of Cuba or Hugo Chavez of Venezuela.

*   *   *

One of the challenges faced by Armando de la Cruz would be getting by existing French and Spanish colonial attitudes in Morocco. His own background in Colombia and his cultural, political knowledge of all Latin America made it easier for him to grasp and understand.

It was a familiar story of conflict.

Morocco dates back to the second millennium and the first known residents were the Berbers. They ruled small tribal states.

As a result, unity was difficult for this northwestern African country, bordered by the Atlantic Ocean to the west and by the Mediterranean Sea to the north.

Geography made Morocco at the same time important and vulnerable. The Strait of Gibraltar was an easy 36-mile water crossing either way from Europe to Africa.

Rome annexed Morocco and made it part of Mauritania to the south and west in A.D. 46. The Arabs arrived in 685 and brought Islam with them.

Immediately, Arabs and Berbers opposed each other until Morocco was invaded by Portugal and Spain.

They put everything in reverse. Together, they invaded Spain 711. But that didn't last long. The old rivalry surfaced again and the Berbers revolted against the Arabs.

The Berbers took control of large parts of Spain in 1086 until they were tossed out in the 13th century.

Direct descendants of Muhammad reportedly pushed their way into Morocco in 1660. Officially known as the Alawite Dynasty, they were members of the exclusive Sheite Islamic Sect.

Morocco's current King Muhammad VI claims to be part of the sect and to be a direct descendant of Islam's founder.

* * *

Even today tension exists just below the surface between Morocco's Islamic government and the West. De la Cruz saw the space as a possible wedge. Moving forward would depend on his ability to make friends and to link with international leftist political groups, organizations and individuals including Islamic extremists.

It was similar to the strategy used by the old Soviet Union in Chile during the 1970s. He learned about details from his father, Daniel de la Cruz. Even though the plan failed then, Armando was positive it could succeed this time.

Working through Cuba's Fidel Castro, the Soviets called on every known Latin American leftist to join in the struggle. Their goal was clear: convert Chile into a second Soviet-dominated Cuba.

It failed because the effort to do so was too much out in the open. From now on, Armando de la Cruz reasoned, public exposure of the current plan would be avoided.

The opposition, he believed, should be given no opportunity to react until it's too late.

For him, there was a glaring example of that truth.

In Chile, because of how all intentions were known early, the Cuban-Soviet effort was stopped. One attempt failed. Another was successful.

The American Central Intelligence Agency [CIA] tried first.

The failed CIA effort gave Chile's top military leader, Augusto Pinochet, time to end the Communist threat on Sept. 11, 1973.

In the end, Chile became one of the most prosperous and democratic republics in Latin America.

Armando's father, Daniel, told him the story. And to this day, de la Cruz was unable to accept the final outcome. If successful now, Chile's failure would be vindicated by what was learned and corrected.

*   *   *

To propel his ambitious drug-slave operation, de la Cruz made a calculated decision to coordinate every business and political transaction through Rabat, Morocco's capital. This northwest African-Muslim nation was a natural buffer zone to navigate through complicated world cultural, language and political layers.

Success would come easier, he reasoned, because most people defined the world through their own culture, language and political views. Recognizing and using such a general defect, his products could move hidden or almost unnoticed from one geographical point to another.

Let this modern-day deception begin in Rabat and roll on from there, he reasoned.

An investigator or anyone interested in Rabat on any level could fall into an easy trap. He counted on that happening nine chances out of ten.

Those nine opinions would say or believe everything is carried on there in a single language, Arabic. A closer examination shows a different reality.

While it is a Moroccan dream to make Arabic the important language and only means of communication in their country and elsewhere, they know and practice a different and sometimes unpleasant reality.

Business is carried out mainly in French and Spanish. And English is becoming the popular language to learn. Until Arabic could be better accepted internationally, it would remain a secondary language even at home.

*   *   *

It was a reality he became aware of in reverse in his home country of Colombia. There Spanish was the language of communication and the language of doing business and everything else. He discovered the same to be true in France and Spain.

There was no general need or pressure to know another language like English even though the United States was just to the north of his country and even though England was part of Europe.

His thinking was simple enough. He reasoned success would be on his side with each country and region faced with the same kind of language barrier.

It was within the language of each country, that culture and politics were defined.

So if all that was true, according to his thinking, the large majority of the world would define their own country by the language they spoke, their own culture and their own definition of politics.

That meant, he reasoned, anyone outside his own country would define another place the same way he or she did at home.

And it was this general error in judgment Armando de la Cruz would attempt to exploit as he moved slaves and drugs from one zone to another. He could be in and out before anyone or any country would understand his logic of deception.

*   *   *

De la Cruz would use the United Nations as a wedge. And once the UN was in control of the world, his version of a single international government would be easier to put in place.

He liked the option because it provided infrastructure suited for governing.

Organized in 1945 after World War II, the UN replaced the League of Nations.

Most important for him to make the plan work was the UN's ability to deal fluently and at ease in six official languages: Arabic, Chinese, English, French, Russian and Spanish.

Such talent was needed to coordinate the 192 UN's member states. Only Kosovo, Taiwan and the Vatican were not part of the world organization. At the right moment, he knew, it wouldn't take much to control them too.

With the necessary languages in hand, according to de la Cruz, his organization like the UN would be better able to take on hard cultural and political matters.

*   *   *

And if de la Cruz wanted to run his operation though Rabat, the capital of Morocco, he had to know more about France and about Charles André Joseph Marie de Gaulle.

In fact, he would use part of the Frenchman's methods to combine with his own ideas to move ahead politically.

Born in Lille, De Gaulle was the second of five children of Henri de Gaulle and Jeanne Maillot. His father was a philosophy and literature professor at a Jesuit college and his mother's family was rich. They were successful entrepreneurs from the industrial region of Lille in French Flanders.

De Gaulle was educated in Paris at the College Stanislas and briefly in Belgium.

He taught at the École Militaire [Military School]; and wrote books and articles about the military. In 1931, he published Le fil de l'épée [The Edge of the Sword, 1960), an analysis of military and political leadership.

During World War One, he was wounded and captured at Douaumont in the Battle of Verdun in March 1916.

Not only was De Gaulle to become a brigadier general, he served as Undersecretary of State for National Defense and War. Opposing France's decision to surrender to Germany during World War II, he urged the French government to move to North Africa and carry on the conflict from France's African colonies.

Failing to convince his military mentor, French Marshal Henri Petain, De Gaulle and other senior French officers fled to London with 100,000 gold francs in secret funds given him by ex-prime minister Paul Reynaud.

Petain chose to cooperate with the Germans as premier of France's Vichy government 1940-44 headquartered in Lyon.

Because of his split with the now German dominated French government, de Gaulle turned to Algeria, Morocco and North Africa or French North Africa. At the time, North Africa was called French North Africa covering Algeria, Morocco and Tunisia.

An even broader definition of North Africa moved beyond Algeria, Morocco and Tunisia to include Egypt west of the Suez Gulf and Libya.

French North Africa became an important World War II battleground between Allied and German forces. Once under control, the war jumped to Europe.

In May 1943, de Gaulle moved his headquarters from London to Algiers following the Anglo-US invasion of North Africa in November 1942.

De Gaulle, once in North Africa, organized the French First Army and invaded southern France to help liberate nearly a third of their homeland occupied by the Nazis.

A few days before Paris was liberated, de Gaulle traveled to France by plane from the French colony of Algeria.

Joining Allied officials, de Gaulle rode in a vehicle near the front of the military force entering the city. Once established in Paris, he praised the French Resistance for its role in liberating France during a radio speech.

At the end of the war, De Gaulle returned to his elitist roots. He wanted to restore France's colonial empire, at one time the second largest behind the British or a control over 8.6 percent of the world's surface. In doing that his mistrust of Great Britain and United States surfaced. He saw them as colonial competitors rather than allies.

It didn't matter that it was the Americans in particular and the English who had liberated a defeated France dominated by German dictator Adolf Hitler.

De Gaulle's appreciation of the two allies should have been even deeper, de la Cruz realized.

*   *   *

De la Cruz learned something else he needed to know if he was going to take over this part of the world. By acquiring knowledge of past history, he felt mistakes made by others could perhaps be avoided.

Or perhaps even more significant, by learning old ways of bluffing the enemy, he could gain control of new territory at a faster clip.

*   *   *

Before World War II started, he found out England and France had an opportunity to stop Hitler and turned it down.

They lost their chance during a 1938 meeting in Munich, Germany. Before the gathering, English Prime Minister Neville Chamberlain and French Premier Édouard Daladier had been warned by Czech Republic president Eduard Beneš.

Benes' and others said the same peril could happen to them if they didn't stand firm against the Germans.

Hitler had demanded that Beneš turn over the western part of Czechoslovakia, Bohemia or Sudeten, where the population majority were of German descent.

At the time, Benes told the British and the French Hitler could be stopped. He said a number of German military officers close to Hitler would take him out.

Their signal to act, Benes said, would be the British and French issuing a public `no' to Hitler's demand to acquire the Sudeten.

Both England and France had a military advantage at the time as a result of the Versailles Treaty ending World War I. Germany's army had been cut to 100,000. France had 400,000 troops.

Instead, British Prime Minister Neville Chamberlain and French primer Édouard Daladier signed a peace agreement, the 1938 Munich Pact with Hitler and Italy's dictator Benito Mussolini in the German city.

After Chamberlain called the pact a "peace in our time" agreement, Germany invaded Czechoslovakia the next year. Sudeten or Bohemia was annexed and declared a German protectorate.

It wasn't long before Germany moved into France. England was also threatened.

*   *   *

De Gaulle's first move to rebuild the French colonial empire immediately following the war was a push for an organization to later be called the European Economic Community (EEC).

He would need German cooperation for the EEC from the start. To do so, the general-president paid the first state visit to Germany by a French head of state since Napoleon.

His gesture paid off in time.

In January 1963, Germany and France signed a friendship treaty or the Élysée Treaty.

De la Cruz learned de Gaulle had made his public announcement of his political intentions for France by starting out talking about Europe.

De Gaulle announced his vision for Europe in a Strasbourg speech in November 1959.

In French he said: "Oui, c'est l'Europe, depuis l'Atlantique jusqu'à l'Oural, c'est toute l'Europe, qui décidera du destin du monde."

Here is the English translation: "Yes, it is Europe, from the Atlantic to the Urals, it is the whole of Europe that will decide the destiny of the world."

In other words, the world's future would be decided without the Americans and British.

*   *   *

De la Cruz knew he would need to resurrect this kind of conflict, defined by the French, to take control of the world.

*   *   *

During a 1959 speech, de Gaulle openly proclaimed his approach. He wanted Europe to stand between the Americans and British in all dealings with the Soviet Union.

Here is how de Gaulle saw the future.

"A European Europe means that it exists by itself for itself, in other words in the midst of the world—it has its own policy."

Later, he added "France has no friends, only interests." He rejected ideologies, international organizations, or multilateral agreements." Instead, he believed in nations and their relative strengths.

He didn't want a repeat of what happened to France after the 1938 Munich agreement. The French, he reasoned, should control all decisions affecting France rather than being forced to ask the Americans and British for help.

In an attempt to strengthen his position, De Gaulle made it clear France would re-establish the French colonial community.

Here is what he meant.

France would extend a hand to help the less fortunate living in all French colonies. The policy was called `mission civilisatrice' in French or its civilizing mission.

If North Africans, as an example, adopted French culture, learned to speak French fluently and converted to Christianity, they could be French citizens and be equal to any resident in France.

* * *

De la Cruz was amused but not surprised at the reaction.

De Gaulle's colonial position was challenged immediately by leaders of French colonies once the war ended in 1945. They didn't expect the French leader to change his view of them just because France had been taken over by the Germans and later liberated.

Leaders of France's colonial land expected nothing else once France was liberated.

The first to rebel were the French associated states of Cambodia, Laos and Vietnam. Then there was Algeria.

When talk failed, war erupted and a full-scale conflict broke out following a series of uprisings in 1954. When de Gaulle relented eight years later, Algeria became independent on July 5, 1962.

Two years afterwards, Morocco and Tunisia, also associate states, became independent.

By the end of the 1960s, most of France's colonies had gained independence. The number had been reduced to one percent of what it was in 1939. The remaining French overseas Departments and territories stayed on because their residents voted to stay with France.

* * *

De la Cruz studied with interest what else happened during the break-up of France's colonial empire.

Despite the huge loss of colonial territory, de Gaulle continued on the path of attempting to make France unique in world politics.

He vetoed the British application to join the European Economic Community (EEC) in 1963 because, according to him, the United Kingdom lacked the political will to be part of a strong Europe.

What he really feared, de la Cruz reasoned if past history was a guide, was Britain being a "Trojan Horse" for the United States.

Publically de Gaulle charged continental European and British economic interests were not compatible.

A year later, he took a more direct slap at the United States.

In September and October 1964, de Gaulle traveled 20,000 miles over 26 days covering ten South American republics. This followed a trip to Mexico the year before.

His announced goal was to expand France's cultural and economic influence. And he was quick to express his resentment of the United States.

And after being re-elected to a second seven-year term as France's president in December 1965, de Gaulle went further in an attempt to secure his country's political importance.

He ordered France's withdrawal from the common NATO military command, but remained a part of the organization.

The North Atlantic Treaty Organization (NATO) was formed in 1949 to oppose the Soviet Union during the Cold War. Headquartered in Brussels, Belgium, NATO members at the start included Belgium, Canada, Denmark, France, Great Britain, Iceland, Italy, Luxembourg, the Netherlands, Norway, Portugal, and the United States.

*   *   *

De la Cruz was amazed. De Gaulle didn't stop there. Three days before the start of the Six-Day War between Israel and the Arab world in 1967, de Gaulle declared an arms embargo against Israel.

France was a major arms supplier to Israel at the time.

De Gaulle then described the Jewish nation as "this elite people, sure of themselves and domineering".

In a letter written to the Israeli government following the Six-Day War, the French leader accused Israel of using unnecessary force to take possession of Jerusalem and so much of Jordan, Egypt, and Syria.

Chapter Fifteen

De la Cruz reaffirmed his earlier decision to make Morocco and Rabat, the capital city, his operational base. From there, he reasoned, it would be easier to maintain contact with an important support group called the Polisario.

The leaders and membership were his kind of people. It all depended on the politics of the person or group leader speaking. They were called terrorists by political opponents. All others referred to them as a necessary liberation force.

It took de la Cruz time to decide on locating in this country occupying such a key and strategic region of northwest Africa. He made the final decision after carefully going over the region's political history.

He concluded his kind of operation there would attract little or no attention.

Simply put . . . there were too many other distractions going on all at the same time to be concerned about this man from Colombia, a far-off land in South America.

And as one of the Barbary States during the 17th and 18th centuries, Morocco was headquarters for pirates operating in the Mediterranean.

* * *

Here was what de la Cruz looked at and really liked. The Barbary or Maghreb Pirates operating in the region were a criminal alliance power block.

He really admired the way they earned money to fund current and future adventures.

They plundered merchant vessels for cargo and raided southern Europe's coastal zones for local residents. Once captured and under their control, they were sold as slaves.

The alliance controlled North Africa and ravaged southern coastal zone of Europe for eight centuries.

Made up of Muslims and privateers or those paid to operate side-by-side with those followers of Islam, they operated separately or together in four countries.

They worked out of organized bases inside and beyond the Mediterranean Sea zone.

Morocco was the western border and Libya the eastern border. In between were Algeria and Tunisia.

* * *

In 1904, France and Spain divided Morocco. France controlled most of what is now Morocco. Spain had the southwest portion or a desert covering 102,703 square miles.

Spain consolidated its control in 1958 by naming the desert the Spanish Sahara. They did so by bringing together two parts, Rio de Oro to the south and Saguia el Hamra to the north.

De la Cruz wanted to be established there for the same reason the others did.

The African desert was geographically well placed and economically important.

It is surrounded by Algeria to the east, Mauritania to the west and south and Morocco to the north. The land was also flanked by the Atlantic Ocean to the west and was near Spain's Canary Islands.

* * *

A group called the Polisario challenged Spain.

Organized and developed by Sahrawis residents of the Spanish Sahara, they rebelled against those who would name their homeland, the Spanish Sahara.

So when Spain turned down their petition to be politically independent, it didn't take long for battle lines to be drawn.

Guerrilla warfare exploded in the 1970s.

At the beginning, there was no match.

Spain's military superiority was too much for the Polisario's force estimated at 800 men and women. Forced out of their desert home, they relocated just across the border in Tindouf in western Algeria.

Once there, their numbers expanded to several thousand armed fighters coming from other parts of Africa. Algeria supplied arms and funding. Their leaders had ambitions of their own.

At the same time, Morocco's King Hassan II sent in a force estimated at 300,000 in 1975. He decided it was time to regain control of their former territory.

With opposition building on more than one front, Spain withdrew in 1976 and the territory was renamed, the Western Sahara.

With the Europeans gone, those left opposed each other.

Mauritania and Morocco decided they wanted control.

Desert residents, the Saharawis, rejected both of those ideas. They wanted independence and to be recognized as the Sahrawi Arab Democratic Republic.

Three years later, Mauritania reached a peace agreement with the Polisario.

Morocco rejected the plan.

To let everyone know they were serious, they seized land given up by Mauritania and began immediately to exert administrative control over the entire region.

After a cease-fire was proposed in 1991, it was decided a referendum was the only way to decide the desert's political future.

The United Nations suggested the Sahara become an autonomous region of Morocco.

The UN's solution was proposed after Morocco opposed a vote on an independence referendum. There was a dispute over voter eligibility.

The Polisario rejected the UN's autonomous region proposal.

A third alternative was also turned down.

When Morocco's King Mohammed VI, who took over for his father, declared in 2002 he would not "renounce an inch of" the Western Sahara.

De la Cruz was amused on learning the UN Security Council called for still a new approach in an attempt to calm down the parties involved. It was a modified version of any earlier suggestion.

According to the plan, the Western Sahara would be declared a semiautonomous region of Morocco for five years.

At the end of that term, voters would have three choices: autonomy, independence or integration into Morocco.

The Polisario said okay.

Morocco refused to consider it.

"Why should anyone be surprised at that?" de la Cruz told a friend.

In an attempt to control the bitter dispute, the UN spent more than $600 million to keep peace in Western Sahara over a 13-year period.

And in 2005, the Polisario freed 404 Moroccan prisoners. They had been imprisoned nearly 20 years and were reportedly the world's longest-held prisoners of war.

"They probably just got tired of holding them," de la Cruz said. "I'm surprised they held them that long. On the other hand, I hope this kind of conflict continues forever. It's better for me."

*   *   *

Also from Rabat, de la Cruz figured he would be in the best place geographically to make contact with al-Qaeda, the world's largest terrorist organization. He felt he could do so there without causing suspicion or trouble for himself at the start. Later, it would not matter.

He selected al-Qaeda over Hamas, Hezbollah and Irish Republican Army (IRA).

While he wouldn't turn down any opportunity to cooperate or work with any of the groups, al-Qaeda . . . in his opinion . . . provided the best overall chance for success.

It was an approach long-used by the old Soviet Union, the grouping together of international leftists.

At the beginning—called international brigades—they fought unsuccessfully against Spain's Francisco Franco. Clashing during Spain's Civil War of 1936-39, Franco got outside help from Germany and Italy.

The Soviet Union, fighting off the Nazi's at the time, encouraged the international brigades to oppose Franco on the battlefield.

Leading up to Sept. 11, 1973, when Chile's Gen. Augusto Pinochet turned back an attempt to convert this South American republic into a second Communist Cuba, the Soviets used a similar tactic. Leftists—from all over Latin America—responded to the take-over call.

Now, Al-Qaeda, was using a similar Soviet strategy.

De la Cruz—like other leftists who never forgave Pinochet for his success against them in Chile—was hopeful al-Qaeda had learned from the Cuban-Soviet failure in South America.

Al-Qaeda or "the base" in Arabic was a network of extremists organized by Osama bin Laden of Saudi Arabia. The group first surfaced to openly oppose Soviet occupation of Afghanistan.

Instead of being called International brigades, volunteers numbering in the thousands from and around the Middle East were called the MUJAHIDEEN. They were warriors fighting to defend fellow Muslims.

In the mid-1980s, Osama bin Laden became the prime financier for the organization that recruited Muslims from mosques around the world. This volunteer force was crucial in driving the Soviets out of Afghanistan.

De la Cruz wanted to learn more about them if contact could be made. Here is what he found out.

*　　*　　*

Bin Laden sought out radical Islamic thinkers to learn how they thought, operated. He was motivated for a simple reason. He wanted U.S. troops out of Saudi Arabia, the birthplace of Islam.

His first moves against his own government and the Americans ended in failure. Payment for his deeds came quickly.

Bin Laden was tossed out of his country in 1991.

From there, he moved al-Qaeda's headquarters to Khartoum, Sudan, west of Saudi Arabia, across the Red Sea and south of Egypt.

It didn't take long for the terrorist organization to launch attacks on U.S. servicemen in Somalia, to the east of Sudan and across to neighboring Ethiopia bordering the Indian Ocean.

Earlier, he had learned not to carry out attacks on his base country. In doing so in Saudi Arabia, he paid a very high price.

*　　*　　*

As part of his new approach, bin Laden issued a "Declaration of War" against the United States in August of 1996.

And here is the part de la Cruz liked best.

It took bin Laden nearly two years to work out an alliance with other terrorist groups to carry out the plan.

They included the "International Islamic Front for Jihad Against the Jews and Crusaders," the Egyptian al-Gama'at al-Islamiyya, the Egyptian Islamic Jihad and the Harakat ul-Ansar.

De la Cruz also discovered al-Qaeda and Osama bin Laden had become virtually synonymous, but bin Laden did not run the organization by himself.

His top advisor and possible successor was Dr. Ayman al-Zawahiri, al-Qaeda's theological leader.

An Egyptian surgeon from an upper-class family, he joined the Islamist movement in the late 1970s.

He was a man with a long history of terrorism.

Al-Zawahiri served three years in prison on charges he was involved with the 1981 assassination of Egypt's President Anwar Sadat.

On release, he traveled to Afghanistan, where he met bin Laden and became his personal physician and advisor. He was likely instrumental in bin Laden's political evolution.

Al-Zawahiri was suspected of helping organize the 1997 massacre of 67 foreign tourists in Luxor, Egypt, and was indicted in connection with the bombing of U.S. embassies in Kenya and Tanzania.

And he was one of five Islamic leaders to sign bin Laden's Declaration of War.

Wanted by the FBI, Al-Zawahiri was sentenced to death in absentia by Egyptian authorities.

* * *

The way al-Qaeda was put together impressed de la Cruz and he knew for sure this was his door of entry on his own terms.

To recruit radicals internationally, al-Qaeda's leaders decided that could be done best through a loosely organized network of cells.

It was at that point in his information gathering process de la Cruz knew how he could best connect with terrorists whether he was really or fully committed to Al-Qaeda or not.

Here was the important point.

The organization's infrastructure was small, mobile, and decentralized. Each cell operated independently.

Here was the key: they don't know the identity of other cells. And they didn't want to know. It was a matter of self protection for one or the other if captured.

For de la Cruz, he could do as he pleased without much concern of al-Qaeda or the leadership. It meant he could establish contact, take advantage of what was available or contribute and then move on.

*   *   *

De la Cruz made his first contact with Al-Qaeda at a well-known open-air coffee shop near where he was staying on Rue AL Mourabittin 17 in the Quartier Tour Hassan on the north side of Rabat.

Of more than passing interest for de la Cruz was the ruins of a mosque started but never finished on the order of the man who founded Rabat, Abou Youssef Yaacoub el-Mansour.

The structure was to be built to honor Islam's victory in Spain at the end of the 12th century. Had it been finished, it would have been the world's second largest mosque.

Today, there are two prominent reminders of the original plan.

One is a reddish-brown 144-foot tall Minaret on the north side of the block. It would have been used to call worshipers to pray.

And two is what could be called a forest of small columns spread out in front of the Minaret.

Nearby is a second historic place, also near where de la Cruz was headquartered.

It was a marble pavilion called the Mohammed V Mausoleum built to honor a very long serving King of Morocco. King Mohammed V was buried there after being in power 52 years, starting in 1909 until his death in 1961.

The second son of Mohammed V, King Hassan II, took over for his dead father and served 38 years until his death in 1999.

He was buried near his father and a brother, Moulay Abdallah, another Mohammed V son.

*   *   *

He learned later his contact was working with militants in Belgium, Iraq, Syria and Sweden and he was recruiting candidates to join Al-Qaeda fighters in Afghanistan and Somalia.

And he showed a strong interest in what de la Cruz was doing in Bogota, Colombia, in South America, Rabat in Morocco and the coastal towns of Toulon in France and Malaga in Spain.

In short, tourism was the perfect cover for his fleet of cruise ships. From those vessels, he reasoned, it would be easy to put slaves ashore, trade in drugs and laundry money.

The African-Caribbean-European-Latin American operation would be headquartered in Rabat, the African capital city of Morocco; and Tortola in the Caribbean British Virgin Islands. And slaves and drugs would be unloaded in two European Mediterranean ports. One was Malaga in Spain and the other was Toulon in France.

His money would be cleaned up during the process of buying and selling, moving from one currency to another and depositing and re-depositing funds in a string of banks.

The Port of Málaga had been in operation since 600 B.C. on Spain's south coast and near Africa to the south.

And the Port of Toulon is in southern France, a perfect tourism attraction with an historic center near the port, filled with narrow streets, small squares and fountains. It was also the home of a French Mediterranean Naval base.

The Toulon harbor is one of the best natural anchorages on the Mediterranean and one of the largest harbors in Europe.

Chapter Sixteen

De la Cruz first saw Abdelkader Belliraj at the Rabat coffee shop, just north of where he lived and near the Mohammed V Mausoleum.

Although he had a general idea of how his operation should work, he realized he needed more background knowledge on how to make it all function properly. Too much trial and error could end the operation abruptly. It could also cost him his life.

His primary vulnerability was operating out of his Latin American environment and in an area where his native Spanish language was helpful but not all the time.

Fortunately for him, Abdelkader Belliraj faced a similar challenge talking with the Colombian and Europeans in general.

Both, however, shared a second language: French, a favorite over English for many Latin Americans; and a more than second language in Arabic-speaking Morocco. Residents there forced to use it to communicate with Europeans who generally spoke little or no Arabic.

So with that in mind, Abdelkader Belliraj was the kind of man Armando had dreamed of knowing for a very long time. From his sources in Colombia, in the northwestern part of South America, he knew Belliraj recently had been in contact with bin Laden, Hezbollah and the Russian mafia.

Having confidence in himself because of long business and political experience in Latin America, his choice of such a vital contact was made after careful consideration and talks with trusted friends.

And just to be on the safe side, he didn't want to stop there.

One significant contact—no matter how good—was not enough. He wanted many more or as many as possible until he had enough information. He would know instinctively when such a moment had arrived.

Although an announced convert to Islam for convenience only, it was his way of opening up an important information door.

If his fictitious religious position held, he reasoned his effort to couple those added contacts with the political left would place him in the best position possible to carry out his major goal: do damage to the West, particularly the United States.

His first step, if possible, would be to play a role to politically unify significant parts of North Africa. If done, it would be easier to penetrate and perhaps dominate parts of Europe.

De la Cruz got his first training and a better understanding of how his current mission should work from the Revolutionary Armed Forces of Colombia or Fuerzas Armadas Revolucionarias de Colombia known as FARC.

Established in 1964 as the military wing of the Colombian Communist Party, FARC was Colombia's oldest, largest, most capable and best-equipped Marxist insurgency.

And de la Cruz felt Abdelkader Belliraj or someone like him could do something else for him. Place him right in the middle of all major Islamic and leftist terrorist movements in Africa and Europe.

He saw the possibility of bringing together Algeria, the Western Sahara and maybe even Morocco, a long shot and perhaps the plan's largest stumbling block.

From there, the Basque country in Spain to the north and Angola to the south could help apply necessary political pressure. Such action was needed, de la Cruz believed, to give his plan any chance for success.

De la Cruz felt he could use to an advantage his Latin American heritage and political background in dealing with two leftist groups in particular, ETA in Spain and the Polisario in Western Sahara or the former Spanish Sahara in the northwestern part of Africa.

*   *   *

Listening to his Islamic connection, Armando de la Cruz learned of two important historic events, both of which had something in common. Those dates referred to battles fought in Europe and both represented two military loses. Those defeats meant an Islamic attempt to control Europe was over.

The first was delivered by Charles Martel, called Charles the Hammer, at the 732 Battle of Tours in Western France on the Loire River.

Martel brought down a Muslim army following the capture of Egypt, North Africa and Syria. His victory also stopped an effort to end Christianity.

The second was another 9-11.

De la Cruz knew of two 9-11s, one in Chile in 1973 and the other in New York in 2001. This new connection with Islam gave him a third one: Sept. 11, 1683.

As part of the Great Turkish War, an Austrian, German and Polish army, commanded by Poland's King of Poland John III Sobieski turned back the Ottoman Islamic Empire's force in the Battle of Vienna.

The King's army was provided by Austria, Poland, Russia and Venice, all members of a Roman Catholic organization called the Holy League.

From then on, Islamic influence in Europe and the world for that matter was never the same again.

At the time, between the 16th and the 17th centuries, the Ottoman Empire had controlled much of North Africa, Southeastern Europe and western Asia.

It was also an Islamic successor to the Eastern Roman Empire governed from Constantinople.

In other words, the Ottoman Empire had been at the center of the Eastern and Western worlds for six centuries.

And now, according to bin Laden, the New York Sept. 11, 2001 twin towers attack date was selected in advance for a reason.

For him, it meant Islam had finally reversed itself following that dramatic Sept. 11, 1683 humiliating loss. Islam was again on the road to being a single combined political and religious power structure following Islamic rules.

And most important, the final goal was now possible: Islam would and now could control all countries or the world.

De la Cruz wasn't sure that was true but he would repeat it as often as necessary to further his own cause and to broaden his contacts with the political left.

*   *   *

His own contact with the political LEFT started in Colombia, his home country in South America. That was pretty solid. And that was made through the Colombian Communist Party, known as FARC, formed in 1964 as the military wing of the Colombian Communist Party.

De la Cruz learned more in Cuba, a Caribbean Communist country, needing a way to buy arms and finance international revolution starting in Latin America.

It turned out to be an exchange. Colombia provided drugs and Cuba earned money to buy arms.

How?

It was done by allowing Colombian drugs to be shipped through Cuba in order to reach the large U.S. market. It was an operation coordinated by Cuba's Interior Ministry, also where Cuban intelligence was headquartered.

All this was handled and coordinated by Fidel Castro as self-appointed head of the Latin America department. Castro, as chief of Cuba's Communist Party, decided it should be a separate part of the Foreign Affairs Ministry.

According to one plan, drugs or cocaine were brought to Cuba by boat and plane. Once on the ground and placed aboard government-owned vans, the drug-loaded vehicles moved to waiting Miami-bound cigar speed boats able to travel as fast as 60 knots.

Small twin-engine airplanes carrying 1,000 to 2,000 pounds of cocaine did have an option. Their cargo could be dropped in secure open water near waiting speed boats.

De la Cruz learned something else in time.

Cuba provided not only weapons but training to Colombia's guerrilla fighters. It was a clear pathway to seeing how Fidel Castro and Ernesto [Che] Guevara of Argentina operated and thought about how to increase the size and scope of world-wide revolution.

*   *   *

To really be successful, de la Cruz knew he had to look beyond Latin America. For him, he had to include Africa. He instinctively knew he needed to know what had happened there before attempting any kind of venture into Europe.

Like what he had done and learned in the Caribbean, he would look to Cuba to guide the way further down the road of spreading international terrorism. The main targets were the industrialized West and the United States.

He was surprised, but not shocked how Fidel Castro had honored African revolutionaries in Cuba. That was how he found out about Cuban involvement in Africa.

On one of his trips to Cuba, he accidently stumbled across a place called: the African Memorial Park. It was built in the Miramar section of Havana.

The park's first statue recognized Angola's first president, Agostinho Neto.

Oliver Tambo was the second.

Oliver Reginald Tambo connected with the Cubans in Angola, where leftists trained to oppose apartheid in South Africa. He had received military training in the Soviet Union.

Also a close friend and associate of Nelson Mandela, Tambo had converted the African National Congress [ANC] into a radical national liberation movement.

He went on to aggressively establish ANC missions in 27 countries including Egypt, Ghana and Morocco.

Cuban support of revolutionary movements in Africa started in 1965.

At one time, there were as many as 200,000 guerrilla fighters and hundreds of instructors in education and sports working in Africa.

Cubans were there to push a Communist-Socialist Revolution. They followed all orders and direction given them by the Soviet Union.

*   *   *

South Africa's president Thabo Mbeki, elected after Nelson Mandela retired in 1999, visited Cuba two years later and said: "Cuba's intervention was decisive in Angola when they and their MPLA [Popular Movement for the Liberation of Angola] allies defeated South African forces in open battle.

"This led the White Regime to back off from Angola and ultimately Namibia and South Africa."

*   *   *

Here is where Cubans were involved.

Angola, the largest key zone in southwest Africa, is bordered by three countries: the Democratic Republic of Congo or the Republique du Congo to the north and east; Zambia to east; and Namibia to the south or the country between Angola and South Africa.

Guinea Bissau, a small country just south of Senegal, is north of Angola.

The third, Mozambique, is in southeast Africa, just north of South Africa.

*   *   *

It was that kind of contact—coupled with all-out backing from the Soviet Union—that placed Cuba not only on the edge of the international leftist revolution but squarely in the middle of it.

*   *   *

So the next step was easy. It seemed to be the perfect match.

De la Cruz would look beyond Latin America, this time to Africa. He instinctively knew he needed to know what happened there before attempting any kind of venture into Europe.

If he was correct, it would be like being issued an entry pass to cross a bridge connecting the Western Hemisphere and Europe.

Like what he had done and learned in the Caribbean, he would look to Cuba to guide the way further down the road of spreading international terrorism.

Chapter Seventeen

First of all he wanted to find out what Fidel Castro did after being ordered by the Soviet Union to move Cuba's Soviet acquired leftist politics beyond the Caribbean in the late 1950s. And he also wanted to know more about Ernesto [Che] Guevara of Argentina who wanted to help spread more of the Soviet Revolution to another part of the world.

Armando de la Cruz thought it best to start understanding Cuban international involvement by taking a look at ETA in Spain and the Polisario in the Western Sahara in Africa.

Both Leninist liberation guerrilla-terrorist movements—organized in the early 1970s by Fidel Castro of Cuba and Ernesto [Che] Guevara of Argentina—followed the same strategy Fidel and Che had learned in adapting Soviet-style politics to the successful 1959 Cuban revolution.

Now the Soviet Union wanted to exert more influence in those two particular zones: one, Western Europe and two, that part of northern Africa. And they would use Fidel and Che in their attempt to get the job done.

*   *   *

Beyond ETA and Polisario, Armando learned Cuban penetration was much deeper.

During a 30-year period, dating from 1965, Cuba touched and supported revolutionary movements in Africa.

The Caribbean island operated in Spain, Algeria, the Sahara Dessert and all three of Portugal's former African colonies: Angola, Guinea Bissau and Mozambique.

Besides being in Namibia, they helped Nelson Mandela come to power in South Africa.

Che Guevara said Cuban support, ordered by the Soviet Union, was necessary to stop the Congo's return to colonial rule.

After becoming politically independent from Belgium in 1960 without leaving the French Community, the Congo was named the Republic of the Congo.

Much of its political movement was centered around Patrice Lumumba, the spark that brought on independence.

* * *

In early 1965, the 37-year-old Guevara, traveled to Africa to offer his knowledge and experience as a guerrilla to the ongoing conflict in the Congo.

His main motive for traveling there, however, was an attempt to avenge Patrice Lumumba's death.

As an admirer of the late Lumumba, Guevara declared that his "murder should be a lesson for all of us."

Using an alias, Ramón Benítez, Guevara was joined by 12 Afro-Cubans on April 24 and another 100 black Cubans shortly afterwards.

He did that for a reason.

Egyptian President Gamal Abdel Nasser, who first met Che in 1959, had warned Guevara his plan to fight in the Congo was "unwise" and doomed to failure.

There was another opinion mixed into his thinking.

According to Algerian President Ahmed Ben Bella, Guevara thought Africa was imperialism's weak link and therefore had enormous revolutionary potential.

Still the Egyptian President's view weighed heavily in his mind.

*   *   *

Nasser was concerned about Che's lack of language skills and his limited knowledge of African culture.

Guevara had some knowledge of Swahili. To cover his linguistic shortcoming he was assigned a teenage interpreter, Freddy Ilanga.

Over the next seven months Ilanga grew to "admire the hard-working Guevara," who according to Ilanga, "showed the same respect to black people as he did to whites."

And despite his attempt to do so, it was not possible to maintain the kind of low operating profile needed in the Congo to foment revolution. It could have been done if he had been able to blend into the cultural landscape.

Instead, he was vulnerable and detectable.

*   *   *

The U.S. government was aware of his location and what he planned to do in advance.

All of Guevara's incoming and outgoing transmissions were picked up by the National Security Agency [NSA] from a floating U.S. Navy listening post.

It was placed in the Indian Ocean near Dar-es-Salaam, the capital of Tanzania, in southeastern Africa and east of the Congo.

From those transmissions, it was learned Che was operating in the mountains near the Congo village of Fizi on Lake Tanganyika, a natural border between the Congo and Tanzania.

With advance information, an attack group working with the Congo National Army moved to stop Guevara.

The attack force was made up of Cuban exiles who had fled Cuba when Castro took over, white South African mercenaries and a U.S. Central Intelligence Agency [CIA] group.

*   *   *

After seven frustrating months, Guevara left the Congo with those Cubans who survived the ordeal on Nov. 20, 1965. This part of his mission had ended in failure as Nasser had predicted.

Later Che blamed his departure decision on his health. He was suffering from acute asthma and dysentery.

*   *   *

After long consideration, Armando decided he needed to review one more time and in more time and in more detail what exactly had happened to Che in the Congo.

Why?

In the end, if he could find adequate answers, a terrorist strategy workable in any of the world's multiple cultures would more likely be possible.

He sensed Che may have attempted to develop a plan largely on his own without consulting anyone.

In other words, he may have given little attention to obvious cultural differences.

*   *   *

Armando determined from the start Che Guevara had wanted to act on a report Belgium would again colonize Zaire or the Democratic Republic of the Congo to provide armed support in Angola, Guinea Bissau and Mozambique.

And it was at that time nationalist Patrice Lumumba first attracted Che's interest in the Belgium Congo in late 1959. He found out Che not only wanted to travel there, but if possible he

165

wanted to take up the leftist political struggle where Lumumba left off.

The Belgium-dominated government had jailed and later released Lumumba after charges of instigating public violence were dropped to allow him to participate in the Brussels Congo conference in 1960.

It was after the Brussels meeting, the Congo became politically independent on June 30, 1960 and Patrice Lumumba of the leftist Mouvement National Congolais became the Congo's first Prime Minister and Joseph Kasavubu of the ABAKO Party became President.

*　*　*

Events had unfolded quickly after Belgium declared the Congo independent.

Within weeks, another political leader Moise Tshombe announced Katanga should be independent of the Congo. Leaders of a second province, South Kasai, announced similar breakaway plans.

Katanga, in the southeast part of the Congo, borders Angola on the southwest, Zambia on the southeast, and Lake Tanganyika on the east.

Zambia in the southeast corner of Katanga is the capital and a farm and ranch zone.

*　*　*

Che was apparently concerned about Katanga and South Kasai.

If left alone, the newly independent Congo could have lost two rich and developed areas, part of the richest concentration of precious metals and minerals on earth.

Many like Che, Armando learned, viewed the move an attempt to create Belgian-controlled puppet-states run for the benefit of mining interests.

Tshombe's decision had the support of Belgian business heads and over 6,000 Belgian troops. Belgium, however, did not officially recognize the new states before independence was declared.

Those Belgian industrial companies mined cobalt, copper, gold, diamonds, radium, tin and uranium.

Once processed, most of the minerals were shipped by rail to other parts of the Congo, Angola and Zambia. A steamer service did the same on Lake Tanganyika between Katanga and Tanzania.

So the decision to bring Katanga and South Kasai together as a single unit, Armando felt, was an answer to Che's concerns. And at the same time, it gave Che a better understanding of why Lumumba and Kasavubu wanted the states to be part of the Congo.

*   *   *

More disruption followed.

Despite change in the Congo, there were more political challenges ahead for Lumumba. All of them were tied to an Army mutiny called by Col. Joseph Désiré Mobutu.

Order was restored after three things happened: Lumumba asked the United Nations [UN] to send in troops, Belgium sent in soldiers to protect Belgian citizens and Colonel Mobutu ordered the military to return to their barracks.

Mobutu acted after Lumumba agreed to his demand to name him Army chief of staff.

At the same time, Lumumba and President Kasavubu blamed each other for not being able to control escalating political challenges.

To make things worse, Kasavubu ordered the dismissal of Lumumba as Prime Minister and Lumumba ordered the dismissal of Kasavubu as President.

During the turmoil, it didn't take long for Lumumba to realize caving into the army leader was a huge mistake despite the fact he had no choice.

*   *   *

A second coup exploded.

There were no deals this time.

Mobutu became Prime Minister and later President of the Democratic Republic of the Congo in 1965.

Immediately, he moved to make the Congo more African by giving the country a new name: Zaïre. And with that same kind of reasoning in mind, he changed his own name to Mobutu Sese Seko.

*   *   *

And he did something else.

Mobutu made another political decision and it had to do with Lumumba himself, an alleged former friend and former political ally.

Soon after becoming President of the Democratic Republic of the Congo or Zaire in 1965, Mobutu accused Lumumba of being pro-communist and placed him under house arrest.

After Lumumba managed to escape and was later recaptured, Mobutu decided it was time to end that kind of possibility from happening again.

Immediately, Mobutu moved Lumumba to Katanga in the southeastern part of the Congo near Angola.

From there Mobutu sent Lumumba to Élisabethville, now Lubumbashi.

It was first announced by the Mobutu government Lumumba had been killed. Later, it was leaked he was brutally murdered. First he was tortured and then executed. Belgian officers reportedly witnessed those final moments.

*   *   *

Protest riots erupted in many parts of the world after news reports were heard and read internationally later about what really took place.

*   *   *

The Soviet Union later honored Lumumba by putting his name on a terrorist training school for Latin Americans in Moscow.

*   *   *

When Che Guevara confirmed Nationalist Patrice Lumumba was dead, he vowed to finish the work started by Lumumba in the Belgium Congo.

Armando wanted to determine exactly how he carried out his promise.

*   *   *

First, he took a general look at the entire Black Continent, starting in the north and working further south. He assumed there was a special economic reason beyond politics for not only backing but fomenting terrorist activity there.

De la Cruz found out the north was rich in iron ore and phosphates and that reality was made more important because it had a long western coastline open to the Atlantic Ocean.

So if their terrorism take-over plan was clear and well defined, Fidel, Che and the Soviets would be in a better position to take control of three important northern coastal countries sharing the Sahara desert.

They were: Algeria to the north and east, Morocco to the north and Mauritania to east and south.

But such thinking, Armando learned, was opposed by Spain.

*   *   *

In an attempt to thwart the leftist threat, Spain considered holding a referendum to allow Sahara residents to decide their own political future.

An interesting series of events unfolded.

Before an agreement could be reached, Fidel, Che and the Soviets attempted to take matters into their own hands by unleashing a leftist guerrilla protest.

The Polisario ignited an armed movement against Spain's hold on the Spanish Sahara in the 1970s. They got what Armando thought was unexpected help when more than 300,000 from neighboring Morocco marched into the territory in 1975.

The Polisario-Morocco coalition on that issue produced results.

A year later, Spain withdrew and the Spanish Sahara got a new name: the Western Sahara.

The conflict, however, didn't end there.

Instead, two Western Sahara neighbors, Mauritania and Morocco announced they would take over the region themselves.

Morocco took charge of the northern two thirds of the Western Sahara and Mauritania settled for the southern third.

Again, the Polisario Front with Algeria's and Cuba's support swung into action by attacking Mauritania's and Morocco's desert strongholds.

At the same time, desert residents unofficially renamed the Spanish Sahara or the Western Sahara. In the future, they said, it would be known as the Sahrawi Arab Democratic Republic.

*   *   *

Armando learned more.

Partial political change did come in 1979.

Mauritania relented to pressure and withdrew its claim on the southern part of the Western Sahara.

Morocco did not.

Instead, the northern neighbor took full control of the Western Sahara and fighting led by the Polisario broke out again. Thousands fled to Algeria.

After a United Nations-monitored cease-fire was declared, Morocco took administrative control of the Western Sahara in 1991.

A later referendum called to decide the Western Sahara's political future failed and so have other UN attempts to end Morocco's sovereignty over the region.

* * *

While Castro and Che remained committed to giving the political left absolute control of the Sahara, they changed directions by moving on to Angola, Portugal's richest colonial possession located further south on Africa's west coast.

It was a relationship that spanned 26 years before ending in 1991.

Armando learned their first contact there was with an Angolan Marxist-Leninist terrorist group, the MPLA or the Popular Movement for the Liberation of Angola [Movimento Popular de Libertacao de Angola].

Again at Soviet urging, Castro played a vital role in expanding the MPLA.

Cubans first trained MPLA guerrillas in 1963 north of Algiers, the capital of Algeria.

It was a natural relationship with the country on Africa's north coast facing the Mediterranean Sea. Algeria had supported their effort in the Western Sahara.

* * *

Armando de la Cruz's search didn't end there.

He learned how Che Guevara later became involved when he met MPLA-leader Agostinho Neto Jan. 5, 1965, in Brazzaville, the Congo's capital and largest city. And it was just north of Angola, where Cuba established a two-year military mission.

Brazzaville was also an example of the thick layer of French influence in this part of Africa.

Dating back to 1910, it was once the capital of French Equatorial Africa, originally called the French Congo.

The zone included four French terrerities: Gabon, Middle Congo (now Republic of the Congo), Chad, and Ubangi-Shari (now the Central African Republic).

Free French forces had used the Congo against the Germans and the Vichy regime during World War II. And in 1946, the region was granted a territorial assembly and representation in the French parliament.

The Congo opted for autonomy within the French Community following a 1958 constitutional referendum.

*   *   *

Out of the Che-Neto meeting, there was another petition.

Che asked Neto to help the guerilla movement against Portuguese colonialism.

Both approaches were approved by Cuba's Communist Party and confirmed by the Soviet Union.

The meeting took place after Cuba had established a military mission in Angola.

*   *   *

After that meeting Cuban support of revolutionary movements in Africa were launched in 1965. It started after Che Guevara declared it was necessary to stop a possible new colonization of Zaire or the Democratic Republic of the Congo.

If Che Guevara could confirm Belgium would again colonize Zaire, he would move to provide or to contribute armed support for the Portuguese colonies of Angola, Guinea Bissau and Mozambique.

*   *   *

So after getting a better look at the entire Black Continent starting in the north and working further south, Armando wanted to determine what occurred exactly when Che arrived with 100 internationalists, called "Columna Uno."

They came to train and to fight with Lumumba supporters in Zaire.

And he learned together in the months ahead they battled the Mobutu government at least 50 times.

After failing to make the kind of major advances Che thought necessary, he elected to regroup for a reason. It had not been possible to form a large enough organization to oppose the government beyond the battlefield.

In an attempt to fill the personnel gap, a second group or column trained in the Congo's Brazzaville.

Named the Patrice Lumumba Battalion, it would be used to strengthen the new Congo government and for emergencies only against the Mobutu government.

If successful, a military part would be added later.

Brazzaville and Leopoldville, now known as Kinshasa, capital of the Mobutu government, were separated by the Congo River, one of the world's longest rivers.

*   *   *

Armando de la Cruz carefully studied Castro and especially Che Guevara, realizing he would need every bit of knowledge and background to carry out a successful operation.

He showed more interest in Che, who like himself, was born and raised in South America, not in the Caribbean like Fidel.

After being trained as a physician at the University of Buenos Aires, Che took part in the 1952 riots against dictator Juan Perón in Argentina, joined agitators in Bolivia, and worked in a leper colony.

He met Fidel Castro and other Cuban rebels in Mexico in 1954 after leaving Guatemala a year earlier following the defeat of Jacobo Arbenz Guzmán's leftist regime.

Guevara became Castro's chief lieutenant soon after the rebel invasion of Cuba in 1956.

After their successful overthrow of Cuban dictator Fulgencio Batista on Jan. 1, 1959, Castro and Che became school teachers, according to Armando.

They taught the basics of revolution to any third-world country, particularly those in Africa wanting a clean break from old colonial ties.

Acting on orders from the Soviet Union, Che and Fidel took action in two key areas, Spain and in the Spanish Sahara in the early 1970s.

Although wanting to understand their entire strategy, Armando was most interested in North Africa. There would be the primary connecting point for his operation into Europe.

After Fidel organized ETA in Spain from Cuba and after Che did the same with the Polarsio in the Spanish Sahara, those declared Spanish revolutionaries came to Havana for training. Those from the North African desert country got their instruction in Algeria.

At the urging of the Soviet Union, their mentors sought to establish multiple copies of Marxist-Leninist governments like what was accomplished on this Caribbean island.

The Soviet goal was to consolidate trade and political control of both using a single tool: terrorism.

De la Cruz wanted to determine if terrorism would be helpful to achieving what he had in mind.

*　　*　　*

In all Armando found out, Cuba sent an estimated 250,000 personnel to fight in the neighboring countries of Angola and Namibia on Africa's deep southwest coast between 1975 and 1988. Namibia was administered by South Africa at the time.

Even though the Soviet Union provided Cuba's military hardware free of charge—valued at over $2 billion for 1982-84—the additional costs of maintaining an overseas army, which included 65,000 Cubans (troops, and military and civilian advisers) spread over 17 African nations, consumed 11 percent of Cuba's annual budget.

*   *   *

Armando also wanted to look at and examine Che's failures if any in Africa.

By learning more about North Africa, his first and most important interest at that moment, he would be in a better position to judge what Che did or did not accomplish there.

He wanted to know how it had developed economically and politically over the years before Che got there.

Trade between Europe and the Western Sahara had a long history.

Portuguese navigators got it started in the 1400s from Cape Bojador on the Western Sahara's north coast.

Later in 1884, Spain claimed the zone as a protectorate, an area extending from Cape Bojador south to Cap Blanc on the border of Mauritania, another West African country.

He learned France became involved when Spain's protectorate boundaries were confirmed and extended by Franco-Spanish agreements.

The first came in 1900. Two others followed in 1904 and 1920.

Later in 1958, Spain moved ahead again.

Two separate desert districts—Saguia el Hamra in the north and Río de Oro in the south—were brought together and named the Spanish Sahara.

Che used the history of those desert zones to move ahead.

The names of those two districts were blended together when Guevara organized the Polisario, the Polisario Front or Frente Polisario, the Spanish abbreviation of Frente Popular de Liberación de Saguía el Hamra y Río de Oro or the Popular Front for the Liberation of Saguia el-Hamra and Río de Oro."

Other Africa nations where Cuba took an interest were Algeria to the north facing the Mediterranean Sea and the Congo, the former Belgium Congo and now called the Democratic Republic of the Congo.

*   *   *

Che had traveled to Africa for two reasons. As Cuba's Minister of Industry, he was there to promote trade. His real motive, however, was to strengthen ties with revolutionary movements.

His first stop was Algiers, the capital of Algeria, on the Bay of Algiers facing the Mediterranean Sea. It is one of the leading ports of North Africa and a commercial center.

From there on Dec. 18, 1964, Che moved to Mali, a landlocked country in West Africa and a part of the Sahara.

It is bordered by Algeria to the north, Mauritania to the west, Senegal located south of Mauritania to the west and by a ring of countries moving east starting with Guinea, followed by Côte d'Ivoire, Burkina Faso and Niger.

Caravan routes have passed through Mali starting in A.D. 300 and Morocco had ruled over it for two centuries.

From 1904 to the present, it moved from being a French colony to being declared politically independent on June 20, 1960. It is now known as the Republic of Mali.

He also met liberation movement leaders from Portuguese colonies including Angola and Mozambique. The Angolans asked for instructors for guerrillas, weapons and money. They asked for military aid and instructors to train militia and troops.

*   *   *

Next was Guinea in West Africa facing the Atlantic.

Becoming politically independent on Oct. 2, 1958, Guinea is bordered by Mali and Senegal to the north; and Sierra Leone, Liberia and Côte d'Ivoire to the south.

Guinea became a French protectorate in 1849.

First called Rivières du Sud, the protectorate was named French Guinea and in 1895 it became part of French West Africa until independence.

On January 24th, a Cuban delegation had traveled to Dahomey or Benin, a thin West African country once called the Slave Coast because Guinea black traders once raided neighbors for slaves to be sold to Europeans.

It became the People's Republic of Benin in 1975.

Niger is located to the north, Nigeria to the east, and Burkino Paso and Togo to the west.

Che was back in Algeria on Jan. 27, 1965.

Before returning to Cuba on March 14, he visited China and Dar-es-Salaam in Tanzania.

*   *   *

De la Cruz learned more.

Shortly after Che Guevara arrived in the Congo, he contacted the newly organized Marxist Simba movement in an attempt to export the revolution by instructing anti-Mobutu Simba fighters in Marxist ideology and guerrilla warfare.

They also collaborated with guerrilla leader Laurent-Désiré Kabila, a Patrice Lumumba supporter.

It didn't take long for Guevara to become disillusioned with the discipline of Kabila's troops, the reason, he believed, his effort in the Congo finally failed.

*   *   *

In his Congo Diary, he later wrote the incompetence, intransigence and infighting of the local Congolese forces were key reasons for the revolt's failure.

At the time, Guevara was also in ill health, suffering from dysentery and acute asthma. And disheartened after seven months of frustration, Che decided to leave the Congo with six other Cubans on Nov. 20, 1965. Six others of his original 12-man group died there.

He had been urged to leave by his comrades and two emissaries sent by Castro.

*   *   *

Che's career as a guerrilla fighter ended in Bolivia in South America two years later where he was wounded, captured, and executed by government troops in 1967.

*   *   *

In another search Armando learned MPLA battle field advisors in the Second Guerrilla Front were trained in Cabinda, a small West African Angolan exclave facing the Atlantic Ocean located between the two Congos.

Once prepared, they moved by land to the First Front north of Luanda, Angola's capital, largest city, main Atlantic port and administrative center.

This occurred between 1965 and 1967 while the leadership of MPLA and the Batallón Lumumba stayed in the Congo's Brazzaville.

Between then until 1974 Cuban solidarity with revolutionary Angolans was recognized at the United Nations and by the Non-Aligned countries movement.

*   *   *

De la Cruz knew without being told the Belgium-French mix helped drive Abdelkader Belliraj's political interest in the region. Besides the old French Congo, there was the former Belgium Congo, now called, the Democratic Republic of the Congo, that extends across most of Angola's northern border.

Chapter Eighteen

Armando de la Cruz took still another look at ETA in Spain and the Polisario in the Western Sahara in Africa.

De la Cruz did so knowing the new review might mean going over information he had covered earlier. It didn't matter, he concluded.

If it meant learning or discovering even the smallest bit of new detail needed to more forward and achieve his political goal, the effort would be more than worth it.

*   *   *

ETA or Euskadi Ta Askatasuna, translated as Basque Homeland and Freedom, operated in the Basque part of northern Spain, or in the provinces of Álava, Guipúzcoa, and Vizcaya.

Those three zones also bordered France just to the north. Because of geography those residents spoke French and Spanish in addition to the Basque language.

The Basque conflict erupted during Spain's 1936 Civil War, when the Spanish government granted the three provinces political autonomy.

Spain's dictator Francisco Franco ended that soon after Basque nationalist leader, José Antonio de Aguirre, was elected president of the autonomous government.

In support of the Basques, the Soviets fought Franco on Spanish soil with leftist militants called International Brigades. They came from many countries including the United States.

After the region again achieved autonomy in 1979, Cuba from Havana helped organize ETA. And ETA was responsible for much of the terrorism that followed later in Spain. A cease fire—without a negotiated settlement—was finally declared by ETA in 1998-99.

*   *   *

ETA and the Polisario were similar.

The Polisario grew out of the second conflict with Spain, only this time the land dispute was centered in North Africa and not in Spain itself.

Before that time, the Spanish Sahara had been ruled as a territory by Spain between 1884 and 1975 and was one of the last parts of the Spanish Empire.

It was then called the Western Sahara, with a scant population of 273,000 covering 102,703 square miles of desert located on Africa's northwest coast.

There was a good reason for interest in the desert zone.

Besides being rich in iron ore and phosphates, it was well placed geographically. The region had a long western coastline open to the Atlantic Ocean and it was near Spain's Canary Islands.

And for those same reasons, three neighboring countries had a very strong interest in the Sahara.

They were Algeria to the north and east, Mauritania to east and south and Morocco to the north.

*   *   *

Multiple attempts were made early to stabilize politics for the Sahara. As of 2011, a workable solution had not been achieved.

At the beginning, even before Spain decided to leave for good, Spain was urged to hold a referendum vote to allow Sahara residents to decide their political future.

Before an agreement could be reached, a guerrilla war erupted.

The Polisario first opened with an armed protest against Spain's hold on the Spanish Sahara in the 1970s. They got help when more than 300,000 marched into the territory from Morocco in 1975.

A year later, Spain withdrew and the Spanish Sahara got a new name: the Western Sahara.

The conflict, however, didn't end there.

Instead, two Western Sahara neighbors, Mauritania and Morocco, announced they would take over the region themselves.

Morocco took charge of the northern two thirds of the Western Sahara and Mauritania settled for the southern third.

Again, the Polisario Front with Algeria's and Cuba's support, swung into action by attacking Mauritania's and Morocco's dessert strongholds.

At the same time, desert residents unofficially renamed the Spanish Sahara, now the Western Sahara. In the future, they said, it would be known by a third name, the Sahrawi Arab Democratic Republic.

Partial political change did come in 1979.

Mauritania relented to pressure and withdrew its claim on the southern part of the Western Sahara.

Morocco did not.

Instead, the northern neighbor took full control of the Western Sahara and fighting led by the Polisario broke out again. Thousands fled to Algeria.

After a United Nations-monitored cease-fire was declared, Morocco took administrative control of the Western Sahara in 1991.

A later referendum called to decide the Western Sahara's political future failed and so have other UN attempts to end Morocco's sovereign claim over the region.

Castro and Che wanted to give leftists absolute control there. This meant the Soviets did that to further complicate the issue.

*   *   *

Little is known about the Western Sahara before the fourth century B.C., when trade with Europe began. It was occupied first by Berbers and later by Arabic-speaking Muslim Bedouins during the Middle Ages.

By the 19th century, Spain had claimed the southern coastal region, called Rio de Oro; and later in 1934 occupied the northern interior region, named Saguia el Hamra.

Spain's protectorate boundaries were confirmed with France's help and extended by Franco-Spanish agreements.

The first came in 1900. Two others followed in 1904 and 1920.

Later in 1958, Spain moved ahead again.

Two separate desert districts—Saguia el Hamra in the north and Río de Oro in the south—were brought together in 1958 and named the Spanish Sahara.

And when Spain departed in 1976, Mauritania and Morocco stepped in and announced they wanted control of the desert territory.

At the time, both countries ended up dividing it.

*   *   *

Che Guevara had organized the Polisario in the name of the indigenous Saharawis who wanted the desert zone to be politically independent.

From neighboring Algeria, when they were unable to gain control of the Western Sahara, the Saharawis proclaimed a government-in-exile.

It was then in 1976 they officially called their proposed country the Saharawi Arab Democratic Republic.

At the time, the move was recognized by more than 50 countries.

*   *   *

Currently Morocco claims and administers Western Sahara, but sovereignty itself remained unresolved, de la Cruz later learned.

*   *   *

Spain abandoned its claim of the desert country for several reasons.

There was international pressure coming from decolonization resolutions presented in the United Nations, internal pressure from the Saharawis and external ownership claims made by Morocco and Mauritania.

*   *   *

Instead of the sovereignty dispute ending there, it lingered for more than a quarter of a century.

*   *   *

A United Nations-administered cease-fire has remained in effect since September 1991.

During that period, repeated attempts to decide the desert's political future failed for a simple reason: Morocco and the Polisario were never able to agree on the wording of a to be voted on referendum.

It was thought an agreement was possible in 1979 when Mauritania agreed to surrender their claimed part of the desert.

In reaction to the announcement, Morocco seized the land claimed by Mauritania to further complicate the issue.

In the absence of any kind of agreement, Morocco and the Polisario Front decided to fight until a cease-fire was reached in September 1991.

According to terms of the agreement, a referendum vote would be held to decide the independence question. And the vote would be supervised by the United Nations [UN].

Despite the agreement, the UN-supervised referendum could not be scheduled for more than a decade.

Besides Morocco's objection to the vote, the major stumbling block was voter eligibility.

In a further attempt to resolve the issue, former U.S. Secretary of State James A. Baker was named a special UN envoy to the Western Sahara.

Instead of an independence referendum, Baker suggested the Western Sahara should consider being an autonomous region of Morocco.

His proposal was rejected immediately by the Polisario.

Later in 2002, King Mohammed VI of Morocco announced he would not "renounce an inch of" the Western Sahara.

According to a new peace plan prepared by the UN Security Council in August of 2003, the Western Sahara could become a semiautonomous region of Morocco for five years.

Afterwards, the council suggested, a referendum should be held to determine independence, autonomy, or integration into Morocco.

Polisario leaders agreed to the plan. Morocco's refused to consider it.

Chapter Nineteen

Jordon Frost and Colt McCoy got out the cruise ship's schedule again.

After departing Cap Haitien, the ship stopped in Las Palmas, Canary Islands, located off Africa's west coast, near Morocco and the Sahara.

"What's the next one?" McCoy asked.

"Rabat, Morocco, followed by Algiers in Algeria and then on to Barcelona, Spain, the first one in Europe."

McCoy added: "For now, I think we'd better concentrate on Rabat before we consider Algeria and the continent."

"Why not consider Las Palmas?" Frost asked.

"On this one I think we have to use a little common sense before moving forward."

"So what does common sense tell you?"

"Because of size, it would be harder to hide foreign women in Las Palmas even though they share a common language, Spanish."

"That means you like Rabat better?"

"Until we get something more concrete, I do."

"Why?"

"It's an easy area to operate in because of the French and Spanish there. While Arabic is the important language, residents there whether they like it or not have to know one of the other two to survive and to do business with their neighbors to the north."

"And how do you know that?"

"I've been there. And because of our time in Puerto Rico, I speak Spanish and some French."

$*$ $*$ $*$

Well after the women are unloaded in Rabat, they have to be housed, probably in a single and perhaps centralized location.

"There are at least a couple of options," Frost volunteered.

McCoy wanted to know immediately about what came next.

"As I see it," Frost said, "they have to be hidden away quickly from public view and from any suspicion of wrong doing."

"And what may those options be?"

"Good question. While you can ask, we have to have something concrete before we can move on."

"Obviously that's true."

"And once we know more about the women, we'll have a better idea about how the entire operation works. That could include connecting points in Africa, Europe and other parts of the Middle East."

"Where do we start?"

"It should be easy enough to determine where the cruise ship docks. Once confirmed, we should have a beginning idea about the Moroccan contacts and beyond."

"Good. Let's leave it at that until we know more."

"And how do we do that?"

"We were extremely lucky about finding out what was going on at Navassa Island. I don't think we can expect a repeat performance in other areas."

"We do have an advantage now compared to then."

"Of course and it's a huge one."

"We can travel there and observe for ourselves. We'll have to be careful, I know. It will, however, be easier moving around there."

"So that means you think, we've also got to be on the ground in Rabat in order to find out more information."

"Yes, I do."

"So how do we get there?"

"I've been thinking about logistics."

"Okay."

"I think it would be better to travel by a commercial airline from New York to Brussels, Belgium."

"Wouldn't it be better to go to London first?"

"Since we'll be using our French to enter Morocco, it would be better and easier to get there through Brussels and then Paris."

"So what airlines do we use, Air France all the way?"

"No, we can travel on American Airlines between New York and Brussels, by train to Paris and by plane again, this time Air France, for the final leg to Rabat."

"That sounds complicated."

"It might be. By taking that route, I believe it will be the easiest and the safest."

"Safest? Will you explain that please?"

"At some point, interested parties might want to know what we are doing and why."

"And you think that will happen the closer we get to our final destination and the closer we get to uncovering how the operation really works?"

"Yes."

"It's likely . . . the entire operation . . . is much broader than just dealing in sex slaves."

"And what could that be?"

"Why not let the investigation give us an answer to that one."

"It's too easy to speculate. Is that what you are saying?"

"Yes, it is."

"Okay. I'm ready. When do we start?"

"As soon as possible, that's when. But we have to confirm a couple of things first."

"And those things are?"

"From here, we have to know a new cruise ship is in service and that a load of women using Navassa Island has been placed aboard."

"So you think we can travel immediately once all of that information is confirmed."

"Yes. Everything will get underway once we know the cruise ship has docked in Haiti and the women have been picked up by speed boats and escorted aboard."

"And how will we know all of that for sure?"

"First, we'll check with the boat owners in the British Virgin Islands."

"Will the man in charge give us that kind of information?"

"I think he might. He will want everyone to know he's still in business."

"Even us?"

"I think so."

"If not we can always resort to visual contacts."

"And the other stuff?"

"We'll talk to the folks who confirmed all of this for us at the start, our contact at the U.S. Embassy in Port-au-Prince."

"That sounds logical."

"It also means something else."

"And what is that?"

"The moment we know the women are aboard ship, we'll leave here and be there on time in Rabat to greet them so to speak."

"And if we fail?"

"We'll stay there until we've successful."

"So far, all of that sounds good and logical to me."

"I have the feeling this could be only the start of a long and frustrating journey."

"Unfortunately, I must agree."

*   *   *

After going over the cruise ship's schedule, Jordon Frost suggested another possibility.

"Why don't we examine the period's history?"

"The period's history . . . ?" Colt McCoy asked. "I don't understand."

"This idea could be called an extreme long shot. And if you called it that I would have to agree."

McCoy came back quickly. "Before I arrive at any kind of conclusion you're going to have to tell me what we're talking about."

Laughing at first, Frost turned serious.

"To figure out what's going on here, we have to know what they are thinking."

"Yes, of course."

"Why don't we look into the history of slavery?"

"Why? I don't understand how that can help us at all."

"As I said Colt, this is the very long shot part of this idea."

"I can only agree with that."

"What I'm thinking may seem to be so outrageous, but these modern-day slave traders could be counting on us rejecting the idea for that very reason."

"So, if that's so, they may be counting on us never figuring out what's going on here."

"Okay," McCoy said. "Let's hear what's on your mind even if what you are about to say may be as far out of the park as you are suggesting."

Gathering his thoughts for a few seconds, Jordon Frost started slowly.

"For the moment at least and with the idea of figuring out what's ahead of us, we should first determine how and where slaves are found and later put in a single group wherever that might be in the Western Hemisphere."

"And once we do that, what will we have?"

"How about reversing the process?"

"Reversing the process . . . ?"

"Yes, absolutely, reverse the process."

"I'm not getting any of this. I am willing to listen."

"Good."

"Well let's hear it."

"Without going into every detail, here is a short summary of how the slave trade started and how slaves ended up in the

Western Hemisphere in such far-a-way places like Brazil and the United States."

Here is a brief historical account as supplied by Jordan Frost.

For three centuries, beginning with the 16th or about 1650 and ending with the 19th or about 1900 slaves were shipped by boat largely from West and Central Africa to North and South America.

The largest number, about 40 percent, came from West Central Africa or from Angola, the Democratic Republic of the Congo and the Republic of the Congo.

When Europeans did become involved at the later date, black Africans marched black African slaves to eight mostly Atlantic coastal loading zones.

It was done that way because white Europeans rarely traveled to Africa's interior. They feared disease and they were concerned about personal safety.

Those involved in the Atlantic Slave trade traveled to Africa from Brandenburg-Prussia, Denmark, England, France, the Netherlands, Portugal, Scotland, and Spain.

A large majority of the estimated 9.4 to 12 million Africans coming to the New World were taken to Brazil. The smallest number arrived in the United States. The others ended up in the British, Dutch, French and Spanish Caribbean.

For ten centuries—from the ninth to the 19th—slaves were sold to Muslim countries.

It all started in 625 when Muhammad started the slave business after capturing enemies during conflicts.

In all, a rough estimate of about 30 million slaves were captured, sold and shipped by land and sea to a final destination.

Most were moved on the trans-SAHARAN dessert caravan route and across the Atlantic Ocean. Others were exported east through the Red Sea and the Indian Ocean.

Slaves were usually acquired as a result of conflicts between African tribes and states. So with so many slaves in hand and with the prospect of having more, Africans decided to turn a negative into a positive.

They would be sold for a profit to the white man in exchange for guns, ammunition and factory made goods.

Here is what one African leader said of slaves and the slave trade in the 1840s.

King Gezo of Dahomey or Benin concluded:

"The slave trade is the ruling principle of my people. It is the source and the glory of our wealth."

In all, 29 African countries had slave traders.

Once captured and once the decision was made to sell them, they were marched to coastal zones. At the end of those marches, they waited in large forts called FACTORIES.

Following each sale, they were loaded onto a waiting ship ready for the Atlantic voyage. An estimated 350 to 600 slaves were crammed onto each waiting ship.

* * *

The first African slaves were brought to the Western Hemisphere in small numbers beginning in 1501. That year, they were placed on Hispaniola shared by the Dominican Republic and Haiti in the Caribbean.

Cuba got four slaves a dozen years later in 1513.

Seventy percent of those brought to the New World worked in sugar cane fields. The remainder helped harvest coffee, cotton, and tobacco.

Slaves were not the only ones traveling to the New World. Another 50 million or more Europeans traveled there in search of a better life.

* * *

Frost added another point.

"On reflection, we can learn something about slavery beyond the fact that it's totally wrong according to any definition."

"And what would that be?" asked Colt McCoy.

"Slavery destroyed culture, language, religion and most of all . . . human possibility."

"Are you talking just about slaves?"

"No I'm not."

"Can you explain that please?"

"It's true, slaves were most affected."

"BUT . . ."

"This slave disease as I like to call it infected any and everyone touched by it."

"Every one . . . ?"

"Yes . . . absolutely."

"Let's put this in simple, understandable terms."

"Okay."

"Simply put, it infected anyone who willingly accepted the notion that any man, woman or child especially a black, man or woman should or could be a slave."

"You actually mean that."

"Yes, I do. I'm talking about the sellers and the buyers, both white and black."

"I have to ask again. You actually mean that."

"Yes."

"Does that include culture, language and religion?"

"How can anyone be a true believer in GOD and think otherwise?"

"What about culture and language?"

"Yes, of course. It also includes something else."

"It's the destruction of human possibility."

"Freedom not control makes that possible. Is that what you're saying?"

"Absolutely, it does."

"So when did we collectively realize that in the United States?"

"This sad practice ended for us on Jan. 1, 1808. And the last country to stop and to end importing African slaves was Brazil in 1831."

In other words, Frost concluded with a summary and more historical statement, the United States outlawed the importation of slaves on January 1, 1808; and Brazil was the last country to ban Atlantic slave trade in 1831.

*   *   *

After all that, McCoy took a deep breath and asked a thoughtful question.

"Is it really over for us?" McCoy asked.

"I don't think so."

"What do you mean by that? I can't believe it if you do."

"Please pay close attention. It's important. I mean discrimination and racism haunts all of us . . . even today."

"All of us? I'm having a little difficulty with that."

"Of course it does."

"Can you please explain?"

"First of all, blacks or African Americans won't let us forget. Second, whites or the remainder us too many times just accept their point of view without question."

"What does that mean exactly?"

"In my view, it means both black and white men or women or all races for that matter are equally capable of racist attitudes."

"And why would that be?"

"All of us have failed to read and know the history of slavery, as an example."

"If I'm reading you correctly, we all . . . regardless of race or nationality . . . are facing the same question now . . . today . . . but from different perspectives or starting points."

"That's a start."

"Yes, it is."

"Starting points? What do you mean by that?"

"Yes, of course. If you are black, Hispanic or white, each one has a starting point. We can't possibly all be the same."

"Why not . . . ?"

"It's just not possible . . . that's why not."

"So what are the differences?"

"Each one has a culture, a political point of view and each one has a language of origin."

"So to grasp what you have just said one has to know something of the other's culture, politics and language."

"Exactly . . ."

"But right now, we're not dealing with race relations. We are faced with finding answers to a much more difficult and complex political issue wrapped in terrorism."

"I know. Unless . . ."

"Unless what?"

"Unless you think this kind of academic race-relations discussion might somehow help with what we're trying to accomplish right now."

For the moment, Frost declined to give McCoy a direct answer. Instead he said: "We are faced with solving a very difficult puzzle."

"Yes, we are."

"And we need correct information immediately if not as soon as yesterday to cross the finish line."

"Without doubt," McCoy responded. "I still want a direct answer to my question."

This time Frost put it this way. "To get close to finding those answers, I suggest the following."

"I think I know more or less what you are about to say. Or at least I hope so."

"We must, in fact we are required, to use those same tools we covered in dealing with race."

"Please go on. I want to hear your exact words on this hot issue."

Smiling, Frost said: "As a first step, we must be able to step beyond our own country's cultural, political and language barriers."

"So far, so good . . ."

"And once we do that we'll be in a position to cross either one or multiple such barriers to find answers."

"About terrorism . . . ? Is that what you are talking about?"

"It is."

"By that you mean we may be required to cross or virtually leap over second or third or more individual cultural, political and language barriers."

"Yes. That's exactly what I'm talking about?"

"Do you think the President and his advisors will understand that in that exact way if we discover something?"

"I think we should avoid, if possible, such academic discussions with our Washington friends."

"One thing's for sure. We don't want a repeat of what we faced during our recent visit there."

"I think we can totally agree on that."

"If we are going to get to the bottom of this terrorist threat we're now facing, we must know the culture and the politics of the enemy."

"And to get inside that kind of thinking, we must be equipped with a second, third or more languages."

"Correct me if I'm wrong. I believe you are saying the following. Any race or nationality faces the same challenge."

"I think we understand each other."

Chapter Twenty

In an attempt to prove his point, Jordon Frost gave a short review of Europe's involvement in Africa.

Colt McCoy asked: "And is Germany a part of what you are about to say?"

"Yes," he responded without hesitation. "In fact before World War One, Germany set the rules for the way Europe colonized Africa."

"So are you also saying Germans were also slave traders?"

"Yes I am. They were involved just like their European neighbors."

Colt McCoy said: "I guess I should have known that. Maybe I did read about such a thing long ago. Right now I admit, I didn't or don't know."

Frost explained it this way: "Slavery is or was a motive for wanting to be in Africa. Germany had no choice so to speak despite Europe's other cultural differences."

He went on to explain.

"It all started when German chancellor Otto von Bismarck organized the Berlin Conference in 1884-85. He did so for a very specific reason."

"And that was . . ."

"It was his attempt to give order not disorder to the colonial process."

"What was the alternative?"

"For Bismarck, it was that or open conflict."

"And what you are about to say does include slavery. Is that correct?"

"Yes. Slavery is always there either said or unsaid."

"This I really want to hear."

Collectively at the time, he said, Europe had added almost nine million square miles or one-fifth of the land area of the globe—to its overseas colonial possessions.

Europe's holdings included all of Africa except Ethiopia, Liberia and Saguia el-Hamra, which latter would be integrated into the Spanish Sahara.

The players were Belgium, Britain, France, Germany, Italy, Spain and Portugal.

Then it all concluded for the Germans.

"War ended Germany's colonial hold on Africa," Frost added. "That may be one reason you might not readily associate Germany with slavery."

McCoy didn't respond. He just listened to what his associate said. His explanation sounded much like what one would read in a text book.

"Germany's Imperial Empire began in 1883 and ended in 1919 after Germany lost World War One.

"During that period, separate German states because of trade called `Zollverein' decided to expand into Africa like their other neighbors.

"Here was the German order of development at home and later expansion into the Black Continent."

McCoy added: "I want to know all of that, obviously."

Frost continued: "First the German European Empire was formed in 1871. That was done by bringing together 22 German states north of the Main River and combining them with three southern states. They were Baden, Bavaria and Württemberg."

Frost concluded: "From there, Germany staked claim to colonies in Africa."

They included German Togoland or part of Ghana and Togo, Cameroon; German East Africa or Rwanda, Burundi, and Tanzania; and German South-West Africa or Namibia.

Starting in the 1880s, Germany became the third largest colonial power in Africa.

Frost added what he believed to be an important point: "In colonizing Africa, Germany took a different approach in one significant area: language."

"What do you mean exactly?" McCoy asked.

"Unlike France, Great Britain and Spain, Germany decided against establishing large colonial German-speaking communities in each colony.

"As a result, there were few or no post-colonial texts left in the German language. And no non-European country made German an official language."

"I see what you mean."

"France's experience was different."

"How . . . ?"

"French is an official language in 28 countries."

"What else should I know?"

"While knowledge of French made it easier for locals to do business and communicate with Europe and the outside world, the language had an unintended down side on the local level."

"This ought to be interesting."

"It is as far as I am concerned," Frost admitted. "For residents who lived under colonial rule, it was more difficult to rid themselves of shaped French colonial mentality."

He added: "France didn't help."

"Can you please explain," McCoy asked.

"Of course I can and I will.

"In the name of the French language and culture, France's government operates 150 institutes and another 1,000 French Alliances or what they call the 'Alliance Francaise' not only in former colonies but worldwide."

Without being asked, Frost added:

"According to a story published in the 'La Croix' French-language newspaper in Paris on April 8, 2010, Bernard Kouchner, Minister of Foreign and European Affairs, and Jean-Pierre de Launoit, President of the Fondation Alliance Française, had this to say:

"Along with our 150 French institutes and cultural centres around the world, it is an invaluable asset for French foreign policy.

"Together they form a cultural network which is unique in the world and goes far to explain the interest which our ideas, innovations and way of understanding the world continue to generate on all continents."

Frost gave another example.

"In Rabat, the capital of Morocco, a former French-African protectorate, two institutes are located within walking distance of each other."

He concluded his thought this way:

"At the height of Europe's colonial African presence, the most important were Portugal's Angola and Mozambique, France's Algeria and the United Kingdom's Cape Colony or South Africa."

Chapter Twenty One

"We're got to know more about what happened to those people not officially listed on the cruise ship passenger list," said Jordon Frost.

Colt McCoy agreed. Listening in silence, he was more than curious about what his partner was thinking.

"You may remember, our first and only visit with William Younger didn't go all that well."

"Yes, I do recall."

"We need more detail about the women and children aboard the vessel. Once we have that we'll pay Mr. Younger another visit."

"I can't argue with that."

"Good."

"Let's look at those stops one more time."

"I'm assuming you mean those ports where the cruise ship visited from start to finish."

"Yes."

"And they are?"

"In all, there were seven ports of call and here they are: Caracas, Venezuela; San Juan, Puerto Rico; Cap Haitien, Haiti; Las Palmas, Canary Islands; Rabat, Morocco; Algerirs, Algeria and Barcelona, Spain.

"Based on that and what we tentatively now know, I think we need to find out more about the Haiti stop."

"Why?"

"I'll state the obvious. It would be easier to get people aboard there than any other port in this hemisphere."

"So your idea is the following. There is less security there and it would be easier to buy off responsible authorities if necessary to get them aboard."

"Yes, I agree. Now, we need to be clear on two general points of reference. Where did these people come from? And from where were they transferred from?"

"Maybe the Coast Guard would be a good starting point?"

*   *   *

Again, they reviewed the report provided them about the ship's sinking. There were no immediate answers or even hints.

Within 24 hours, they were talking to the Coast Guard in San Juan, responsible for all Coast Guard missions in the Eastern Caribbean area.

Frost consulted with the Coast Guard captain of the San Juan port, James Madison. He asked him a direct question. "Has there been increased activity of any kind along the north coast of Haiti?"

"No more than usual."

"What about in the general area?"

"We just got a tip about some kind of activity near there."

"Where . . . ?"

"Have you ever heard of Navassa Island?"

"Navassa Island . . . what are you talking about?"

"It's a small, uninhabited Caribbean island. And it is an unorganized unincorporated territory of the United States."

"I've never heard of it."

"Its two miles square and is located south of Cuba, east of Jamaica and west of Haiti."

"And how far is that from Cap Haitien?"

"It's a couple of hundred miles, more or less . . . an easy trip. The island is close to a lot of places."

"Can you explain that please?"

"Of course . . . to repeat Navassa Island is near Cuba, Jamaica, and Haiti. It's a largely unknown crossroad or what might be called a strategic location."

"I see."

"Its 100 miles south of the U.S. naval base at Guantanamo Bay, Cuba, and about one-quarter of the way from Haiti to Jamaica in the Jamaica Channel."

"Do people live there?"

"No and that's probably one reason you haven't heard of it."

"So what's there?"

"Not much, mostly coral and limestone. It's similar to another island I'm sure you are more familiar with."

"And where would that be . . ."

Cutting off his sentence, he said: "The topography and ecology is similar to Mona Island in the Mona Passage, between the Dominican Republic and Puerto Rico."

"I do know that one."

"I knew you would."

"So what goes on there, if anything? I'm talking about Navassa Island."

"It's used by Haitian fishermen largely and others who camp there en route to somewhere. Otherwise, the island is uninhabited. One can anchor offshore. There are no ports or harbors."

"Who discovered this unknown place or did it suddenly just appear out of nowhere?"

"Believe it or not, Christopher Columbus did in 1504. It was later claimed for the United States in 1857."

"So what's the Coast Guard's interest?"

"We are obviously very interested. The island is part of an Exclusive Economic Zone or EEZ. And it's a part of the Caribbean under U.S. jurisdiction, meaning the Commonwealth of Puerto Rico, Navassa Island and the U.S. Virgin Islands."

"Is there anything else? . . ."

"Yes. Here is our responsibility. Our Search and Rescue Operational zone for the Eastern Caribbean Sea area covers the Dominican Republic and the Lesser Antilles islands chain."

"Earlier you said something about a tip."

"Yes, I did."

"Can you explain please?"

"I can, but I'll need permission from Washington before I can tell you."

"That sounds fine to us. When can we meet again?"

"Would tomorrow at this same time be okay with you?"

"Perfect."

Leaving the office, Frost and his partner, Colt McCoy, were excited. They felt they had perhaps found their most promising lead. They also called Washington to alert them of the upcoming U.S. Coast Guard request.

*   *   *

At the appointed hour, Frost and McCoy walked into Capt. James Madison's office. His secretary gave them immediate entry.

"I see you are who you say you are," the captain said.

"Good, so let's get down to business."

"I'm ready."

"So what do you know?"

"Something happened there and we think it could be important."

"Can you explain that?"

"We've heard reports speed boats have been spotted near Navassa Island."

"Do you have more detail?"

"No. Hopefully, we'll have more shortly."

"While we're here, can you give us a little more about the island itself?"

"Yes. The island is ringed by vertical 30-to-40 foot white cliffs and is covered by trees."

"I assume Coast Guard helicopters have flown over Navassa one or more times."

"Yes . . . that's true."

"Does that mean those trees could be covering up something?"

"That's all together possible."

"When do you think you might know something?"

"Maybe later today . . . tomorrow should be the very latest."

"We'll contact you then."

"Not a problem."

*　　*　　*

Back at their office, Frost told McCoy, "I think we have enough information to more or less figure out what's going on here."

"You do?"

"Yes, I do."

"Okay. I'm ready to hear what you have to say."

"We know Navassa is small and isolated, that the island has a good amount of tree cover and it's close to Haiti. And the Coast Guard reports speed boats have been spotted recently near there."

"What's next?"

"We also discovered unaccounted for bodies of women were found in the hold of a sunken cruise ship near Puerto Rico."

"So?"

"It all means, if I am correct, those ladies could have been brought from somewhere in a speed boat and loaded onto the doomed boat that had docked overnight at Cap Haitien before moving on."

"Is that possible?"

"I think it is."

"But first we have to confirm for sure why those speed boats sighted by the Coast Guard near Navassa Island were there in the first place."

"Yes, that's true. Otherwise, nothing makes sense."

"Maybe it does."

"I don't understand."

"We got an unconfirmed report recently that Colombian drug dealers may have found a new route to move drugs into the United States."

"I remember."

"Without doubt . . . in the past . . . that's been done through Central America and Mexico."

"True. But as that route closes down, a big question remains to be answered."

"And that is . . ."

"Maybe speed boats are involved somehow."

"I thought we were talking about women, not drugs."

"We were and still are without doubt. I'm just wondering if both could be connected to speed boats."

"I think it's time to get back to our man at the Coast Guard.

"Good idea."

*   *   *

Hours later they were in the Coast Guards captain's office.

"I'm glad you are here. I have something to report. It may not be what you are looking for, but it might be."

"Good," Frost said. McCoy nodded in agreement.

"Speed boats reportedly are being used to transport drugs to Miami."

"And the drugs are coming from where . . . Colombia?"

"Yes."

"And the drugs are being picked up where?" they asked.

"In Cuba . . ."

"In Cuba . . . ?" The response startled both Frost and McCoy momentarily.

"Yes, Cuba . . ."

After gathering his composure, McCoy asked. "And how do drugs reach Cuba?

"By plane . . ."

"By plane . . . ?" Frost asked. "Are you sure?"

"As sure as I know we're seated at this table across from each other having this conversation."

"It's that sure?"

"Yes."

"Then if planes, drugs and speed boats are in the area, other criminal options are good, if not very good."

"And what does that mean?" the Coast Guard captain asked.

"What I'm about to say will have to be confirmed."

"You've got my interest. What do you mean exactly?"

"There's a good chance women are kidnapped in South America and shipped as sex slaves to Europe."

"And how would they go about doing that?"

"If I'm right, easy . . ."

"You've got my interest. Please go ahead."

"They may be placed aboard speed boats and taken to a waiting cruise ship docked at Cap Haitien on Haiti's north coast."

"Like the one that sank near Puerto Rico?"

"As you know unaccounted for bodies of women were found in the sunken vessel."

"I remember."

"We thought you would."

"So you are saying the following. Speed boats are forced to wait in Cuba for drug ships to arrive by plane from Colombia. So during idle time, they could be used to ship other cargo to a nearby cruise ship."

Frost added: "I think that's what we've got to confirm or disprove."

"I agree," the Coast Guard captain said. "If that's true, our Caribbean mission has just been expanded by quite a bit."

"And so has ours," Frost said.

*   *   *

Each agreed to investigate starting immediately using their own resources and to report findings to each other as well as to immediate superiors.

Chapter Twenty Two

"Do we dare go there?"

"Where?" asked Jordon Frost.

Colt McCoy responded quickly. "How else are we going to know what's going on?"

"You've lost me. Please explain what you are talking about."

"Navassa Island . . . that's what."

"I see." Admittedly, he had not thought of the possibility.

"Whatever we do, I think we have to see this place for ourselves," McCoy said.

"Why?"

"It's small and we think we now know something may be going on there."

"There's another thought."

"And what might that be?"

"Because of the island's size, we could be putting our lives in extreme danger."

"Can you explain that please?"

"If discovered any option to protect ourselves would be drastically reduced."

"So you think that means, whatever we decide, we have to use a lot more care than normal."

"Yes. And it's unlikely we'll be able to observe everything we will need to see from a Coast Guard cutter."

"Then what do you suggest?"

"Captain Madison mentioned something we ought to consider."

"And that is . . ."

"Haitian fishermen stop there, sometimes for the night . . . often longer."

"So you think we ought to go with them?"

"Maybe . . . It's only a thought, a possible suggestion."

"There's also a negative."

"I don't understand."

"If we are with them, it might draw too much attention to ourselves."

"How so . . . ? I don't understand."

"Anyone thinking is likely to ask the obvious question. Why are we there? That's when things could really turn dangerous."

"Good thought. I might have a solution."

"Ok, I'm listening."

"I have a contact at the U.S. Embassy in Port-au-Prince," Haiti's capital.

"And what might this contact do for us?"

"He might be able to get one of the fishermen to tell us or to find out what we need to know."

"That's a great idea if it works.

"If not, we'll go to plan B, whatever that might turn out to be."

*   *   *

Within two days after contact had been made with Haitians living and fishing out of Dame Marie, a small village on a peninsula extending west from Port-au-Prince, they got a report.

Once they were told what Frost and McCoy wanted, the investigators found out much more than they ever expected to turn up in such a short time period.

Here is what they told the Embassy's political official, who spoke Creole and French, the two languages spoken in Haiti.

In recent weeks, empty speed boats had come to Navassa Island and left carrying women. While they didn't know a final destination, they reported the craft always headed to the northeast across the Caribbean Sea.

Questioned for more detail, the Haitians said the speed boats had been arriving routinely every two weeks in a well coordinated operation. And almost immediately, about 40 women were placed aboard four waiting speed boats.

The women had been brought to Navassa Island aboard a single plane capable of landing at sea.

It took less than an hour to complete the transfer.

* * *

Their next step was to contact U.S. Coast Guard commander James Madison in San Juan and to report to him what the Haitians had told the U.S. Embassy contact.

"If true, this is very important and frightening information," he told Frost and McCoy. "I don't think it will take long to confirm or discount that kind of report."

"How long . . . ?" Frost asked.

"I should know something within two days."

"Today is Monday. Let's meet again here at this same hour on Wednesday."

"Agreed," Frost said. McCoy nodded his head in agreement.

* * *

The three men met again at the agreed on hour and date.

"Your Haitian fishermen obviously have provided important information. And to be truthful with you, I'm very disappointed the Coast Guard was not aware of such a report."

Frost added quickly: "Perfection simply does not exist Captain Madison. Please don't feel bad about this or overly responsible."

"Thank you," he said. "I appreciate your words more than I can adequately say." He then added: "We must do a better job. And I promise you that will be the case in the future. Too much is at stake."

McCoy cut in after the Captain's last remark. "Besides confirming our information, do you have anything else to report?"

"Smiling," he said. "I certainly do."

Frost and McCoy waited patiently for his reply.

"The speed boats arrived off the north coast of Haiti just after midnight. On arrival, the women were placed aboard the cruise ship you mentioned to me before."

"And how did they do that?" McCoy asked.

"My answer may surprise you."

"Maybe, maybe not . . . Let's hear what you have to say."

"The boats one at a time pulled up beside the cruise ship and unloaded their cargo."

"In other words, they boarded like regular passengers. Is that what you are saying?"

"Yes. Instead of being escorted to the upper levels of the ship, they were placed in the cargo or lower parts of the vessel."

Frost added: "Your information tells us how those women got abroad the sunken cruise liner and why they remain unidentified."

"Exactly," Captain Madison said.

*   *   *

McCoy added: "We still have unanswered questions."

Speaking with a more confident tone of voice, Captain Madison said: "Perhaps I can do better this time around." It was as if he was anticipating the kind of questions he was about to be asked.

"Here's hopefully a simple one," McCoy said. "Where did these speed boats and planes come from?"

Captain Madison replied: "That's an easy one. They came from Cuba."

"Cuba?" asked Frost. "I don't understand."

"It all has to do with the drug traffic."

"I thought we were talking about women here, not drugs," McCoy said.

"Actually, we're talking about both at the same time."

"Both. Can you explain that?"

"I would be happy to."

"We've listening."

"Actually, we've been working on this for months and I believe we finally have at least some answers."

"Good."

"Drugs are being shipped into the United States."

"How . . . ?"

"On speedboats, the same ones used to transport the women."

"The drugs and the women . . . were shipped from where?"

"Both have the same origin, Colombia."

"Let me see if I understand you correctly."

"Okay."

"Both the women and the drugs were transported directly from Colombia to Cuba."

"Yes."

"So what happened or what happens next?"

"Drugs are shipped to Miami in the speedboats from Cuba. And while waiting for a new load of drugs, they were used to ship women from Navassa Island to the cruise ship docked at Cap Haitien."

"Is a single plane like you describe large enough to carry drugs and the women?"

"Yes. A single plane can hold 40 women and a normal drug shipment."

"Tell us how all this happens."

"En route to Cuba, the plane's first stop and drop off point is the uninhabited U.S. island, of all places. Once in Cuba, the second stop, the drugs are unloaded."

"I want to backup a moment. I want to understand exactly what's happening here. I thought you said speed boats carried the women to Cap Haitien."

"I did."

"What does that mean?"

"There are many speed boats and they are all used in the total drug-women operation."

"We're listening."

"That means part of what amounts to a fleet of speed boats are used to carry drugs from Cuba to Miami and the others transport the women to Haiti."

"So that means the speed boats are rotated."

"Yes."

"Why?"

"To make it more difficult for folks like us to spot and to figure out exactly what they are really up to."

Frost then asked: "When were you able to put all of this together?"

Captain Madison was a little slow with an answer this time around. Finally, he did.

"To be frank, the information you provided did the trick."

"Really . . . ?" Frost asked.

McCoy was also having difficulty understanding what Captain Madison had just told them.

"We would have figured it out eventually. I'm sure of that. Your input speeded up the process."

"We're glad."

"And so are we. Thank you very much."

*   *   *

Back in their San Juan office, Frost and McCoy realized they had part of their answer. Now, they had to figure out what happened to the other women once placed aboard other cruise ships.

Before going ahead with the second part of their investigation, Frost called Washington to tell the president what they had found out so far.

"We'll get back to you as soon as possible once we know more."

Chapter Twenty Three

Here is another part of Africa's past that interested Armando de la Cruz.

* * *

North Africa, Morocco in particular, played a key role in the development of international slave trade. It all started when Arabs brought Islam into Morocco in 685. It was relatively easy to take over a divided country.

Being one of several Barbary States was another part of Morocco's history that helped. From the 17th to the 19th centuries, Morocco's geographical location made it a logical PIRATE base to attack Mediterranean trade.

In the 19th century, pirate attacks from Morocco were ended by Europe. Once done, it became an important economic trading zone.

In northwest Africa, it was the closest connecting point between Africa and Europe. They were just short of 10 miles apart.

* * *

What had happened in Morocco was part of a larger European conflict, de la Cruz learned.

From the time of profitable slave trading, Europe's interests shifted to nation building. As a first step, Britain and France aggressively moved to acquire colonies and protectorates in Africa.

With Britain and France spending so much energy and time attempting to control Egypt, it gave Germany an opportunity to move into Africa.

The ongoing conflict contributed to World Wars One and Two.

*   *   *

All of Europe had turned to imperialism. The expansion of political power was the easiest and most inexpensive way of broadening influence and power.

Armando de la Cruz wanted to know why.

He learned wars were costly and Europe was pretty much claimed and divided.

So if a European country was interested in Empire building, Africa was the closest and most obvious alternative to do just that.

Germany had another incentive.

If Germany could acquire colonies, it could or would be as dominant as France and England on the world stage.

And here is what Germany accomplished between 1884 and 1920.

In short, the Germans accomplished what their leaders had in mind. Their zones of influence were labeled German East and West Africa.

In the EAST, the Germans controlled Tanzania, Rwanda and Burundi, Kenya, Mozambique, Namibia and part of Botswana.

And in the WEST they claimed Cameroon and Togo.

*   *   *

France and Spain countered the German move. Together they joined forces with the British in an attempt to stop them from acquiring Morocco.

In the end, all four accepted the same terms as had been agreed on earlier. Called the Madrid Conference, German investments were assured protection.

During the first 1880 Madrid Conference in Spain, Europe and the United States had agreed to help bring a splintered Morocco together and to help it develop as an important trade link between the two continents.

Successful at the beginning, the concept began to crumble in 1904. Too many countries wanted to control the trading point for themselves.

In secret, France and Spain agreed to partition Morocco. Their agreement was called ` the Entente Cordiale'.

With a growing fear of Germany wanting to take over that part of Africa, Great Britain secretly agreed on a deal with France and Spain.

The English would not oppose them in Morocco, if they would give the British a free hand in Egypt. Such an agreement, all three believed, would place them in a stronger position to face down Germany.

When France moved to make Morocco a French protectorate in 1905, German Emperor William II traveled to Tangier and declared support for Morocco's political integrity.

A year later, at German insistence, the Algeciras Conference was called to consider the Moroccan question.

All parties agreed to readopt the earlier Madrid Conference, favorable to France and Spain. There was one other important part of the agreement.

German investments in Morocco would be protected.

With the pact in place, France moved to steadily annex territory during a claimed pacification process.

That was done with France's ability to patrol Morocco's border with Algeria. Both France and Spain were also allowed to police Morocco.

Another conflict with Germany surfaced in 1908 when the German consul in Casablanca gave refuge to French Foreign

Legion deserters. It was later settled by the Hague Tribunal in the Netherlands.

Moving forward to the second Madrid meeting, German leaders said they would allow France and Spain to patrol Algeria's border and to police Morocco.

And finally on Nov. 4, 1911, Germany agreed to a French protectorate in Morocco in exchange for French territory in equatorial Africa.

The French used the agreement to their advantage. In the name of pacification, the French pushed ahead to annex Morocco outright.

The next year, France and Spain moved to divide Morocco into four protectorates: French Morocco, Spanish Morocco, a Southern Protectorate of Morocco and the international zone of Tangier.

Rabat became the capital of French Morocco or nine-tenths of the country and Tétouan was named the capital of Spanish Morocco.

The Southern Protectorate of Morocco was administered as part of the Spanish Sahara and the international zone of Tangier stayed under French military rule until 1925.

*   *   *

With France and Spain working confidently to control the Northwest African country, they were challenged by a new opponent: Morocco itself.

Morocco began opposing European rule between 1921 and 1926. And after a nationalist movement was launched in 1934, the French crushed a revolt in 1937.

*   *   *

In another dramatic move, Spain's General Francisco Franco used Spanish Morocco to carry out a successful revolt against Spain's government in 1936.

*   *   *

Other events followed, all related to the start of World War II.

After World War II started in 1939, Germany attacked France on June 5, 1940 and victory came four days later.

France's defeat resulted from a series of bad judgment calls.

Rather than oppose Germany from the start, the prime ministers of France and Great Britain, Édouard Daladier and Neville Chamberlin, respectively, elected to appease Germany by agreeing to the 1938 Munich Pact.

Negotiated in Munich, Germany, without the presence of Czechoslovakia, it gave Germany the right to annex the western part of Czechoslovakia called Sudetenland where ethnic Germans lived.

Later the Munich Pact was called the Munich Betrayal. After the Germans took control of Sudetenland, it didn't take long for them to take over all of Czechoslovakia.

And mistakenly France relied too much on what was called the Maginot Line, concrete fortifications built along their common borders with Germany and Italy.

Germany invaded Belgium, flanked the Maginot Line, and conquered France.

*   *   *

After France's defeat, Prime Minister Paul Reynaud wanted to move government to North Africa, and continue the war from there.

The view was opposed by Vice-premier Philippe Pétain and commander-in-chief, General Maxime Weygand. They insisted government remain in France and share the misfortune of its people and that's what happened.

*   *   *

When France surrendered on June 22, 1940, not only to Germany but also Italy, an armistice was signed between the old competitors.

218

Pétain, as last Prime Minister and a reactionary by inclination, blamed the Third Republic's democracy for France's quick defeat.

France—under German direction—would be governed administratively from the city of Vichy, southeast of Paris in central France.

A second armistice was needed after Italy's army, directed by Benito Mussolini, successfully invaded France June 10, 1940.

According to treaty terms, Germany occupied northern and western France, the Vichy government was responsible for the remaining two-fifths of the country and Italy controlled a stripe of France bordering Switzerland and Italy.

Once Petain took charge of the Vichy government, meaning he was willing to collaborate with the Germans, his position was opposed immediately by long-time friend General Charles de Gaulle.

In challenging the legitimacy of the Vichy government, de Gaulle fled to England where he directed his country's affairs from London.

* * *

Although under German control, the Vichy government was assigned time-consuming tasks to free Germany for planning and carrying out an attack against Germany's other long-time competitor, Britain.

German dictator Adolph Hitler expected the same kind of quick success there as he had experienced in France.

* * *

Here is what the Vichy government willingly did for Hitler and Germany.

Vichy had civil jurisdiction over the whole of metropolitan France and its African colonies. This action relieved Germany of administering French territory.

The plan had a secondary but important goal.

If implemented correctly, it would have been virtually impossible for the French to oppose Germany militarily or otherwise from North Africa.

*   *   *

Hitler moved to further drain France economically.

The Vichy government was ordered to pay for maintaining Germany's 300,000-man occupation army. The daily cost was 20 million Reichmarks.

In southern France, Germany did allow the Vichy government to maintain a small army to defend French territories including Morocco from Allied assault.

*   *   *

All of Hitler's careful planning ended Nov. 8, 1942 when the Allies invaded North Africa.

When all resistance in Algeria and Morocco ended three days later, Hitler annulled the 1940 armistice, Germany occupied all of France and the Vichy government was drastically reduced.

Immediately on May 30, 1943, De Gaulle moved his provisional government from London to Algeria.

De Gaulle relocated it a third time in June 1944 when the Allies' invaded France.

After the Liberation of Paris in August, the Provisional Government of the French Republic (GPRF) was recognized on Oct. 23, 1944 by the Allies as France's legitimate government.

Refusing to accept defeat, the Germans relocated the Vichy government to Germany where a French government in exile was established on Aug. 20, 1944.

The French-German arrangement ended in April 1945 when the war ended.

Chapter Twenty Four

Armando de la Cruz wanted to know more.

Spain was a part of Europe's struggle for power and world influence. It was the kind of competition between neighbors like Britain and France that never seemed to end.

Geography played an important role. Europe and Africa, to the immediate south, are separated by the Mediterranean Sea. The closest point, the Strait of Gibraltar, is a body of water that separates the two continents by just under 10 miles.

It was an obvious step, consolidate and expand power in Africa, the closest nearby and very large continent. Spain was north of it and Morocco was just to the south.

History tells more of the story.

*   *   *

The Kingdom of Spain—to become the most important in Europe and perhaps the world for almost three centuries—was launched in 1492.

It all started after Islam's nearly 700-year domination ended and after the bringing together of two large parts of the country, the Kingdom of Castile and the Kingdom of Aragon.

And to consolidate power further at home, Spanish monarchs Ferdinand and Isabella ordered the Spanish Inquisition directed by Tomas de Torquemada to expel Jews and Muslims who refused to become Roman Catholics.

After early service as a monk at a Catholic Dominican monastery, de Torquemada became advisor to Ferdinand and Isabella before being named Inquisitor General in 1483.

Starting in 1478 and ending in 1834, the Inquisition by de Torquemada's order first moved on `crypto-Jews' and then `crypto-Muslims' or those thought to still secretly practice their faith after publically claiming otherwise.

Baptized non-Catholic Christians were also investigated but most were released after questioning.

With that done, Christopher Columbus discovered America to launch the largest colonial effort the world had ever known.

* * *

De la Cruz had a special interest in how Spain developed, being from Colombia, a part of Latin America controlled by the Spanish until it became politically independent in 1819.

* * *

Instead of attempting to expand their world power like what Britain and like what France would do later, Spain took a different route almost by accident.

Queen Isabel and King Fernando were desperate for a competitive edge after their expensive war against North African Islamic Moors.

So they accepted a risky proposal presented them by Italian adventurer Christopher Columbus following a two-year negotiation period. It was the same plan that had been rejected earlier by Portugal.

Talks were slowed down in part because Spain was broke. Private Italian investors provided half of the financing. The monarchs ordered the royal treasurer to make up the difference by shifting funds from existing accounts.

If successful, Spain could perhaps gain a larger slice of Asia's spice market currently controlled by Arab and Italian traders.

There were other reasons to seek a sea route.

Land travel had become more difficult after the Ottoman Turks conquered Constantinople in 1453. With a better one, it would be easier to acquire colonies in Africa and elsewhere.

In return for such an outlandish accomplishment, Columbus demanded knighthood, to be appointed Admiral of the Ocean Sea, made the viceroy of any new lands and be given ten percent of any new wealth.

In the end, for what seemed to be more than just surprising, Columbus launched not one but four voyages to the New World, not Asia.

Those trips also exploded a very large false assumption about world geography. Instead of being flat, it was round.

He started the first historic trip with three vessels under his command: La Niña, La Pinta and the Santa Maria.

* * *

What this seemingly crazy and risky Columbus 1492 strategy provided Spain was more than it could ever have dreamed or planned for over time covering nearly four centuries.

It was in fact too large to control or to handle over such a long period.

Columbus made it possible for Spain to expand across most of present day Central America, the Caribbean islands, and Mexico; much of the rest of North America including the Southwestern, Southern coastal, and California Pacific Coast regions of the United States; and though inactive, with claimed territory in present day British Columbia Canada; and U.S. states of Alaska, Washington, and Oregon; and the western half of South America.

The Spanish Empire began to break apart in the early part of the 19th century. Those former colonies, particularly those in South America, wanted to be politically independent of Spain.

What Columbus had started was finally put to an end by the United States following the Spanish American War of 1898. Cuba, Puerto Rico and the Philippines were the last pieces of Spain's New World and Empire that had become too much to handle.

Of those three, only the U.S. Commonwealth of Puerto Rico elected to remain part of the United States. The other two, at their own request, became politically independent.

*   *   *

A year after 1898, Spain sold its remaining Pacific islands—the Northern Mariana Islands, Caroline Islands and Palau—to Germany and Spanish colonial possessions were reduced to Spanish Morocco, Spanish Sahara and Spanish Guinea, all in Africa.

*   *   *

While Columbus sailed west to open the New World, Spain moved south just across the Mediterranean Sea to control five sea-port towns on Africa's north coast between 1497 and 1510 for two reasons.

Catholic Monarchs and Spanish regent Cisneros wanted to block any future Islam interest in Spain and Europe forever. The move south into Algeria and Morocco was expected to generate more political power and wealth.

Those sought out port towns were Algiers, Mazalquivir, Melilla, Oran and Peñón de Vélez de la Gomera.

*   *   *

During all the growing and shrinking of the Spanish Empire, an established language and culture were left behind as permanent reminders of past glory. This was true even in Puerto Rico where residents have been U.S. citizens since 1917.

And it was a long-ago but a present-day footprint of past competition and conflict that still exists between the two European colonial expansionist powers, England and Spain.

For a modern observer, the two languages are a silent but speaking 21st century evidence of what two countries had achieved over centuries.

English from England and Spanish from Spain are there, but ironically those countries can no longer claim to be the largest country for those spoken languages. They are in a real linguistic sense, a victim of their own success.

For England that distinction moved to the United States and for Spain it is claimed by Mexico. As both England and Spain were European neighbors, so are Mexico and the United States in the New World or the Western Hemisphere.

There is another achievement.

Both languages are perhaps the world's two most important.

While figures may be difficult to come by, there are enough available provided by government census offices to show native Spanish speakers barely outnumber native English speakers by 329,000 to 328,000.

The numbers change dramatically when second-language speakers are added. At that moment, English vaults ahead to 1.8 million when all world nationalities add it as a second language.

It does so because more people believe it to be the best speaking tool to carry on international business and to be able to move ahead in international politics.

While significantly up, Spanish drops behind to 495,000.

*   *   *

Armando de la Cruz also wondered if he needed to speak a second language. Besides Spanish, he felt it would have to be English or French.

*   *   *

225

After English and Spanish, there is the French language, spoken as the official language in 29 countries. It is used in seven others although not officially. It is there for the same reason, France's intent to spread in Africa, the Americas and Asia, and Oceania.

It is ranked as the world's fourth language behind Chinese, with 1.3 billion native speakers largely Mandarin but also Cantonese.

And English and French are the only languages spoken on the five continents.

Native Arab speakers rank fifth worldwide with 221 million. When bilingual or second speakers added on, the figure moves to 326 million.

* * *

France's move to acquire colonies began in the 1600s and ended in the late 1960s. Only the British were more successful in the 19th and 20th centuries.

At its peak in the 1920s and 1930s, the French Empire covered about five million square miles or 8.6 percent of the world's surface.

The French language and culture, however, remained even after those political relationships ended.

French thus became the fourth-most spoken European language, behind English, Spanish, and Portuguese.

* * *

De la Cruz reviewed and looked a bit more at what he felt he should know about the French.

France established colonies in North America, the Caribbean and India. And in the 19th century, the French moved on to Africa and South East Asia.

France's colonial empire began in 1605 in Nova Scotia, Canada and Samuel De Champlain founded Quebec or New France, but also Canada, 1608.

In 1699, French territorial claims in North America moved south to Louisiana and to the West Indies in the Caribbean. A settlement in French Guiana began in 1624 and the colonies in Guadeloupe and Martinique were founded in 1635.

Those colonies were built and sustained by slaves brought there from Africa.

France's most important and richest Caribbean colonial possession was established in 1664, when the colony of Saint-Domingue or Haiti was founded on the western half of the Spanish island of Hispaniola.

It was the plan to make it the capitol of everything French in the western Hemisphere.

*　　*　　*

The largest French possession was the Louisiana Territory and it was vast.

And when the United States acquired the land it doubled the country's size at a cost of less than three cents per acre. It makes up about 23 percent of current U.S. territory.

New Orleans—the starting point of U.S. interest—was turned over on Dec. 20, 1803. The remainder of the territory was transferred by France to the United States on March 10, 1804, during a St. Louis ceremony in Missouri.

As it turned out, Napoleon decided to sell after France tried and failed to establish control and slavery in Haiti. Following the devastating defeat, Napoleon dropped plans for New World Empire to be headquartered in Port-au-Prince, Haiti.

The Louisiana Purchase contained all or part of 14 current U.S. states and two Canadian provinces.

This included Arkansas, Missouri, Iowa, Oklahoma, Kansas, Nebraska, parts of Minnesota that were west of the Mississippi River, most of North Dakota, nearly all of South Dakota, northeastern New Mexico, the portions of Montana, Wyoming, and Colorado east of the Continental Divide, and New Orleans.

It also contained small portions of land that would eventually become part of two Canadian provinces, Alberta and Saskatchewan.

* * *

French colonial expansion was not limited to the New World.

In West Africa, the French began to establish trading posts along the coast Senegal in 1624. And between 1673 and 1739, four colonies were fixed in India: Pondicherry Yanam, Mahe and Karikal.

Others came in Indian Ocean: Réunion, Mauritius and the Seychelles.

France invaded Algeria in 1830.

Back in the Western Hemisphere, Napoleon III attempted to establish a colonial-type protectorate in Mexico at the time of the U.S. Civil War from 1861 to 1867.

U.S. President Andrew Johnson forced the French out by invoking the Monroe Doctrine.

In southeast Asia, Napoleon III established French control of Cochinchina or southern Vietnam including Saigon in 1867 and 1874, as well as establishing a protectorate over Cambodia in 1863.

From Cochinchina, the French took over Tonkin or northern Vietnam and Annam or central Vietnam in 1884-1885.

French Indochina was established in 1887 when Cambodia and Cochinchina were united. Laos was added in 1893 and so was Kwang-Chou-Wan in 1900.

In 1849, a French concession in Shanghai lasted until 1946.

* * *

Back in North Africa, France made Tunisia a protectorate in 1881.

Gradually, French control was established over much of Northern, Western, and Central Africa by the turn of the century (including the modern nations of Mauritania, Senegal, Guinea, Mali, Côte d'Ivoire, Benin, Niger, Chad.)

French West Africa was created in 1898 by unifying all West African territories.

The Military Territory of Chad in 1900 and Morocco became a French protectorate in 1911.

The French also established colonies in the South Pacific, including New Caledonia and established joint control of the New Hebrides with Britain.

*   *   *

The French made their last large colonial gains after World War I in Syria and Lebanon and Togo and Cameroon.

In each colony during the late 19th and early 20th century, France made its intention known with a clear motto: "Three colors, one flag, one empire."

All Africans agreeing meant they had accepted 'la mission civilisatrice' or the civilizing mission.

Africans could then be civilized after adopting and accepting French culture, speaking fluent French and converting to Christianity.

Their reward would be French citizenship, including the right to vote.

*   *   *

After World War II her colonial universe began to unravel.

French authority was first challenged in Algeria and Vietnam and by the end of the 1960s, most of France's colonies were politically independent.

There were exceptions: Guadeloupe and Martinique in the Caribbean and French Guiana on South America's north coast. All three became a part of France as overseas departments.

Chapter Twenty Five

Armando de la Cruz took special interest in knowing about pirates operating out of North Africa.

He learned Mediterranean pirates enslaved those captured—both black and white—following raids.

Called Barbary Pirates, an alliance of Muslims and privateers, they operated out of the region for eight centuries.

Their aim was to conquer and to enslave not only Christians but the entire world.

* * *

De la Cruz discovered the pirate tradition took hold as a result of a severe difference of religious belief between Christians and Islam.

This conflict first exploded when European believers were told by Islam they would no longer be welcome in Jerusalem to worship at Christ's birthplace.

Besides that, Islam proclaimed, the Christian belief of Jesus' death on the Cross near there was fictitious.

So Islam's claim on the city was far more significant, according to what de la Cruz found out and what he had to say he believed if ever questioned.

* * *

Armando then could state—once he had all the facts straight—what made Jerusalem important to Islam and what it had to do with Muhammad, Islam's founder.

* * *

According to Islam, Muhammad making what only could be described as a 'miraculous journey' to Jerusalem made the city too significant to share with anyone or any group including Christians.

Here was the story.

Muhammad made a two-stop trip in one night with the angel Gabriel.

Starting at the Al-Aqsa Mosque in Mecca, their first stop was at the Al-Aqsa Mosque in Jerusalem. Once there he led prophets Adam, Moses, and Jesus in prayer.

During a second stop, Mohammed toured heaven and hell, where he spoke with earlier prophets, Abraham, Moses, and Jesus.

There in the heaven part he led them again in prayer.

Once back in Mecca, he gave a detailed description of Jerusalem for those who doubted his story.

* * *

Reflecting for a moment, de la Cruz concluded: "That would be a difficult experience to top. Maybe Islam has a point."

Armando felt now he better understood Islam's conflict with Christians and that he was in a stronger intellectual position of "sounding convincing when necessary."

Anyway Armando de la Cruz was now fully aware of Islam's reasoning for wanting to establish sole ownership and control of the Holy City and the Holy Land.

* * *

At the same time, De la Cruz was able to draw another conclusion about Islam.

Mohammed's 'miraculous journey' or dream-like flight to Jerusalem was more significant than the Christian claim over the city.

They alleged Jesus Christ was born and died there on a Cross near there.

And it was this sharp difference of vision—the Muhammad trip and Jesus Christ—that caused believers in Muhammad to spare no effort in their mission to stop all Christians from traveling to Jerusalem for any reason.

* * *

Armando de la Cruz did wonder why it took Islam so long to challenge Christians, who had traveled to Jerusalem as pilgrims for hundreds of years.

Islam finally took a position, he concluded.

Seljuk Turks, new and fanatical converts to Islam, faced off against some 7,000 Christian pilgrims en route to the Holy Land in 1065.

Organized by Roman Catholic bishops, they had gathered in Germany to travel as a single group.

After defeat the pilgrims did respond to Islam.

Byzantine Empire forces, formed in the Greek-speaking Eastern Roman Empire, confronted the Islamic force in the Battle of Manzikert in 1071.

Islam won, Armando discovered. And the loss was devastating for Christians.

Not only was the Roman Empire's Eastern Emperor captured, his army was scattered.

* * *

There was more to the story.

Islam delivered another major blow to Christians in Asia Minor, their main source of troops and revenue.

After Asia Minor was lost, Western princes and the Roman Catholic Pope asked for soldiers to help regain lost territory.

De la Cruz learned the plea launched what is known in history as the CRUSADES.

Roman Catholic Pope Urban II called for the First Crusade to regain the Holy Land in 1095.

Preaching at the Council of Clermont, he called for all Christians to take up the cross for a cause that promised material and spiritual rewards.

At the end of Pope Urban II's emotion-filled speech, the crowd responded with repeated shouts: "God wills it." The response became a Crusader battle cry.

* * *

In all, seven Crusades were organized between the 11th and 13th centuries in the struggle with Islam over Jerusalem.

The First Crusade was the most successful.

A force of 5,000 knights and infantry captured Jerusalem, the Holy City.

The attack was launched from Constantinople, where the army gathered coming from France, parts of Germany, and Norman Italy.

* * *

De la Cruz learned something else.

Christian public opinion was further inflamed by tales of alleged Turkish mistreatment of Christian pilgrims.

* * *

Islam used force to keep the dispute alive and obviously this was the part that most interested Armando de la Cruz.

The Barbary Pirates—the armed part of Islam—were based in North African ports of Tunis, Tripoli, Algiers, Salé and others in Morocco. This stretch of North Africa became known as the Barbary Coast.

Their attack zone against Christian nations was a large one.

Starting with the Mediterranean, it extended south along West Africa's Atlantic seaboard and into the North Atlantic as far north as Iceland.

De la Cruz learned pirates destroyed thousands of British, French, Italian and Spanish ships, the primary targets.

European coastal towns were also included.

Between the 16th to 19th centuries, pirates captured an estimated 800,000 to 1.25 million white Europeans and made them slaves.

Pirates collected more slaves after plundering seaside villages in Italy, Portugal and Spain. They didn't stop there. Other countries, Britain, France, the Netherlands, Ireland and as far away as Iceland and North America, got the same kind of cruel and violent attention.

Long stretches of coastline in Spain and Italy were almost completely abandoned until the 19th century.

All slaves, including Christians, were sold at Islamic-controlled slave markets in Algeria and Morocco.

*   *   *

Politically, the Barbary pirates also opened the door for the Ottoman Empire's 400-year presence in North Africa.

It all started when they took control of Algiers in the early 16th century and after they made that country's port city of Algeria the center for everything done in the Mediterranean.

Once firmly established, the Ottoman Empire was launched.

*   *   *

Besides knowing about the Barbary pirates, De la Cruz knew he had to learn more about the religious side of this equation if at any time his Islamic faith was questioned or doubted.

Such an understanding was also important, he realized, to grasp the depth of the conflict.

So after learning about the pirates he felt he had to know more about Jerusalem, a point of serious and obvious difference between Christians and Islam.

*   *   *

Here is why he had to examine this ancient Jewish spiritual and political capital dating back 10 centuries.

It was there the most significant event ever recorded in human history occurred. This was the Christian position.

And that was the coming of Jesus Christ, born a Jew, who was crucified, buried and resurrected on the outskirts of Jerusalem.

The city located in the center of Israel, bordering the eastern edge of the Mediterranean Sea, was part of the Roman Empire ruled from Rome at the time.

By going through back data, de la Cruz also realized the conflict reached far beyond Jerusalem. While the city remained extremely important, he learned defining Jesus was the hot issue.

De la Cruz's research showed another difference between Christians and Islam. And that was how the life of Jesus ended.

Christians believe Jesus died on a cross. Muslims believe someone else died in his place.

Why?

According to de la Cruz, they had no choice but to see it that way if as they believed Jesus was not the son of God. That being so Muslims can and could not accept the Biblical description of his death.

And they could and do not believe he was resurrected to live again three days after his reported death.

*   *   *

There was another point of difference.

If not the Savior of Mankind, according to Islam, Armando de la Cruz had to ask the obvious question.

"Who was this man called Jesus?"

Muslims called him a prophet like all others written about in the Bible and the Koran. And if a prophet, according to Islamic tradition, he and all other prophets were Muslim.

Muslims do believe, however, Jesus' was born of the Virgin Mary and that he lived as a prophet to restate what is termed 'divine religion.'

His miracles and his serving the 'Lords Supper' to the disciples near the end of his life are also recorded in the Koran.

And both agree he will return at the end of time to judge all people.

*   *   *

Besides Islam, Jerusalem and Jesus were challenged by Rome.

Leaders there reacted to any real or perceived political question of their rule over large parts of Africa, Europe and the Middle East.

Their reason was Jesus being called by many `King of the Jews.'

For them, the word `King' meant this man wanted to be the political leader of Israel and perhaps beyond.

*   *   *

He might also want to seize spiritual control of Rome and the Empire. They were Roman Pagan. It was the only approved worship allowed or permitted at the time.

*   *   *

So if successful in both the physical and spiritual parts, they reasoned, the man called Jesus could mean a Jewish takeover not only of Rome but the entire Roman Empire.

* * *

So when Roman Emperor Tiberius Julius Caesar Augustus allowed Jesus to die on the cross like a common criminal, he acted out of self interest, of Rome and of the Pagan Roman Empire.

* * *

In other words Armando de la Cruz concluded the God-Man Jesus had upset Rome's leadership big time.

Chapter Twenty Six

Here is what Roman Emperor Tiberius; Roman Prefect of Judaea Pontius Pilate; Rome; and the Pagan Roman Empire feared.

Jordan Frost and Colt McCoy decided to review this part of their belief as a necessary part of their investigation.

Breaking it down into simple terms as quickly as possible, they felt they had to review what Pilate witnessed as the ranking Roman official nearest the conflict.

As Prefect of the Roman province of Judaea under the Emperor Tiberius, he was the one who dealt most directly in the final authorization to put an end to this perceived political threat.

They were unable to conceive or to believe Jesus was about giving hope to all people including Romans regardless of race, language or world geographical location.

It was simply too large a concept to digest outside of their own cultural vision or beyond their own definition of politics.

In other words, the only possible motive for this man called 'King of the Jews' would be to replace them and to take total control of everything Roman.

So with that in mind the next step—for them—would be the only logical and rational decision: declare him guilty as charged.

If guilty, as Pontius Pilate believed him to be, Jesus had to suffer the harshest penalty of the day.

His death on a cross near common criminals would serve as the only possible consequence to anyone or any group holding or planning political domination of the Roman Empire.

*   *   *

Frost and McCoy, as impossible as it might have been for them, tried to imagine the painful thought process undoubtedly endured by those Roman leaders.

In the end, they realized this was an extreme example of what could happen to world leaders or even the most common man's ability to think correctly under extreme pressure.

They had made the mistake of not being able to conceive or even imagine what their role could be or should have been in the final stages of such a world-changing event.

Their final decision, based on what they perceived was to protect themselves and the Roman Empire, allowed this God-man Jew to die on the cross like a common criminal and to be buried.

His resurrection undoubtedly sent all of them—beginning with Pontius Pilate—into total confusion and wonder, perhaps second guessing as to what faulty decision making had produced.

*   *   *

Frost and McCoy considered the possibility this part of their review might produce a kind of Roman thinking process. If so, they would be a step closer to finding the person or persons most responsible for the sinking of 'The Caribbean.'

*   *   *

Here was what Rome believed to be a disturbing message, a position Frost and McCoy were aware of. They decided to review it anyway.

On those days after his death, burial and resurrection, now more than 2,000 years ago, God through his son, Jesus Christ, gave each man and woman who lived before that date and all who lived afterwards an opportunity to have a permanent, non-breakable relationship with God.

According to Jesus as recorded in the Bible, each person accepting Jesus as savior was saved and was transformed or born again. The first birth was physical. The second was spiritual.

So when anyone said `yes' to Jesus or to his heavenly father, he or she was granted and assured eternal life. From that moment on they would be with him now in this life and later in paradise or heaven forever.

And it was in the asking and the admission of personal sin that any individual would be granted salvation. Making a choice, by saying either `yes' or 'no,' was the key to what Jesus said.

Saying `no' meant a person's position would be respected and accepted and they would be permanently separated from God.

According to the Bible, separation meant being cast into HELL.

And that word, as horrible as it sounds, might not be enough to define such a reality.

Being permanently cut off from Jesus Christ might be more painful than HELL.

In other words, God could have and did have the power to insure a permanent relationship for all people. Instead, he gave each living human the opportunity to select.

The power in the giving and in the accepting of such a clean-cut decision is awesome to think about, maybe close to impossible.

Beyond the accepting or rejecting part there is nothing any individual or institution can suggest to anyone to help earn or secure such a relationship.

"Good Works," as an example, is a natural result of acceptance.

Doing "Good works" before the final decision is made means nothing or is not a prescribed way for any man or woman to earn a permanent bond with Jesus Christ and his father.

Such a profound individual selection to either be with or to be separated from God is possible only after what happened on the CROSS outside of Jerusalem.

At that moment, Jesus assumed the burden of all sin or error committed by all men and women before and after that point in time.

All by himself, he paid the price for all accumulated sin and that price was DEATH.

It had to be done in that specific way to provide salvation and a forever spiritual relationship with Jesus and his father.

The name of Jesus was not and is not a myth.

His father was God and his mother was flesh and blood. It was God's way of creating a man who walked the earth for 33 years without committing one single error or yielding to one temptation in thought or deed.

It was done that way so any man or woman could touch, see and hear him talk. Such a collective testimony of what was to come and what did occur was recorded in the 66 books of the Old and New Testaments of the Holy Bible.

There were those who saw in person this perfect God-Man walk, teach and preach among them. And those imperfect men and women who followed could read and hear about what happened and also learn how to become one with him.

It was in fact the only rational way for God to make such a presentation believable and acceptable to all men and women. It had to be done that way for the imperfect man or woman to receive such an eternal gift.

There was absolutely nothing he or she could do by themselves to earn such a relationship. To put it in such a category would do away with the meaning of the cross. It would be saying each individual would be attempting to do what Jesus did to earn salvation.

Simply put: we CAN NOT.

*   *   *

It's for that reason, the city of Jerusalem, is historically important. And it's for that reason so many have attempted to control and dominate it as a way to become closer to God.

If such a goal could be achieved they could perhaps better associate themselves with that world-changing event, to better understand and to project what happened that day on the CROSS.

Jerusalem's history reflects the point.

*   *   *

It first had been made the Jewish or Hebrew spiritual and political capital by King David with the building of the main Jewish Temple on Mount Moriah ten centuries before Jesus was born as a Jew.

Jerusalem because of its political and spiritual significance had been attacked and dominated by foreign powers on more than one occasion until it had been taken over and controlled politically by the Roman Empire from Rome.

Roman Emperors did everything possible to dominate and to knock out anyone thought a threat to their rule. Those Pagan leaders in a Pagan Empire feared Jesus and his talk about God's kingdom.

For Tiberius Julius Caesar Augustus, the Roman Emperor at the time, it was a decision he did not want to make. Sent back to Pontius Pilate, Pilate opened the way to crucify Jesus on the Cross.

While Pontius Pilate gave the actual order, he did so at the insistence of Jewish high priests, who did not believe Jesus was legitimate. Jews, until this day, are still waiting on the arrival of the Real Messiah.

Another Roman Emperor Titus, left unsettled by Jesus and his teachings, destroyed the ancient Jewish Temple in Jerusalem and damaged much of the city 70 years later to both punish and discourage Jews.

Why?

Those first followers of Jesus were Jews.

*   *   *

It took a while for Rome to change its mind about Jesus.

All of that started when Constantine the Great moved the Roman Empire's capital from Rome, Italy, to a new city, Constantinople in Turkey, a more centralized geographical location.

Rome had begun to lose importance and the empire itself would later split into East and West. Italy itself, however, would not recover from the down grading of the city until the 19th century.

Constantine, the top and unchallenged Imperial authority over religious matters and over the state, ruled all of Christianity would be recognized throughout the Roman Empire.

As leader of all things Roman, Constantine decided Christianity by his definition would also be Roman. So the state began to refer to all Jesus believers as members of the Roman Church.

And it didn't take Constantine long to move the Roman church's starting date retroactively back nearly 400 years to make the ruling complete. Roman Paganism was not eliminated.

So the Roman Catholic Church officially started in Constantinople 391 AD, not in Rome following the death, burial and resurrection of Jesus Christ in Jerusalem.

Christians met alongside Jewish believers and those who declined to be Roman Catholics worshipped in hiding. They were as much illegal as all Christians were before Constantine moved to legalize Roman Christianity.

Once established and a historical church record began to be revised, Roman Church leaders would proclaim the first Roman Catholic Pope to be Peter, one of Jesus' 12 disciples.

Historically, the title of Pope was an honorary title used for any bishop in the Western part of the Roman Empire. In the Roman East, it was used only for the Bishop of Alexandria.

From the sixth century, the Imperial Chancery of Constantinople reserved it for the Bishop of Rome, a practice firmly in place by the 11th century.

* * *

Jesus was born and raised in the center of conflict, the Roman Empire, today part of Albania, Algeria, Armenia, Bosnia and Herzegovina, Bulgaria, Croatia, Cyprus, Egypt, France, Georgia, Greece, Gibraltar, Israel, Italy, Jordan, Kosovo, Lebanon, Libya, Republic of Macedonia, Malta, Montenegro, Romania, San Marino, Serbia, Slovenia, Spain, Syria, Tunisia, Turkey, Ukraine and Vatican City.

During its existence of more than a thousand years the Empire remained one of the most powerful economic, cultural, and military forces in Europe, despite setbacks and territorial losses, especially during the Roman—Persian and Byzantine—Arab Wars.

* * *

Jerusalem quickly became a city of religious turmoil. It was no longer an issue just between Christianity and Pagan Rome.

It became wider and more complicated.

Each side was driven by their way of defining God. The Roman Empire sided with the Roman Catholic Church against Islam.

According to Islam, Muhammad's miraculous journey to Jerusalem was more important than the Christian belief of Jesus' death on the Cross.

And for that reason, the city was important to Islam.

* * *

Here is what happened later.

Armando de la Cruz reviewed what he thought he had fixed in his mind to be doubly sure of what had taken place during that period.

He believed the mental process, even if it meant a repeat of some of the basic history, was necessary to grasp as best as possible what it meant to be a pirate in those days.

And above all, he felt the need of having some idea of what motivated them.

* * *

By the tenth century Roman Catholic bishops had organized mass pilgrimages to the Holy Land to worship at the birth place of Christ in Jerusalem.

The largest, an estimated 7,000 pilgrims, started out from Germany in 1065.

For Islamic leaders such a public expression and action was unacceptable and could not be tolerated.

As a result, they ordered and succeeded in taking control of the city and blocking Roman Christian pilgrimages all in the name of Islam.

There was an immediate reaction.

In 1095, Pope Urban II proclaimed the First Crusade to regain the Holy Land to protect the right to travel and to worship in Jerusalem.

Preaching at the Council of Clermont, he called on Roman Christians to take up the cross and fight.

In response to his impassioned oration, the crowd shouted: "God wills it." The expression became their Battle Cry on their successful march on Jerusalem.

From the eleventh century to the end of the thirteenth, there were seven major crusades waged against Muslins.

The First Crusade was the most successful of the seven.

Composed of feudal nobles from France, parts of Germany, and Norman Italy, they had a force of 5,000 knights and infantry by the time they reached Constantinople.

The next stop was Jerusalem.

Besides retaking the Holy City, they took control of a narrow strip of land stretching from Antioch to Jerusalem. Named the Latin Kingdom of Jerusalem, it included parts of Syria and Palestine.

Muslims retook the region in 1291.

*　　*　　*

After taking control of Jerusalem, Islam wanted and did move to expand its influence over more territory.

It did so by creating a power block called the Ottoman Empire, one of the largest and longest lasting in history.

A major success was the ending of the Byzantine Empire or the Roman Empire as the major power in the Eastern Mediterranean.

The Ottoman Empire reached a peak in the 1500s, extending from the Balkans and Hungary to the gates of Vienna.

It covered much of the coastal strip of North Africa, parts of Arabia, Bulgaria, Egypt, Greece, Hungary, Jordan, Lebanon, Macedonia, Palestine, Romania, Syria and Turkey.

The Empire began to decline after being defeated during a naval battle in 1571 between Christians and Ottomans near Lepanto, Greece.

It declined further during the next centuries, and was effectively finished off by the First World War and the Balkan Wars.

Chapter Twenty Seven

Jordan Frost and Colt McCoy made a decision. They would travel to Rabat, Morocco's capitol, as soon as possible for a definite reason.

Once they got word the cruise ship carrying the women slaves was en route, they would be in a better position to track them on arrival at this North African port city.

Frost and McCoy agreed they would be in a better place not only to follow them on arrival but to see what would happen next.

There would be a number of questions to be asked and then answered.

1. Where were the slaves sold? In Rabat or in some other city or country on the African continent.

2. What would happen to the slaves once sold?

3. Who were the buyers? They would need to know if they were Islamic extremists or just regular folks.

4. And how much would be paid for the slaves? Would they be sold on an individual basis or in groups of two or more?

"The moment we know the women are aboard ship, we'll leave here and be there on time in Rabat to greet them so to speak."

*   *   *

From the time they knew Rabat would be the cruise ship's first African stop after picking them up in Haiti, Jordan Frost and Colt McCoy concluded Morocco would be the starting point to find those responsible for the cruise ship, "The Caribbean," just off of Puerto Rico's northwest coast.

"So it was now time to get on site information," Frost said. And McCoy agreed.

*   *   *

They arrived on an Air France flight that took off from the Charles de Gaulle Airport north of Paris and landed two hours later at the Rabat-Salé Airport about five miles north of Rabat.

Jordan Frost and Colt McCoy learned the airport was used by the U.S. Army Air Force during World War II and that it had served as headquarters for the fifth and 316th Air Divisions of the U.S. Air Force's Strategic Air Command (SAC) during the early part of the Cold War.

Immediately, a cab took them to their hotel, the Tour Hassan Meridien, in the center of town near the city's administrative offices and the U.S. Embassy.

*   *   *

On arrival, Frost and McCoy were greeted by a shocking article in a French language newspaper, 'La Gazette du Maroc,' or the Gazette of Morocco.

The story they saw and read was not buried in some obscure corner of the publication.

Instead, it was blasted across the front page of the edition published on May 15, 2008.

Here was the headline: CONCURRENCE EXTREMISTE or Extremists Meet.

At the bottom of the page was another headline: Les Talibans 'Evangelistes Battent le Pave' or 'Taliban Evangelicals Battling in the Streets.'

Sandwiched in between the two headlines was a picture showing the inside of the Rabat International Church.

And inside the newspaper, in a special section called 'Evangelisme' or Evangelism, there was a smaller sized picture showing a larger view of available seating inside the church.

* * *

Their first order of business was to find it and to confirm the story as true or false.

So immediately a search for the Rabat International Church was launched. Their effort was successful.

Located near the Rabat Ville train station in the center of town, the church was the gathering place for 40 dominations from up to 25 nations of all continents and all races.

And on Sunday morning, services are conducted in three languages: English, French and Korean.

* * *

At the same time, Frost and McCoy realized what they had read was something more than an attack against a single church in Rabat.

They concluded this was a much broader battle against Christianity, the only reason so much space was used on the front page and inside sections of the newspaper.

* * *

249

Instead, it was a blunt verbal outburst, a warning against Christian missionaries operating in the Middle East and the United States following the Islamic attack on New York's World Trade Center on Sept. 11, 2001.

Terrorist Osama bin Ladin later claimed responsibility for launching the deadly operation.

While avoiding the mention of bin Ladin by name in connection with the attack killing 3,000, the newspaper suggested foreign missionaries were unfairly attempting to blame Islam and Muhammad.

But instead of taking the U.S. government on directly, the newspaper took issue with missionaries mostly from the United States.

According to the newspaper, it was calling public attention to what had been until now "an underground and secret operation."

And as of today, they "are in the streets for the first time to recruit new evangelicals" in the North African country.

In other words, the written report said, "Morocco has been invaded by an army of missionaries" as ordered by the recently announced "International Year of Prayer for Morocco."

*   *   *

Frost and McCoy were even more surprised when the Moroccan newspaper referred to missionaries as the 'Evangelical Taliban.'

Up until then they had thought of the Arabic word "Taliban" only as a proper name for an Islamist militant and political group.

According to the newspaper, this 'Evangelical Taliban' had been sent to destabilize Islam in the Arab world in the following countries:

Algeria, Bahrain, Egypt, Iraq, Jordan, Kuwait, Lebanon, Morocco, Oman, Qatar, Palestine, Saudi Arabia, Tunisia and United Arab Emirates.

*   *   *

Frost and McCoy knew instinctively the attack was directed most at Southern Baptist missionaries operating in all of those Middle Eastern countries.

They recalled that barely two months after the attacks on the World Trade Center and Pentagon, a record number of new missionaries—124—were appointed by the Southern Baptist International Mission Board [IMB].

"The September 11th catastrophe didn't cause any of them to drop out," Frost remembered. "Those new missionaries scattered to every point on the compass . . . to all 15 of the regions where the IMB works."

They also realized this new verbal, written attack meant they, the missionaries, would have to work more carefully in predominantly Muslim countries.

*   *   *

According to the International Mission Board, Southern Baptists support 5,444 missionaries in Africa and around the world.

And that effort resulted in 565,967 new annual believers outside of North America.

For that reason, according to the newspaper, there was ample reason to openly attack Christianity.

Frost and McCoy repeated those dramatic missionary figures to themselves and openly once they realized maybe for the first time how much each one of them were willing to put on the line—starting with their lives—to spread the Gospel of Jesus Christ.

According to the International Mission Board, Southern Baptists support 5,444 missionaries in Africa and around the world.

"What does the law [of Morocco] say about all of this?"

It was clear.

Any attempt by a missionary to guide or to encourage a Moroccan Muslim into accepting Jesus Christ as his or her Lord and Savior would be rejected.

Why?

Such action would be in "violation of the [Islamic] faith" and would be considered to be "a direct affront to Islam."

And according to the newspaper, such action would be called an attempt "to create discord" and a move by the United States to REMODEL the Middle East.

Violators "exploiting the weakness of the locals" could be fined and sentenced to six months in jail.

And if it could be determined a missionary and a church were connected in anyway, the church could be closed up to three years.

*   *   *

Frost and McCoy discovered the Rabat International Church and a nearby Roman Catholic Church had something very much in common.

According to law, non-Islamic houses of worship could not be identified by a name-plate, a sign or anything else on their buildings' exterior.

In other words, a causal passerby walking or driving by those buildings would not know church services were being or would be held inside.

There was more.

According to law, only foreign nationals could attend services in either one of those churches. It made clear a native of Morocco was forbidden to attend them or to become a Christian.

To make sure the law was respected, a policeman dressed in long colorful Arabic clothing stood outside on all days of worship but especially on Sunday or the Sabbath Day.

*   *   *

Here was a worrisome figure for the newspaper and Morocco's government in general.

In all an estimated 40,000 Moroccans have converted to Christianity and another 15,000 have done so but had elected to keep the decision private.

The report said about 80 percent of the total numbers were Evangelicals and 20 percent were Roman Catholic.

Most of the missionaries serving in Morocco operated primarily in Casablanca and Rabat, the country's two large cities.

And 20 North Americans, according to the news story, were ordered to leave the country between 1995 and 1999.

Violators, according to Morocco's penal code, could be sentenced to six months in jail and fined for disturbing the faith of a Muslim or causing a Muslim to convert to another religion.

The law was needed in an attempt to stop missionaries from "exploiting the weakness of the locals," or the law itself.

*   *   *

After reading the story, Frost and McCoy reflected for a moment why Southern Baptist missionaries risked everything to come to this part of the world.

It was because they were directed to come by 'The Great Commission.'

And each time they read or referred to it in the future they had even a greater respect for those called to serve on the mission field, especially after reading the news story in the Rabat newspaper.

From that moment forward and more often now, they read and thought of the Great Commission found at the conclusion of Matthew, the first book of the New Testament, chapter 28, verses 19 and 20.

It says:

"Go therefore, and make disciples of all the nations, baptizing them in the name of the Father and of the Son and of the Holy Spirit, teaching them to observe all things that I have commanded you; and lo, I am with you always, even unto the end of the age. Amen."

*   *   *

Frost and McCoy also recalled and reviewed what Article XI of the Baptist Faith & Message had to say about the "role of missions in the life of a Christian."

It says:

"It is the duty and privilege of every follower of Christ and of every church of the Lord Jesus Christ to endeavor to make disciples of all nations.

"The new birth of man's spirit by God's Holy Spirit means the birth of love for others.

"Missionary effort on the part of all rests thus upon a spiritual necessity of the regenerate life, and is expressly and repeatedly commanded in the teachings of Christ.

"The Lord Jesus Christ has commanded the preaching of the gospel to all NATIONS.

"It is the duty of every child of God to seek constantly to win the lost to Christ by verbal witness undergirded by a Christian lifestyle, and by other methods in harmony with the gospel of Christ."

*   *   *

"So what do you think?" Frost asked McCoy.

"About what . . ."

"Former Southwestern Baptist Seminary President Russell Dilday and four prominent Cooperative Baptist Fellowship [CBF] members recently said something about Southern Baptists."

"And that was . . ."

"They shared a similar conclusion: The SBC now can be compared to ISLAMIC EXTREMISM" or to those responsible for the World Trade Center Sept. 11, 2001 attack in New York City.

McCoy said: "In my view, they unfortunately demonstrate a lack of knowledge about Islam. Their statement reflects that."

"I agree," Frost said. "It's a common failure of many. It's extremely difficult for many, including these GOOD MEN, to look for truth outside their own cultural and language zone."

Reflecting a moment, McCoy said: "I couldn't have said it any better than that."

Chapter Twenty Eight

The institution of slavery extends back beyond recorded history. It was important for Armando de la Cruz to review how it had developed.

In ancient Egypt slave labor was used to build temples and pyramids and it was practiced by the ancient Hebrews, according to Bible passages.

It was an established institution in Greece.

During the period of the Roman Empire, there were more slaves in greater numbers as wealth increased. They were used in the theater, in gladiatorial combats and prostitution.

Having slaves became a mark of luxury.

Most of them were foreign. Some were highly educated and were employed as instructors.

As the number of conquered provinces grew, so did the number of slaves.

The introduction of CHRISTIANITY toward the end of the Roman Empire had no effect on the abolition of slavery, since the Roman Catholic Church at that time did not oppose the institution.

Slavery flourished in the Byzantine Empire, and the pirates of the Mediterranean continued their custom of enslaving the victims of their raids.

For de la Cruz, this was an extremely important point.

*　*　*

Here is what Armando de la Cruz looked at next. He wanted to know in more detail how Islam felt about the question.

He understood there were at least two versions.

One is Islam does not tolerate enslaving human beings. According to this moderate version, it eradicated slavery thanks to principles set in motion by Muhammad.

There is another view.

Islam institutionalized slavery. Taking slaves was started by Muhammad and the practice continues discreetly today.

*　*　*

De la Cruz decided he liked the second version best and it would be the one he would take seriously.

It functioned over 13 centuries.

During that time it was called a divinely-sanctioned practice. In other words, it was considered to be in complete harmony with the spirit of Islam.

Yes, it can be said Islam made life better for the average slave.

Muhammad, however, intended it to be a perpetual institution. That was the part de la Cruz really liked and that was the part he wanted to be most associated with.

The process started when Muhammad was forced to move from Mecca to Medina.

To defend himself and his beliefs, he allowed, authorized and encouraged the taking of slaves as "booty" or as a reward for followers fighting against enemy Arab tribes.

Later Muslim rulers—following Muhammad's example— took black Africans, non-Muslims and other black Muslims as slaves of all those living in conquered territory.

All of this was recorded long before slave ships sailed for the New World. And slavery continues to this very day.

*   *   *

De la Cruz learned more.

Islamic jurisprudence and the Koran say the taking of slaves is divinely sanctioned. Muslim rulers found support in the Koran to define 'jihad,' as part booty and part slavery.

Islam allows Muslims to make slaves—black and white—out of anyone including Christians and Jews and their children captured during raids on tribes or open warfare.

Muhammad started the practice in Saudi Arabia after gaining power and moving to Medina.

Even today the slave population in Saudi Arabia has been estimated at 450,000.

And public slave auctions are no longer held regularly, only in an alley in Mecca.

From there slavery spread like a cancer.

*   *   *

"Why?"

It was a question de la Cruz needed to ask and a question that needed to be answered.

Here is what he thought was correct, an account he liked best.

*   *   *

Muslims are encouraged to live like Muhammad, who was a slave owner and trader. This was to be de la Cruz's excuse or reason to say he had converted to Islam.

According to records, the leader of Islam captured slaves in battle, had sex with his slaves and instructed his male followers to do the same.

Besides such action being sanctioned by the Koran, it receives additional support from the Hadith, a collection of the traditions of Muhammad, including his approval of what was said or done in his presence.

From the Hadith:

Bukhari (80:753)—"The Prophet said, 'The freed slave belongs to the people who have freed him.'"

Bukhari (34:351)—Muhammad sells a slave for money. He was thus a slave trader.

And in the . . .

Bukhari (72:734)—Some contemporary Muslims in the West, where slavery is believed to be a horrible crime, are reluctant to believe that Muhammad owned slaves. This is just one of many places in the Hadith where a reference is made to a human being owned by Muhammad. In this case, the slave is of African descent.

Muslim 3901—Muhammad trades away two black slaves for one Muslim slave.

*   *   *

In even more practical terms, here is how de la Cruz determined how it works.

Muslim rulers found and find support for the practice in the Koran. The key is 'Jihad,' a word meaning many things including the taking of slaves.

Here are two general rules:

1. Anyone captured during war time or open conflict. The numbers grew as Muslim armies conquered more land. This includes Christians and Jews.

2. And the children of slaves will be raised as slaves.

And later, if black slaves were not transported to the New World, they were sent to the MIDEAST or kept by other black Muslims.

Muslim warriors thought then and think today they were doing women and children a favor by taking them off the field of battle and assigning them to lives of servitude.

This was the position Armando de la Cruz would not only accept but would embrace.

Caliphs, the Islamic equivalent of Roman Catholic Popes, were active participants. They maintained harems of young girls and women numbering hundreds, sometimes thousands.

Those sexual slaves were captured in places like Europe, Hungry and India.

After Muslim armies attacked and conquered Spain in 711, they took thousands of slaves back to Damascus in Syria including the key prize of 1,000 virgins. Muslim rule ended in 1492.

Three million Hungarians were taken over a 150-year period in the 1500-1600's.

An estimated 200,000 Hindus in India were captured and transported to Iranian slave markets in a two-year period alone, 1619 to 1620.

Another 400,000 slaves were shipped to the Western Hemisphere.

When European slave ships began trips to the New World, a Muslim slave broker or a black slave trader gathered and brought them to key points on Africa's west coast.

From there, slaves were brought out to waiting ships on canoes. It had to be done that way. There were no seaports at the time to load or unload cargo of any kind.

Fear of disease and the unknown also deterred Europeans from going ashore until later.

*   *   *

Deciding to back up a little, de la Cruz wanted a better history of how Islam used slavery.

After Islamic forces captured and held a large part of Spain for 700 years before 1492, they transported thousands of slaves back to Damascus, Syria, in the Middle East.

Muslims took black Africans centuries before the first slave ship sailed to the New World.

If not sent to the New World, black slaves were moved to the Middle East, where they were acquired by Arabs or other black Muslims.

An estimated three million Hungarians were taken and placed in slavery between 1500 and 1600.

Another 200,000 Hindus in India were transported to Iranian slave markets between 1619 and 1620.

Some 400,000 others were shipped to the New World.

As slavery became lucrative and wide spread, slave markets were opened for business in every city in the Islamic world.

Islamic Arabs maintained a network of slave trading and used slave markets in China, India and Southeast Asia.

They brought in Turkish slaves from Central Asia, slaves from the Byzantine Empire, white slaves from Central and East Europe, and black slaves from West and East Africa.

And now slave auctions reportedly have gone underground in Saudi Arabia. This is where he learned and confirmed what he had heard earlier that such deal makings are now confined to an alley in Mecca.

*   *   *

Here is how Islamic slavery is kept alive and functioning today. De la Cruz paid close attention to this part of the drama.

Slave traders pose as Muslim missionaries. They invite those willing to listen to travel with them to visit Islam's Holy Places and to learn the Koran in Arabic.

Once they cross the border into Saudi Arabia they learn the real truth. Instead of being missionaries, they are people of deceit and they learn too late the point of their false missionary message.

They lure both blacks and whites into slavery.

White slaves have more value.

Here is a part of what happens to those accepting such a false message of hope. They do so because of desperate living and working conditions for themselves and for family members.

Slaves are tortured, young boys are hobbled and family land seized.

*   *   *

De la Cruz learned something else. It was not a single invention of Islam or Black Africans.

Millions of men, women and children around the world are still forced to live as slaves. Threatened by violence they could be recruited by individuals, governments or political parties and forced to work.

Human slave traffickers have created an international market, now thought to be the second largest world criminal industry. The first is believed to be drugs.

It involves the transport and trade of men, women and children from one area to another.

For girls and women, it can take the form of early and forced marriages. And too many times rape and physical violence becomes a part of the equation.

Eastern European women become prostitutes, children are moved between West African countries and men are forced to work as slaves on agricultural estates in BRAZIL in South America.

An estimated 126 million children alone are forced into child labor.

A family with a sick child can be tricked into taking a loan to cover the cost of medicine. And to repay the debt, family members are forced to work long hours, seven days a week, up to 365 days a year.

They might receive basic food and shelter in for work, but the debt can never be paid. Instead, it might be passed down for generations.

*   *   *

The British, Dutch, French, Portuguese and Spanish further developed the African slave trade during the 15th and 16h centuries. And their main market was the Western Hemisphere, not Europe.

At the beginning Portuguese and Spanish enslaved Indians in Latin America and the West Indies. When they revolted or escaped, Europe's traders turned to black Africans.

In the Western Hemisphere, slaves were first used in the Caribbean and in South America. Slavery later spread to what is now the United States.

A Dutch ship brought the first slaves to a British settlement, Jamestown, Virginia, in 1619.

By the 1640s slavery was well established in Virginia, followed by Massachusetts. Later, slavery would spread to Britain's other North American southern colonies.

A clear majority of slaves moved West were shipped to Brazil followed by what would eventually become the U.S. southern bloc of states.

*   *   *

Here is how the trade cycle worked.

De la Cruz learned slave ships would transport goods including rifles and military gear to West Africa for slaves.

Once brought to Caribbean ports, slaves were exchanged for farm products before making the return trip home.

In many zones the number of slaves grew large.

In French Saint-Dominque, later to be named Haiti, slaves evolved into the republic's majority population.

When the United States became independent of the British in 1776, slaves made up about one-fifth of the population.

*   *   *

In modern times, millions of men, women and children around the world are slaves despite being banned in most of the countries where it is practiced.

It is prohibited by the 1948 Universal Declaration of Human Rights and the 1956 United Nations Supplementary Convention on the Abolition of Slavery, the Slave Trade and Institutions and Practices Similar to Slavery.

Another 600,000 and 800,000 people, mostly women and children, are trafficked across borders worldwide.

The number includes between 14,500 and 17,500 persons brought to United States.

Here is how it works.

False promises play a key role. They are told anything to get them out of their country or origin. Those offers range from a good paying job to marriage.

Those believers—again willing to do anything to escape their plight—too many times get caught in prostitution, pornography and other forms of commercial sexual exploitation.

Others end up in slavery-like labor conditions in factories and fields.

Besides that there is more.

Victims suffer physical and emotional abuse, rape, threats against self and family, passport theft, and physical restraint.

* * *

Two African countries, Sudan and Niger with large Hindu or Muslim majorities, have slaves as is true in all major offending countries. Two others are Mauritania and Mali. In both, Arab Muslims forcibly take land and enslave black Muslims.

An estimated 14,000 people have been abducted since 1983 in Sudan. This is denied by the Sudanese government.

Denials, however, have only increased the profitability of slave dealings as a commercial enterprise, according to one published report.

An organization called Anti-Slavery International [ASI] has estimated seven percent of Niger's population or 870,000 are slaves.

This occurs even though slavery is prohibited by the constitution.

*   *   *

According to ASI, slave conditions exist in other countries.

Hundreds of boys between four and 10 are forcefully taken in South Asia and brought to the United Arab Emirates.

In three other nations, India, Nepal and Pakistan, millions of men, women and children into slave working conditions.

Others in Indonesia, bogged down in poverty with no opportunity on any level, look for work in Asia. Once there, they are exploited and turned into virtual slaves.

Many female migrant domestics are exposed to trafficking and slavery.

According to the U.S. State Department, the trafficking of people is defined as modern-day slavery and "is among the fastest growing criminal activities, occurring both worldwide and in individual countries."

That means they are forced, defrauded or coerced into sexual or labor exploitation.

Victims suffer physical and emotional abuse, rape, threats against self and family, passport theft, and physical restraint.

*   *   *

De la Cruz also learned 14 countries do not fully comply with the minimum standards of the U.S. federal Trafficking Victims Protection Act of 2000 (TVPA).

They are Bolivia, Burma, Cambodia, Cuba, Ecuador, Jamaica, Kuwait, North Korea, Qatar, Saudi Arabia, Sudan, Togo, United Arab Emirates, and Venezuela.

*   *   *

Just a short while ago, a group of Negro pastors in the United States formed an organization to combat Islamic slavery of blacks, both Muslim and non-Muslim in Africa.

The information can be confirmed in the August 1997 issue of Charisma Magazine and in the Nov. 17, 1997 issue of Christianity.

The group is called "Harambee" and is affiliated with the Loveland Church in Los Angeles, CA.

Dr. Charles Jacobs, head of another organization, the American Anti-Slavery Society headquartered in Boston, does the same thing.

Chapter Twenty Nine

Over 13 centuries, Islam institutionalized slavery, calling it a divinely-sanctioned practice. It was in complete harmony with the spirit of Islam. It was a point that impressed Armando de la Cruz and it was one he reviewed again and again for a reason.

He wanted to be historically correct if ever questioned by Muslims about his belief. In his mind, there could be no room for the slightest error if he wanted to carry his plan forward in this key area of North Africa.

Such a mistake, he realized, could cost him his life.

Yes, his research showed, it can be said Islam made life better for the average slave. And that Muhammad moved to make this improved status perpetual.

It all started—a piece of information he had known for some time—when Muhammad was forced to move from Mecca to Medina.

*   *   *

Again de la Cruz reviewed past information.

To defend himself and his beliefs, Muhammad allowed, authorized and encouraged the taking of slaves as "booty" or as a reward for followers fighting against enemy Arab tribes.

Later Muslim rulers—following Muhammad's example—made slaves of black Africans, non-Muslims and other black Muslims living in conquered territory.

All of this was recorded and took place long before slave ships sailed for the New World.

De la Cruz learned slavery continues in Africa to this very day and it was a practice he wanted to maintain and to help spread to all parts of the world.

Arabs went beyond the capture and the sale of black African slaves from West and East Africa. Besides the establishment of slave markets in every city in the Islamic world, traders reached out to markets in China, India, and Southeast Asia.

They also acquired Turkish slaves from Central Asia, slaves from the Byzantine Empire and white slaves from Central and East Europe.

* * *

From there, de la Cruz learned to his delight, human trafficking or slavery has moved to every world country, regardless of socio-economic status, history, or political structure.

In other words, slave traders or human traffickers operate internationally.

Millions of men, women and children around the world are forced to lead lives as slaves.

Although this exploitation is often NOT called slavery, the conditions are the same.

People are sold like objects, forced to work for little or no pay and are at the mercy of their 'employers'.

Women from Eastern Europe are bonded into prostitution, children are trafficked between West African countries and men are forced to work as slaves on Brazilian agricultural estates in BRAZIL.

There is a difference between slavery and other human rights violations. A slave is:

1. forced to work;

2. owned or controlled by an 'employer', usually through mental or physical abuse or threatened abuse;

3. dehumanized, treated as a commodity or bought and sold as 'property';

4. and physically constrained or has restrictions on freedom of movement.

*   *   *

What types of slavery exist today?

This is something de la Cruz needed to know and to learn about really well. It didn't matter, he realized, how many times the information had to be reviewed and gone over again and again.

Here are two of the most common ways to trick families and women.

One, loans are offered to parents in need to cover the cost of medicine for a sick child. In return, they work seven days a week, up to 365 days a year, to repay a debt that never ends.

Many times the debt is passed on for generations.

Another way and perhaps most common are forced marriages.

Women and girls married without choice can end up living lives of servitude and enduring physical violence.

Others are illegally recruited by individuals, governments or political parties and forced to work.

Trafficking may involve the transport and trade of children, men and women from one area or country to another.

An estimated 126 million children worldwide work and are held in slave conditions.

*   *   *

Early slave traders moved in a triangle. They started out in Europe, sailed to Africa and then to the New World before returning home.

After leaving ports in Britain and France loaded with goods to exchange for slaves, they traveled to Africa's west coast. There they acquired slaves in exchange for goods brought from Europe.

Slaves sent to the New World were generally shipped to a port like the one in the now U.S. Virgin Islands and later to include others in New England.

From there in the Caribbean or West Indies, slaves were moved to British colonies in North America and to South America largely to Brazil.

For the return trip back to Europe, ships carried farm products.

Chapter Thirty

By this time in his thinking, Armando de la Cruz had grown to like the idea of slavery and he believed he could expand on it today after his review of how it was done years ago in different parts of the world.

For now, he would try to make it work in North Africa before moving on to Europe where the business would likely be more lucrative.

De la Cruz decided to pattern his move in that direction by using an old tradition: pirates.

*　　*　　*

Here is how it operated.

Mediterranean pirates enslaved those captured—both black and white—following raids, moving the slave tradition forward.

Called Barbary Pirates, an alliance of Muslims and privateers, they operated out of North Africa for eight centuries.

It all started during the Crusades in the 11th century and continued on until the early part of the 19th century.

Based in North African ports of Tunis, Tripoli, Algiers, Salé and others in Morocco, this stretch of North Africa became known as the Barbary Coast.

Their attack zone was a large one. De la Cruz liked the working space.

Starting with the Mediterranean, it extended south along West Africa's Atlantic seaboard and into the North Atlantic as far north as Iceland.

Pirates destroyed thousands of British, French, Italian and Spanish ships, the primary targets.

European coastal towns were also included.

Between the 16th to 19th centuries, pirates captured an estimated 800,000 to 1.25 million [white] Europeans and made them slaves.

Pirates collected more slaves after plundering seaside villages in Italy, Portugal and Spain. They didn't stop there.

Other countries, Britain, France, the Netherlands, Ireland and as far away as Iceland and North America, got the same kind of cruel and violent attention.

Long stretches of coastline in Spain and Italy were almost completely abandoned until the 19th century.

All slaves, including Christians, were sold at Islamic-controlled slave markets in Algeria and Morocco.

Politically, the Barbary pirates opened the door for the Ottoman Empire.

After the capture of Algiers in the early 16th century, they established a pirate center there with a single idea in mind: seize as much land as possible bordering the Mediterranean.

Over the next 400 years, they gained control of North Africa and formed the Ottoman Empire.

*   *   *

A giant shift in the way slaves were bought and sold by the British, Dutch, French, Spanish and Portuguese had begun by the end of the fifteenth century.

The Portuguese were the first to carry out slave raids using appalling brutality for nearly five centuries off Africa's west coast.

But after bringing captured slaves home to Portugal as early as 1440, it was determined more money could be made selling them in the Western Hemisphere and not Europe.

At the beginning, the Portuguese then the Spanish captured slaves in Latin America and the West Indies like they had done in Africa.

All of that changed when those slaves who knew their own territory escaped or revolted.

Faced with such a stark reality, European slave traders discovered the demand for transplanted Africans changed sharply.

There was a reason why.

They were easier to control away from their African homes.

* * *

It was not the first time Africans had been captured and brought west.

A Dutch ship brought the first ones to British Atlantic coast settlements at Jamestown, Va., in 1619.

The raising of coffee, rice, sugar, tobacco, and much later, cotton, made African slaves valuable in North America's southern colonies.

* * *

Armando de la Cruz's aim was to modernize the taking, maintaining and trading of slaves in any world country, regardless of socio-economic status, history, or political structure.

For him, it was an opportunity waiting to be exploited. And if successful without being stopped, he would become a very rich and powerful man.

His goal was to convert slavery into the world's largest criminal industry.

While at the moment such a move would seem to be close to impossible, he would be patient taking it a step at a time.

He figured if he could control at least one major domestic market, it would be easier to dominate human trafficking internationally.

Once done, according to his thinking, it would be quicker to move back or into each domestic market until he was the world's leading or number one human trafficking trader.

Such a move, if done correctly, would also give him enormous political power. Money combined with politics would better position him to move against the United States, his number one enemy.

By bringing down his main opponent, it would be easier to control Europe and eventually the world.

*   *   *

De la Cruz had started slowly in an attempt to control the world slave market. He began the operation in Colombia located on the northwest coast of South America.

It started in the eastern half of the country, a low jungle-covered plain and inhabited mostly by isolated tropical-forest Indian tribes.

The region served as a training ground for acquiring slaves. Theirs was a society suited to slave labor for men, women and children.

Once he acquired slave taking and trade skills, he would attempt to apply what he had learned internationally.

*   *   *

He felt more than justified in doing what he was doing. 'After all slavery is not new,' he said to himself over and over again.

There was not a time in history without slavery. He found the same reference again and again.

In his studies, he discovered they were used in ancient Babylonia, in the Tigris-Euphrates civilizations and in ancient Persia.

Slave labor built temples and pyramids in ancient Egypt and they were used by the ancient Hebrews. It was established in Greece.

After the Fall of the Roman Empire, slavery flourished in the Byzantine Empire and Mediterranean pirates continued the age-old custom of enslaving the victims of their raids.

At the beginning, Armando learned both ISLAM and CHRISTIANITY accepted slavery.

It became a standard institution in Muslim lands, where most slaves were African in origin.

'And if those folks used slavery,' Armando said again and again to himself, 'there's no reason I can't improve on it.'

It didn't matter to him that slavery was now rejected in the civilized world.

His aim was to have slavery fully accepted and respected again.

*   *   *

Armando still wanted to know more and to review much of what he had covered before to be sure his knowledge of past slave history was current and clearly marked in his memory.

Here was still another overall part of his learn-and-repeat process about slavery.

The British, Dutch, French, Spanish, and Portuguese were all involved in lucrative African slave trade during the fifteenth and sixteenth centuries.

The Portuguese were the first to carry out slave raids using appalling brutality for nearly five centuries off Africa's west coast.

And they first brought their captured slaves back to Portugal as early as 1440.

It was quickly determined, however, more money could be made selling slaves in the Western Hemisphere and not Europe.

This shift in trading habits had begun by the end of the fifteenth century.

At the beginning, Portuguese then the Spanish moved to enslave the natives of Latin America and the West Indies but that didn't last long.

Those first slaves who knew their own territory escaped or revolted.

This resulted in an increased in the demand for transplanted Africans, who were easier to control away from their native countries.

*   *   *

And here was how he thought he could reestablish slavery to its once accepted status.

In Colombia, he improved on two important skills learned by studying the past: deceit and trickery.

More often than not parents living in poverty needed medicine for children.

Announcing he was willing to help, De la Cruz offered loans. Those unable to cover the debt were forced to work long hours, seven days a week, up to 365 days a year.

At the beginning, they were provided basic food and shelter as 'payment' for work. As it worked out, many could never accumulate enough cash to pay off the loan.

And more times than not, he worked to have those loans passed on to relatives or other family members. And if possible, they would be carried on by several generations one or more future generations.

Besides loans, there were other roads to slavery.

Early and forced marriage was his main vehicle to bring women and girls under total control.

De La Cruz approached men in a different way. They were offered jobs that didn't exist. When they rebelled, they were threatened. The next step was slavery.

His idea was to create a profitable slave class. When enough were gathered, they were ready for international transport and trade. And once in his total control, they would be moved across state lines and country borders.

Out of their home environment, language and cultural zones, they would be easier to control, work and sell.

It didn't take long to upgrade his thinking. While trading men and women was good, children could be better. He learned again the potential number ranged upwards to at least 126 million.

*   *   *

To move further forward successfully, he realized the approach to the business of modern slavery had to be modified in a key area.

The word 'slave' would be eliminated from his vocabulary for a reason.

Slavery was against the law.

It had been prohibited by the 1948 Universal Declaration of Human Rights and the 1956 United Nations Supplementary Convention on the Abolition of Slavery, the Slave Trade and Institutions and Practices Similar to Slavery.

So his approach became the selling the idea of opportunity to those he wanted to enslave and it worked.

Eastern Europe provided most of his acquired prostitutes once these women moved out of their countries, children needing homes were trafficked between West African countries and men looking for work were easily moved to agricultural estates in BRAZIL.

In the end, they all ended up as slaves.

*   *   *

He needed to know how to keep them all quiet and he readily passed on what he had learned to others who wanted to trade with him across the world.

De la Cruz, skilled in the use of mental and physical threat, preached his methods to willing students wanting to control slaves over long time periods.

If those methods didn't work, he was willing to use physical constraint to protect his investment.

*　*　*

Slaves sent to the New World were generally shipped to a port like the one in the now U.S. Virgin Islands and later to include others in New England.

From there in the Caribbean or West Indies, slaves were moved to British colonies in North America and to South America largely to Brazil.

And the shipping in of black African slaves sometimes dramatically changed local population percentages.

French Saint-Domingue, later to become Haiti, was the most dramatic. Slaves there became the majority.

And in the United States, by the time the Declaration of Independence was declared in 1776, one fifth of the population was black or enslaved.

*　*　*

And here is the part Armando liked best. Slavery is still practiced and it was the part he wanted to improve on most.

According to one organization, "millions of men, women and children around the world are forced to lead lives as slaves."

That's what he learned from Anti-Slavery International [ASI], founded in 1839 as the world's first international human rights organization.

Contemporary slavery, according to ASI, affects people of all ages, sex and race despite being banned by law and the constitutions in most countries.

To go further, Armando had to know those laws in order to get around them.

So he reviewed existing laws.

They include the United Nation's [UN] Slavery Convention in 1926, the International Labor Organization's Forced Labor Convention of 1930, the Universal Declaration of Human Rights in 1948 and the 1953 protocol amending the Slavery Convention signed in Geneva on Sept. 25, 1926.

Others are:

The UN's Supplementary Convention on the Abolition of Slavery, the Slave Trade and Institutions and Practices Similar to Slavery in 1956 and the International Labor Organization's Abolition of Forced Labor Convention in 1959.

And the U.S. federal "Victims of Trafficking and Violence Protection Act of 2000" was enacted to "combat trafficking in persons, especially into the sex trade, slavery and involuntary servitude . . ."

Despite those laws, 11 workers from Mexico were allegedly brought to northern New York State and kept in near-slavery.

In the Sudan, slavery is still practiced. An estimated 14,000 have been abducted since 1983. This allegation is denied by the Sudanese government.

Sudan, in northeast Africa, is the largest country on the continent, measuring about one-fourth the size of the United States.

Anti-Slavery International [ASI] reported slavery was rampant in Niger, in West Africa's Sahara region.

About seven percent of the population—some 870,000 in all—born into slavery will remain slaves as adults.

And interestingly enough, according to Armando, major offending countries have large Hindu or Muslim majorities.

Here are three of them:

1. United Arab Emirates [UAE]—Child trafficking: Although illegal to employ a child under the age of 15, hundreds of boys between four and ten are trafficked from South Asia to the UAE.

2. India, Nepal and Pakistan—Millions of men, women and children are slaves in those countries. Anti-slavery laws exist but are not enforced.

3. Indonesia—A lack of protection for female migrant domestics makes trafficking and slavery possible.

Chapter Thirty One

Morocco's geography made it important, the reason Jordon Frost and Colt McCoy turned their interest in that direction. Located on the African side of the narrow Strait of Gibraltar, it was and remains the closest connecting point between Africa and Europe.

And that may be a reason, the name Morocco is easily recognized in six languages. They are:

1. Arabic
   a. al-Mamlaka al-Maġribiyya, meaning "The Western Kingdom;"
   b. Al-Maġrib [Al-Maghred], a shorter version: "The West";

2. English, Morocco;

3. French, "Maroc";

4. Medieval Latin, "Morroch",

5. Spanish, "Marruecos";

6. and Portuguese, "Marrocos".

And for that reason—meaning its location—Morocco was the target for takeovers over a very long period of time.

Frost and McCoy reviewed the history together.

Rome started in 46 AD. Arabs bringing Islam followed in 685.

After Arabs and Berbers were kicked out of Spain in the 13th century, Portugal and Spain invaded Morocco.

During the 17th and 18th centuries, Morocco was a Barbary State and was pirate headquarters for those attacking Mediterranean traders.

European powers showed a collective interest in colonizing Morocco beginning in 1840.

In 1904, France and Spain divided the country into French and Spanish zones.

France had most of Morocco and Spain held a small southwest portion to be called the Spanish Sahara.

Germany showed an interest in the mineral-rich country beginning in 1905. And following the Algeciras Conference in 1906, Morocco's sultan maintained control of the land and France's privileges were cut back.

In 1912, Morocco's sultan Moulay Abd al-Hafid accepted a French protectorate status for his country.

When the French replaced Sultan Muhammad V with his uncle, nationalists protested and Muhammad V was returned to power in 1955.

A year later, France and Spain recognized Morocco as an independent state.

After Muhammad V's death in 1961, he was succeeded by King Hassan II, his son.

In the 1990s, King Hassan launched "Hassanian democracy," meaning he retained ultimate power while allowing what was called "significant political freedom."

In August 1999, King Hassan II died after 38 years on the throne and his son, Prince Sidi Muhammad, was crowned King Muhammad VI.

Muhammad VI has pledged to make the political system even more open, allow freedom of expression and support economic reform.

He also advocated more rights for women, a position opposed by Islamic fundamentalists.

* * *

Morocco's occupation of the Western Sahara, once called the Spanish Sahara, had been repeatedly criticized by the international community.

In the 1970s, tens of thousands of Moroccans crossed the border into Spanish Sahara to back their government's contention that the northern part of the territory was historically part of Morocco.

Spain, which had controlled the territory since 1912, withdrew in 1976, creating a power vacuum that was filled by Morocco in the north and Mauritania in the south.

When Mauritania withdrew in August of 1979, Morocco overran the remainder of the territory. A rebel group, the Polisario Front, has fought against Morocco since 1976 for the independence of Western Sahara on behalf of the indigenous Saharawis.

The Polisario and Morocco agreed in Sept. 1991 to a UN-negotiated cease-fire in exchange for the holding of a referendum to decide the issue.

Morocco has opposed the referendum from the start.

In 2002, King Muhammad VI said he "will not renounce an inch of" Western Sahara.

* * *

As a result of his announcement, terrorist attacks were launched.

On May 16, 2003, terrorists believed to be associated with al-Qaeda killed 33 people in several simultaneous attacks.

Belgian, Jewish and Spanish buildings were bombed in Casablanca.

* * *

Less than a year later, on March 11, 2004, ten explosions aboard four commuter trains in Madrid, Spain, killed 191 passengers from 17 countries three days before Spain's general elections.

Moroccans were involved.

Jamal Zougam and three other members of Morocco's radical Islamist Combat Group were trained in Jalalabad, Afghanistan.

The Combat Group provided logistic support to al-Qaeda in Morocco in four key areas:

1. A place to live,

2. False Papers,

3. Marriage,

4. False identities for travel to Europe.

* * *

After a 21-month investigation of the Madrid train bombings, Spanish judge Juan del Olmo concluded Jamal Zougam of Morocco planned the attack.

* * *

The attack date was selected in advance to deliver a clear political message and that was to link it to the Sept. 11, 2001 Islamic Extremist attack in New York City.

On that day, 3,000 were killed when two American Airlines passenger jets were hijacked and slammed into Wall Street's World Trade Center twin-tower buildings.

On March 25, 2005, Spanish prosecutor Olga Sánchez declared the bombings occurred exactly 911 days following the Sept. 11, 2001 New York City attack for a reason.

She added "local al-Qaida groups" selected the date as another remembrance of the Islamic Extremist New York attack.

* * *

Of the 28 defendants later to be tried, 21 were found guilty on a range of charges from forgery to murder.

Two others were sentenced to more than 40,000 years in prison. Spanish law, however, limits actual time served to 40 years.

* * *

Authorities also said a wave of suicide bombings struck Casablanca in March and April 2007. They were not certain, however, if the attacks were related.

* * *

There were two suspects: Abdellatif Bekhti and Abu Nidal.

* * *

Abdellatif Bekhti, a dual citizen of both Belgian and Morocco, was thought to be an informant because of his Islamic Militant connections, his political ties and his alleged criminal background over a long period.

During the 1970s, Belliraj was reported to have been a sympathizer of Ila Al Amam, a Moroccan Marxist-Leninist clandestine organization. It is now known as the Annahj Addimocrati Party.

He had connections with Mustapha Moatassim, who 20 years later became one of the founders of the Al Badil Al Hadari Party.

It was a small legalist Islamist party with a close relationship with the Far Left Parti Socialiste Unifié [Unified Socialist Party] and Moroccan human rights organizations.

Moatassim and another party leader were arrested along with Belliraj in February 2008. Immediately afterwards, Morocco's government disbanded the party.

During the 1980s, Belliraj was an activist of the Arab section of the Belgian Christian trade-union, led by Pan-Arabist Moroccan Lekbir Nouri.

Nouri and other party members travelled often in the Middle East to solidify political ties and to raise money from oil-rich Arab regimes. Two of those countries were Libya and Iraq.

Both Belliraj and Nouri allegedly embezzled large amounts of Iraqi and Libyan funds for personal use in 1989.

Belliraj and other members of the Arab section members met with Ayatollah Khomeini of Iran in 1981.

* * *

With that kind of background, Belliraj became an informant for the main Belgian intelligence agency, called the Sûreté de l'État, starting sometime during the 1990s.

They accepted him for another reason, his speaking knowledge of Arabic and French.

Belliraj reportedly was able to successfully provide authorities with large amounts of information about Al Qaeda.

And less than two weeks before the Sept. 11, 2001 twin-towers attack in New York City, it was believed he had dinner with the operation's chief planner, Osama bin Laden.

It has also been alleged that he may have been an informant for the U.S. Central Intelligence Agency [CIA] and for Morocco's secret service.

* * *

His official connections, however, didn't guarantee immunity from the law.

In Belgium alone during the 1980s, Belliraj was convicted of assault and battery, breach of trust, arms trafficking, embezzlement and trafficking in false Moroccan passports.

How was he able to do that?

Belliraj reportedly had inside connections with Morocco's three consular offices in Belgium. One was in Brussels, the capital; and the other two were in Anvers and Liege.

Later, a Belgian-Moroccan gang organized the successful hold-up of a Brinks agency at Kehlen, Luxembourg on April 17, 2000. They took 17-million Euros.

Luxembourg, one of the smallest countries in Europe, is southeast of Belgium, south of France and west of Germany.

After the hold-up, Belliraj was arrested, charged and sentenced to 20 years in a Luxembourg jail in January 2003.

During the next two months, with his gang's help, he escaped and took refuge in Morocco.

There he was arrested again, along with other members of the "Belliraj network."

Authorities there took action after learning Belliraj had successfully laundered 2.5 million Euros or a portion of the money taken in the Brinks holdup.

Later Belliraj was found guilty of arms smuggling and planning terrorist attacks in Morocco.

* * *

Belliraj and 37 others were arrested and accused of stockpiling weapons for terrorist attacks in Morocco in

January and February 2008 and those arrests were made public Feb. 18, 2008.

Again Belliraj denied the charges, claiming the weapons were stored to support Algerian Islamic radicals.

On June 27, 2009, following a long Salé, Morocco, Criminal Appeal Court trial, Belliraj was convicted of "plotting terror attacks in Morocco, holdups in Europe, large-scale money laundering projects and arms trafficking."

Salé is a town on the northeastern edge of Rabat, the African's nation's capital. It was also a known haven for pirates.

Belgium's Justice Minister Jo Vandeurzen tried and failed to have Belliraj tried in Belgium for the crimes he allegedly committed there between 1986 and 1989.

Belliraj was sentenced to life in prison following what was described as perhaps Morocco's highest profile terrorism case.

*   *   *

Although denied by Abdellatif Belliraj, he allegedly committed a series of murders between 1986 and 1989. And for three of them, Belliraj reportedly was paid $300 by Abu Nidal.

Some were claimed in Beirut by a group called 'Soldiers of the Right.'

In the 1990s, Belliraj allegedly became involved with international criminal and terrorist networks, working as a "money man."

At one point, Belliraj admitted to a series of crimes. Later, through his attorney, he recanted those "confessions."

In an open letter, published by the Belgian newspaper Le Soir in August 2008, he claimed to have been tortured by Moroccan police.

Those alleged confessions included the admission of six murders.

1. Raoul Schouppe, 65, a Brussels grocer and a former warrant officer in the Belgian Air Force, July 28, 1988.

2. Marcel Bille, 53, an alleged client of Moroccan male prostitutes, Aug. 16, 1988.

3. Abdullah Ah-Adhal El Hasi, 36, an imam and manager of the Brussels Islamic and Cultural Center, March 29, 1989.

4. Salem Bahri, 48, El Hasi's assistant, for allegedly objecting to Iran's Ayatollah Khomeini's fatwa against Indian-born English novelist and critic Salman Rushdie, declaring Muslims should kill Rushdie for defaming Muhammad and insulting Islam in the 1988 novel, Satanic Verses, March 29, 1989.

5. Samir Gahez Rasoul, 24, a chauffeur for the Saudi Arabian ambassador to Belgium, June 20, 1989. He was a collateral victim of a shot fired at a Saudi diplomat.

6. Joseph Wybran, 49, a Belgian immunologist and leader in the local Jewish community, Oct. 3, 1989.

*   *   *

Others thought he was a hit man for the Abu Nidal Organization [ANO], a secular—not Islamic—international terrorist group used by Libya, Iraq and Syria to attack Arab, Israeli and western targets.

Known as one of the world's most dangerous terrorist organization in the mid-1980s, ANO carried out operations in 20 countries, killing about 300 people and wounding hundreds more.

ANO was named for Sabri al-Banna, a Palestinian terrorist called Abu Nidal.

Other ANO names were the Fatah Revolutionary Council, the Arab Revolutionary Brigades, or the Revolutionary Organization of Socialist Muslims.

*   *   *

Morocco's Interior Minister Chakib Benmoussa Morocco charged there was a direct link between organized crime and terrorists.

Benmoussa came to that conclusion two weeks after the government announced the arrest of 35 members of a cell led by Abdelkader Belliraj.

The arrests, according to Benmoussa, were the government's most important move against terrorism since 2003.

At that time, a suicide attack left 45 dead in Casablanca, Morocco's largest city.

* * *

Morocco's report surprised Belgium's intelligence.

Why?

Belgium authorities reported they had monitored Belliraj and other suspects for years without finding evidence of terrorist involvement.

They concluded if Moroccan accusations were confirmed, the case could rock not only their but Europe's counter-terrorism community for two reasons.

One, it would mean the Belliraj network could become perhaps the most glaring example of direct ties connecting organized crime and terrorism.

Two, and perhaps the most important, it would confirm a connection between Shiite and Sunni Muslim radical groups.

The question was whether the Moroccan allegations had real substance.

Of the 35 arrested in Morocco, the suspects included a correspondent for Hezbollah's al-Manar TV based in Beirut, Lebanon, a self-proclaimed "Station of the Resistance" against Israel.

Hezbollah, meaning "Party of God," is tied financially and politically to Iran and Syria. The group's paramilitary wing is a resistance movement throughout much of the Arab and Muslim worlds.

The detained news personality was a Shi'a or Shia Muslim, one of two Islamic groups. The largest, Sunni Muslims, totals between 80-to-90 percent of the world's 1.57 billion Muslim population. Shia is estimated to be 10-to-20 percent of the total. There are a number of smaller parts.

* * *

Jordon Frost and Colt McCoy felt it important to understand the following:

After Muhammad's death in 632, a split erupted within the Islamic community when there could be no agreement on a single leader, called the Caliph.

Those sharp differences produced two groups, the Sunnis and the Shias.

Today, Sunnis are a majority in most Muslim communities in Africa, the Arab world, southeast and south Asia and China.

Shias are the majority population in Azerbaijan, Bahrain, Iran and Iraq; and they are the largest religious group in Lebanon.

Violent conflict between the two groups continues today from Pakistan to Yemen and is the most common element of friction throughout the Middle East.

Another sharp leadership Islamic division was launched by the late Osama bin Laden sometime between August 1988 and late 1989.

His group, named Al-Qaeda or al-Qa'ida, meaning "the base" or "the foundation," is a global militant Islamist group.

Al-Qaeda is intolerant of non-Sunni branches of Islam and their leaders regard liberal Muslims, Shias, Sufis and other sects as heretics and have at times attacked their mosques and gatherings.

Two others are Fatah and Hamas, both Palestinian political groups.

Fatah is the largest faction of the Palestine Liberation Organization (PLO).

Its goals are to establish an independent democratic state with complete sovereignty of all Palestinian lands and to make Jerusalem its capital city.

*   *   *

The land known as Palestine today has gone through a number of stages including political change over time for a simple reason.

It was a major trade route connecting Africa, Asia and Europe.

And it is a religious center for Christianity, Islam and Judaism.

As part of the Ottoman Empire starting in 1518, it was occupied by Britain during World War One.

And under English rule, called the British Mandate, boundaries were determined after the War. At the time, Palestine included the Gaza Strip, the West Bank and present day Jordan.

Egypt and Jordan captured and occupied East Jerusalem and the Gaza Strip-territories after the 1948 Israeli war of independence.

Until 1948, Egypt and Jordan controlled the Palestinian territories of the West Bank, also called East Jerusalem and the Gaza Strip. That ended with the 1967 Six Day War.

Israel regards East Jerusalem as part of Israel as a result of annexation in 1980. It includes Jerusalem's Old City and some of the holiest sites of Christianity, Islam and Judaism including the Al-Aqsa Mosque, Church of the Holy Sepulchre, Temple Mount and the Western Wall.

The Gaza Strip in particular was historically and politically important for Africa, Asia, and Europe. Located on the Mediterranean Sea, it was a trading crossroads for Africa, Asia, and Europe.

The West Bank is surrounded by Israel on the west, Jordan to the east across the Jordan River and the Dead Sea to the southeast.

It stayed that way until the 1967 Six Day War.

Part of the international community and the Palestinian Authority regard East Jerusalem as part of the West Bank and part of the Palestinian territories or Occupied Palestinian Territories.

Like many other territories in the area, it has a long history of occupation by foreign powers.

*   *   *

On Nov. 15, 1988, the Palestine Liberation Organization's (PLO) National Council (PNC) declared Palestine to be a state with Jerusalem as its capital.

The PLO announcement was made in Algiers, the capital of Algeria, not in Jerusalem. Algiers is the capital of Algeria, on Africa's north coast.

Why there?

Jerusalem and the surrounding territory is controlled by Israel.

Despite that political reality, many countries recognize the State of Palestine. Others announced they welcomed this step without declaring recognition.

This process started on Oct. 28, 1974 when the Arab League meeting in RABAT, Morocco's capital city, declared the PLO as the "sole legitimate representative of the Palestinian people and reaffirmed their right to establish an independent state of urgency."

Morocco also provides the State of Palestine embassy space in Rabat without charge.

*   *   *

Here are the other two Palestinian political groups, Fatah and Hamas.

Hamas or Palestine's Muslim Brotherhood is a political party that governs the Gaza Strip, a narrow strip of land southwest of Israel. Egypt is to south and the Mediterranean Sea borders the west coast.

The strip's 1.6 million population—mostly Sunni Muslim—has been in turmoil since the 1948 Arab-Israeli War.

Hamas' 1988 charter calls for Israel and the Palestinian Territories to be replaced with an Islamic Palestinian state.

And Hamas was founded to specifically carry out the charter's mandate.

After the formation of a Hamas-led cabinet on March 20, 2006, tensions surfaced between Fatah, the largest faction of the Palestine Liberation Organization (PLO), and Hamas.

Mahmoud Abbas, PLO chairman, was chosen as President of the proposed "State of Palestine" by the PLO Council on 23 November 2008.

At one point, Fatah commanders refused to take orders from the government after the Palestinian Authority [PA], an administrative office, launched a campaign against Hamas. Those actions included abductions, assassinations and demonstrations.

In reaction Hamas leader Mohammed Nazzal, in a statement to Al Jazeera's news network, accused Abbas of leading an effort to isolate the Hamas-led government.

At the time, Israeli intelligence warned Abbas that Hamas had a plan to kill him at his Gaza office.

* * *

Here were the major goals of the competing groups.

Hamas sought to liberate Palestine and do away with Fatah.

Fatah sought to declare Jerusalem capital of the proposed Palestinian state and to eradicate all Zionist influence including anything cultural, economic, military or political.

Both Fatah and Hamas are part of Islam, the world's second largest religion. Christianity is the first.

* * *

Besides the 35 arrested in Morocco, police raids found an arms stockpile including AK-47 assault rifles, Skorpio machine pistols, Uzi machine guns and detonators.

It was called the largest terrorist arsenal ever seized in this northwest African country.

After the arrests and the arms seizure, authorities moved to end a small Islamist party called al-Badil al-Hadari or translated means the Civilized Alternative.

They claimed there was a strong connection between the party and the Belliraj network.

Those captured Belliraj network members were charged with using terrorist acts as part of a plan to undermine public order.

*　　*　　*

Morocco's Interior Minister Chakib Benmoussa said network targets included government ministers, high officers of the Forces Armees Royales or Morocco's Armed Forces and Jewish Moroccans.

Benmoussa added the Belliraj network had contacts with al-Qaeda in Afghanistan, the Groupe Islamique Combattant Marocain (GICM) and the Algerian Groupe Salafiste pour la Predication et le Combat (GSPC).

The Belliraj network also trained in Lebanese Hezbollah camps in 2000.

*　　*　　*

Benmoussa said terrorism remained a major concern.

Why?

The threat of terrorism is likely to go up in Morocco as jihad is spreading in North Africa.

Later 14 were killed and 20 were injured by an explosion inside the Cafe Argana in Marrakech, a large city south of Rabat, the North African nation's official news agency reported.

An Interior Ministry statement called the cafe blast a criminal act. The eating place was described as a major tourist destination where locals and foreigners mingled.

$*$ $*$ $*$

As a step toward better controlling such acts, Morocco could become a world counter-terrorism center, according to Benmoussa.

To prove the point, he said an international Combat Nuclear Terrorism meeting was held in Rabat, Morocco's capital.

Russia and the United States co-chaired the gathering also attended by members and representatives of the Group of Eight—Canada, France, Germany, Italy, Japan, Russia, the United Kingdom and the United States.

Others present came from Australia, China, Turkey, Kazakhstan and Turkey.

The government of Morocco and the International Atomic Energy Agency (IAEA) attended as observers.

Chapter Thirty Two

Jordon Frost and Colt McCoy reached the same conclusion: It's time to end our study, find and arrest the Barbary Lion.

Here is what we know: he is working with a series of terrorist organizations, he's dealing with slaves, and cruise ships.

Although he claims to be a believer in Islam, "I don't believe he is. It's just a cover."

"Why do you say that?"

"Here's where our knowledge of English, Spanish, Latin America and the United States come in."

"I agree but explain it to me anyway."

"Agreed . . ."

"I'm listening."

"Why did this occur near Puerto Rico and say not in the Mediterranean somewhere?"

"I think the answer is a simple one. Our terrorist is most likely to be from somewhere in Latin America."

"And I believe your conclusion is absolutely correct."

"I have another question."

"I'm listening."

"Why would Islamic extremists accept such a decision?"

"For a very simple reason, I believe. They like the idea of having a contact like him from this part of the world."

"Why?"

"I think their reasoning is probably simple enough. They want the ability to strike their number one enemy, the United States."

"So that could mean the following. If he could sink a ship with 900 aboard near Puerto Rico, a U.S. Commonwealth, he would be in a good position to carry out a similar attack like occurred in New York City on Sept. 11, 2001."

"And in my opinion, your conclusion is absolutely correct."

*   *   *

"Do we now have enough information about our terrorist?"

"I believe we do."

"Can you explain that please?"

"I just received new information from a contact in Rabat," Morocco's capital city.

"And what did this informant say?"

"There is a man who speaks French with a Spanish accent."

"So where do you believe he is from?"

"His accent tells us he is likely to be from Colombia, in South America."

"Are you sure?"

"Yes I am."

"Again, are you sure? Everyone in Latin America speaks Spanish. Am I not correct?"

"You are. But Colombians are known for the quality of their Spanish. Apart from that, they speak slower and more distinctively than anyone else in the zone."

"Are you sure?"

Rather than answer the question directly, he said: "The Cubans are the fastest talkers. Mexicans speak with a sing-song in their voice. And the Spanish folks from Spain pronounce their 'th's' in a particular way."

"Are you saying it's possible to identify anyone's country of origin just by hearing them speak their language?"

"Yes, I am. It's like hearing someone from the eastern part of the United States and from the South even more so."

"So one might say this is what we're dealing with here."

"Yes."

"So a man with a Colombian accent has been identified in Morocco."

"Yes, that's true."

"Do we know the name of the town or city in Morocco?"

"This man operates in Rabat."

"Do we have an address for this terrorist?"

"Yes, we do."

"What is it?"

"Our man, identified as Armando de la Cruz, has rented Apartment Four, in the Rommana Residence, in the Quartier Tour Hassan or the Tour Hassan Quarter of Rabat."

"Since you apparently have so much information, I'll ask you something dumb."

"Please go ahead."

"Do we know Senor de la Cruz's telephone number?"

"We do and it is 037-26-19-33."

"I can't believe what you have just told me."

*   *   *

"So what's our next move?"

"I think we should call the President and let him handle it from there."

"Your suggestion sounds good to me."

*   *   *

They did and within 24 hours they learned Senor de la Cruz had been arrested.

And shortly afterwards, he confessed to authorities at the U.S. Embassy in Rabat that he had organized, planned and carried out the sinking of 'The Caribbean' off Puerto Rico's northwest coast."

[END]